Henry John Walker is Senior Lecturer in Classical and Medieval Studies at Bates College, Lewiston, Maine. He is the author of *Theseus and Athens* (1995) and *Memorable Deeds and Sayings: One Thousand Tales from Ancient Rome* (2004).

'This fascinating book by classicist Henry John Walker sheds new lights on the beloved yet enigmatic duo of the Indo-European pantheon: the Vedic Aśvins, known in Ancient Greece as the Dioskouroi, Castor and Pollux. Never remote, always nearby, the riders are summoned to save drowning sailors, succor losing armies, repair maimed sacrifices, and heal the sick. Surprisingly, Walker argues that this altruism is a symptom of their marginal, even lowly status among the gods. Why is their nature so hard for modern scholars to grasp? What was the 'strange gap' that separated them from the other gods? Richly researched, Walker's answer is startling: seduced over a hundred years ago by J. Rendel Harris's theory of global 'Dioscurism', we have been distracted by their twinship and thus blind to their powerful theological ambiguity. Eternally adolescent cowboys, 'outlaw', 'almost slave', the twin horse gods never grow up. The author skillfully shows that although born as a pair, they perpetually dwell between opposite poles – childhood and adulthood, soldiers and warlords, tribalism and universalism, death and life, humanity and divinity and the hideous diseases they cure and the radiant immortality they share with the Sun Goddess, their sister, friend or bride. *The Twin Horse Gods* offers a welcome cautionary tale about the dangers of oversimplification when it comes to the interpretation of myth. The book re-introduces us to familiar deities by awakening us to their complexity. Ancient gods had histories, personalities, and multiple allegiances; they were not archetypal cartoons, and their fraught destinies often baffled even those who worshipped them. But perhaps, thanks to Walker's rich and informative book, we are a step closer now to understanding their endless, magnetic appeal.'

Kimberley Patton, Professor of the Comparative and Historical Study of Religion, Harvard University

'*The Twin Horse Gods* is rich in old stories and new ideas about everything in its title – twins, and horses and gods – and much more. It tracks this ancient Indo-European pair through India, Greece, and Rome, and in each place upsets reigning scholarly theories, arguing for their importance as social outcasts and friends of human underdogs as well as the healers and eternal youths we knew they were. They are much more peculiar and interesting and important than I realized before I read Henry John Walker's book.'

Wendy Doniger, Mircea Eliade Distinguished Professor of the History of Religions, University of Chicago

THE TWIN HORSE GODS

THE DIOSKOUROI IN MYTHOLOGIES OF THE ANCIENT WORLD

HENRY JOHN WALKER

BLOOMSBURY ACADEMIC
LONDON • NEW YORK • OXFORD • NEW DELHI • SYDNEY

BLOOMSBURY ACADEMIC
Bloomsbury Publishing Plc
50 Bedford Square, London, WC1B 3DP, UK
1385 Broadway, New York, NY 10018, USA
29 Earlsfort Terrace, Dublin 2, Ireland

BLOOMSBURY, BLOOMSBURY ACADEMIC and the Diana logo
are trademarks of Bloomsbury Publishing Plc

First published in Great Britain 2015 by I.B. Tauris & Co Ltd
Paperback first published by Bloomsbury Academic 2021

A catalogue record for this book is available from the British Library.

A catalog record for this book is available from the Library of Congress.

ISBN: HB: 978-1-7845-3003-7
PB: 978-1-3501-9780-0
ePDF: 978-0-8577-2441-0
eBook: 978-0-8577-3808-0

Series: Library of Classical Studies, volume 11

Typeset in Garamond Three by OKS Prepress Services, Chennai, India

To find out more about our authors and books visit
www.bloomsbury.com and sign up for our newsletters.

To Sarah
the sun goddess
born in the east
and moving west

CONTENTS

PREFACE

This is a book about the young twin horse gods of Ancient Greece and Vedic India, about the stories that celebrated their achievements and the rituals that were performed to honour them. These myths and rites did not exist in isolation, so this book also discusses Greek and Vedic attitudes to riding horses and driving chariots, to young men in general, and to the important women in the story of the horse gods, Saraṇyū, Sūryā and Helenē. The heroines of the story make us aware that a woman could have some independence in an ancient society and that she did control reproduction. The low status of young horsemen in early society will cast light on the different parts played by kings and priests in India, and even on the difference between priests who recite prayers and priests who do physical work. In Greece, the horse gods will be seen as the patrons of young Spartan men who are becoming full citizens, and as approachable gods who can be invited into anyone's home, or called upon in times of trouble; but their ambiguous status as neither adults nor children, as neither distant gods nor mere humans, will make us wonder about the nature of gods and men.

The stories and rituals and social structures of a people form a coherent whole that helps them to establish who they are and enables them to make sense of their world. So a study of two young horse gods will introduce us to the whole world of Vedic India and Classical Greece, because their role in each world will affect every other part of its system. Simple stories and rituals will therefore raise important questions about that world, and the answers that the Greeks and Indians provide are neither exotic nor primitive. I find myself constantly amazed by the sophistication of these people, who had so little in material goods, and thought so hard about the world. I hope I have managed to convey some of that wonder in this book.

My own background is in Ancient Greek, so I approach Sanskrit as an amateur who started to read it very late in life. I would like to thank two great and generous Vedic scholars, Michael Witzel and Ganesh Umakant Thite, for spending so much of their time in a brave attempt to teach me Sanskrit. I hope they will not be too greatly outraged at the strange plant that grew from the seeds of their knowledge, but I also hope that the love they have for the Vedic world will shine through these pages, however much I may have accidentally misrepresented it.

Above all, I want to show that however long ago they may have lived, the thought of the Vedic Indians and the Ancient Greeks is very lively and very much alive. I want to inspire my readers to turn to the ancient texts that are reflected through the distorting mirror of this book.

I would like to thank my editor, Alex Wright, for having faith in this project and helping me to produce this book. Finally, as always, I would like to thank my colleagues at Bates College and my family for taking care of me.

SPELLING AND PRONUNCIATION

In the case of Greek authors and place-names, I have followed the traditional practice of librarians and mapmakers, and I have translated them into Latin, so that it will be easier for the reader to find the places on maps and the authors in library catalogues. Otherwise, I have used the Ancient Greek spelling. Since this book is about the Greek and Indian imagination, I wanted to present their thoughts in their own words.

The vowels in both languages are pronounced as in most languages except modern English: long ā as in English 'grand', long ē as in English 'great', and long ī as in English 'machine'. Sanskrit ṛ is a vowel, as in the slow, ironic pronunciation of the 'r' in English 'great' [girreat], so Sanskrit *ṛta* is pronounced [irrta]. The consonants g and s are pronounced hard, as in English 'girl' or 'see' (never soft as in 'gin' or 'ease'). Sanskrit c is pronounced like English 'ch', Sanskrit ś and ṣ are like English 'sh'.

CHAPTER 1

HORSES, TWINS AND GODS

Introduction

The Capitol of Rome is dominated by the famous equestrian statue of the emperor Marcus Aurelius. There was originally a defeated enemy under the raised leg of his horse, but even without this prostrate victim, nobody needs to tell us that Marcus Aurelius must have been a very powerful and important man.[1] We understand the statue's message almost instinctively, because this message has been delivered to us so often. In ancient Athens, a horseman (*hippeus*) was an aristocrat;[2] in ancient Rome the Equestrians were just below the Senatorial aristocracy.[3] Even today, the capital cities of the world are filled with kings and generals on horseback, who do their very best to imitate the imperious gaze of Marcus Aurelius: Henry IV commanding the Seine, a brittle Charles I bewildered by the traffic around him, a very aristocratic George Washington overlooking the undemocratic grandeur of Commonwealth Avenue. These powerful men stare over our heads – we are literally beneath their notice. And this is how we expect things to be. For 3,000 years, the horseman has been a powerful image of the aristocratic gentleman. In German, a gentleman is a 'rider' (*Ritter*); in the Romance languages, he is a 'horseman' (*caballero*, *cavaliere*, *chevalier*). To this day, English-speakers describe well-mannered men as 'horsemanlike' (*chivalrous*), and Germans describe them as 'riderlike' (*ritterlich*). So we expect horsemen to be better than us and to rule over us. The ancient Roman statue of Marcus Aurelius is an early example of this image of the ruling horseman, and the countless imitations it has inspired still speak to us.[4]

There is, however, a very different image of horsemen on the same Capitol in Rome. At the very edge of the terrace, overlooking the city of Rome, standing in front of the emperor, are two statues of young men with horses. Most of us tend to ignore them because, even if they loom over us as we climb up the Capitol, they disappear from our field of vision as soon as we reach the top. Michelangelo has ensured that our gaze is instantly drawn to the statue of the emperor by the very design of the Capitol itself. We also dismiss these two sculptures because even though they show men with horses, they are not equestrian statues. These young men are not riding their horses; they are leading them by the reins. We could almost mistake them for servants of the emperor, holding fresh horses for him in case he should decide to change his mount. These young men are, however, vastly superior to the emperor himself. They are the ancient Roman Dioscuri, the young sons of Jupiter himself, the twin horse gods, Castor and Pollux.

The contrast between the equestrian statue of the emperor and the sculptures of the horse gods reveals an ambiguity in our attitude to horses. We are brought up to admire them as symbols of aristocratic power, but we also know that they are farm-animals and require a lot of care. A statue of a 'great leader' on horseback might be considered a fine and noble thing, but not too many people would like to work as a stable-boy. We readily understand why cleaning out the stables of Augeias was regarded as one of the impossibly difficult Labours of Hēraklēs.[5] It is surprising, therefore, to find that the horse gods are ready to perform such a lowly task as looking after their own horses. This surprise is reinforced by the stories told about the horse gods.

There is a nice anecdote from ancient Rome that brings out the contrast between the aristocratic world of the horse rider and the humble world of the horse gods. An ordinary Plebeian called Publius Vatinius was going to Rome, when the horse gods rode up to him and told him that the Romans had won a great victory overseas. Vatinius rushed into the Senate to report the good news, but 'he was thrown into jail for insulting the majesty and dignity of the Senate with such a silly story'. Later, of course, the Senate had to apologize for its mistake.[6] This story draws a powerful contrast between the aristocratic arrogance of the senators, who were outraged that this humble citizen would dare to intrude on their meeting, and the friendly behaviour of the horse gods, who thought it perfectly natural that they should deliver their very important message to a very ordinary Roman.

If we are to understand the horse gods, we must lay aside the 3,000-year-old notion that horse riding is for kings. Instead, we must adopt the attitude of the Bronze Age and see it as a very lowly activity, suitable only for cowboys and messengers.[7] This attitude survived into the historical period of the Greek world, where the Dioskouroi are modest and helpful gods, and are very close to ordinary people. In the Bronze and Early Iron Ages of Vedic India, where they are called the Aśvins, we find that the young horse gods have similar characteristics. They are quick to come to the rescue whenever anyone is in trouble, and they are especially ready to help the old, the weak, the humble. For thousands of years the character of the horse gods remains the same. They distance themselves from the high and mighty, and instead they behave like very helpful messenger boys, who are only too eager to come to the assistance of anyone they may meet, as they wander around the world.[8] They are the gods of working people; in fact, they are so close to ordinary people that doubts are raised about their status as gods in the myths of India and Greece. They are almost too human.

Twins

Why are the horse gods like this? Why are they so helpful to people? Oddly enough, the answer that has often been given to this question is that they are twins. The Indians always referred to them as 'the two horse gods' (*aśvinau*), using the dual form of the noun to emphasize that they were a pair. The Greek story of their birth made it clear that the Dioskouroi were twins. The Romans explicitly referred to the horse gods as 'the Twins' (*Gemini*), and they are still honoured by that name in the night sky. According to many scholars who have written about the horse gods, the mere fact that they are twins explains everything about them.[9] These scholars believe that there are certain universal features shared by all twins in the mythical and religious views of every culture, so the character and careers of our horse gods are quite predictable from the very fact that they are twins. In effect, they believe that all human beings have reacted to twins in the same way, that this universal fear of twins is 'the oldest religion in the world'.[10] Their grand theory about twins is known as 'Dioscurism'.

The most striking thing about Dioscurism is not its content, which consists of extraordinary and implausible generalizations, but rather its general acceptance by the scholarly world. The theory of Dioscurism was developed at the beginning of the twentieth century by the biblical scholar Rendel Harris. His theory was accepted by anthropologists,[11] he is quoted with respect by scholars who write on the subject of the horse gods,[12] and his work is still cited with approval in the 2005 edition of the *Encylopedia of Religions*.[13] Harris started off by studying Christian legends about twins, and he was particularly fascinated by the Syrian *Acts of Thomas*, which stated that St Thomas and Christ were twin brothers.[14] They possess what Harris believed to be the essential features of 'Dioscuric' twins: they both have the same mother, but one twin is human and the son of a man, whereas the other is divine and the son of a god. Harris rejected this legend as a pagan survival, as an attempt to assimilate Christ and St Thomas with the Dioskouroi.[15] Given the popularity of the Dioskouroi, this was a plausible explanation, but then Harris went on to explore the origin of the divine twins themselves, and in two vast anthropological studies[16] he concluded that they had developed from taboos surrounding real human twins. According to Harris, this fear and worship of human twins was the original religion of the world, and it was the origin of most religious beliefs except his own.[17] He called this religion 'Dioscurism', and in this he was followed by his student Krappe, who significantly titled his synopsis of Harris's theories, *Mythologie Universelle*.[18] Harris ultimately concluded that this great universal rival to Christianity was itself based on a primitive Trinity, which consisted of the Thunder-God and his two 'Assessors',[19] the divine twins.[20]

Harris firmly believed that every tradition relating to twins could be attributed to this worldwide religion of Dioscurism, as is clear from the conclusion to his *Cult of the Heavenly Twins*:

> We have now taken our rapid survey of what may, perhaps, be described as the oldest religion in the world; a religion which is still extant in some of its simplest and most primitive forms, though, of course, it will very soon disappear.[21]

His work also betrays a strong sense of indignation against the practitioners of Dioscurism. Since twin infanticide was practised in some parts of Africa, his crusading zeal against this imaginary religion is understandable, but his tone is invariably mocking and offensive, even when there is no question of infanticide. His followers may not share his indignation or his belief in a single, worldwide Dioscuric religion, but they do accept the idea that there are certain universal practices and attitudes toward twins. In effect, they deny the existence of the 'oldest religion in the world' but accept the universality of its beliefs. This is the tragic flaw of Dioscurism, because what Harris and his followers are in fact describing is not a single, universal set of beliefs, but rather an extremely diverse variety of beliefs and practices relating to twins.

Given this variety, it is of course very easy to come up with coincidences between individual practices and beliefs found in one or more societies throughout the world, but these coincidences do not constitute a universal, underlying pattern. Modern anthropologists who study twins have rightly drawn attention to the extraordinary diversity of African beliefs, even 'among peoples who live side by side'.[22] Some scholars have suggested that twin infanticide is not a separate phenomenon from infanticide in general,[23] but the harsh reality is that infant twins (just like infant girls) are regularly put to death or left to die because their desperately impoverished mothers cannot afford to raise them and because they are considered to be a manifestation of supernatural evil.[24] There is no such thing as Dioscurism or a single universal approach towards twins; there are hundreds of diverse attitudes, each one peculiar to its own society.

The followers of Harris organized his meandering works into a system. The ethnologist Sternberg in 1916, the folklorist Krappe in 1930, and another folklorist, Ward, in 1968, formulated the general principles of Dioscurism:[25]

(a) Dual paternity: twins are born when a human mother sleeps with a god and with a man.
(b) Twin tabu: the mother and her twins are banished from society, if not murdered.
(c) Magic powers: twins have superhuman powers, but their divine status is dubious; they use their powers to benefit the human race, they rescue people and promote fertility.

It would be absurd to claim that any of these three beliefs is accepted throughout the world, but it might be worthwhile asking whether they are found in India and Greece. They would, after all, provide us with one way of explaining why the twin gods are so helpful to ordinary human beings, because the three beliefs are interconnected. If one of the twins was human, and if both of them were banished from normal society, they would naturally sympathize with people of low or dubious status who have been abandoned by their fellow men. Harris believed that these principles applied to all twins, human twins as well as twin gods, but we shall find that the 'primitive' beliefs of the Indians and Greeks are rather more sophisticated than his own, and that they are quite capable of distinguishing between earthly twins and heavenly ones.

Double Paternity

Several pairs of twins are mentioned in the *Ṛgveda* (*RV*), but not one of these twins is the child of a human woman, and not one of them has two fathers. The parents of all the gods, Dyaus and Pṛthivī (heaven and earth) are twins (*yamiyā*, *RV* 9: 68, 3a); their daughters, Night and Dawn, are also twins (*yamiyā*, *RV* 3: 55, 11a). The first human beings, Yama and his sister Yamī, are once again twins (*RV* 10: 10), and they are the children of the goddess Saraṇyū and the mortal Vivasvant (*RV* 10: 17, 1c). Both Yama and Yamī are, of course, mortal. Finally, the divine Aśvins are also the twin sons of the same couple (*RV* 10: 17, 2c). As we shall see later, there are other versions of these stories in which Night and Dawn are sisters but not twins, and where the Aśvins are not even brothers; but the stories I have mentioned make it clear that twins do not require an extra father. In every case the twins are the offspring of one father, and the status of the twins is identical – either both twins are divine or both twins are mortal.

There is, in fact, only one case where two fathers produce children from one mother. The gods Mitra and Varuṇa see the very attractive Apsaras Urvaśī and cannot restrain themselves from ejaculating into a pot. The pot acts as a surrogate womb,[26] and from it the two babies Vasiṣṭha and Māna Agastya are born. Urvaśī is their mother because they are 'born from her mind' (*RV* 7: 33, 11b).

> They poured their combined semen into the pot;
> from the middle of it Māna came up,
> from it they say that the *ṛṣi* Vasiṣṭha was born.
> (*RV* 7: 33, 13b–d)

This story does not conform to the pattern of Dioscurism because all three parents are divine, and Vasiṣṭha and Māna Agastya are the sons both of Mitra and of Varuṇa,[27] and surprisingly they are not regarded as twins or even as brothers![28] As far as mythical twins are concerned, one father may beget twins, and two fathers may beget singletons.

When we turn to everyday twins, we find that Harris underestimated the biological knowledge of Vedic Indians. They associated the birth of twins with the problem of the mule. They realized that mules could not reproduce, and that the ability to produce mules was given instead to horses and donkeys. The reproductive power of the mule has, therefore, been distributed among other animals. The male ass is *dviretas* ('with double semen'), meaning that he can produce either an ass or a mule.[29] The *Taittirīya Saṃhitā* (*TS*) (7: 1, 1^2) explains it as follows:

> He (Prajāpati) followed the mule, took its semen, and placed it in the ass. Therefore the ass has double semen.

The *Taittirīya Saṃhitā* goes further, however, and declares that mares are also *dviretas*, since they can produce either a horse or a mule:

> He placed it in the mare. Therefore the mare has double semen.

This makes it clear that the word *dviretas*, in spite of its obvious etymology, is not restricted to males alone and means something like 'doubly reproductive'. Finally, the *Taittirīya Saṃhitā* declares that the reproductive capacity (*retas*, semen) of the mule is also granted to humans (*prajāsu*), and this is why they can produce twins:

> He placed it in humans. Therefore twins are born.

Instead of having the ability to produce one offspring belonging to either of two species, like a mare, human mothers can produce two offspring belonging to the same species. The capacity to produce the additional offspring (a mule or a second child) lies in human nature itself, not in multiplying the number of fathers. Twins are born because of this 'double reproductive capacity' (*dviretas*), not because of double paternity.[30]

The story of Vivasvant and Saraṇyū reveals that the ability to produce twins rests with the mother alone. When Vivasvant sleeps with her, he begets twins each time (Yama–Yamī and the Aśvins), but when he sleeps with Savarṇā, he has one son only, Manu. So twins have nothing to do with paternity, not to mention double paternity. The same attitude (which happens to be biologically correct) is also found in the medical texts of ancient India. Whether a woman has twins or not depends on the condition of her body, not on the father (or fathers). The action of the breath (*vāyu*) inside her body determines whether she will give birth to twins or a singleton.[31]

In Greece the situation is similar. The most important twins in the Greek pantheon are Apollōn and Artemis, and they are the children of Zeus and Lētō.[32] Both of their parents are divine, and Apollōn and Artemis are gods too. In the *Iliad*, there are three pairs of men who are explicity called twins (*didumoi*, or *didumaone paide*), and in two of these cases Homer specifies that there is one human father alone.[33] In the third case, they are the sons of the god Poseidōn and a mortal woman Molionē, though she is actually married to the human Aktoriōn.[34] All three sets of twins are mortal heroes.[35] As a final example, the Spartans believed that their unusual dual monarchy was created when the twins Eurusthenēs and Proklēs inherited the throne, but these twins had only one father, Aristodēmos, and one mother, Argeia.[36] Since both their parents were human, these kings were human too.

If a god and a human sleep with the same woman, the result will not necessarily be twins. Thēseus, for example, has a human father, Aigeus, the king of Athens, and a divine father, Poseidōn, the god of the sea. Even some historical characters enjoy such double or ambiguous paternity: Alexander the Great had a human father, Philip II, the king of Macedonia, and a divine father, Zeus, the king of the gods. As in India, double paternity is neither necessary nor sufficient for begetting twins.

There are, however, two cases of Dioscurism in the myths of Ancient Greece: the birth of Hēraklēs and his twin brother, and the birth of the Dioskouroi themselves. Both these cases are highly unusual, because normally the offspring of a divine parent and a human parent is a mortal hero, but Hēraklēs and one, if not both, of the Dioskouroi are gods.[37]

Alkmēnē, the human mother of Hēraklēs, sleeps with Zeus and with her human husband Alkaios on the same night. Hēraklēs is the son of Zeus, the insignificant Iphiklēs is the son of Alkaios. Hēraklēs is unique among the Greek heroes (twins and singletons alike), in that he becomes a god after his death. As Pindar puts it, he is a 'hero god' (*hērōs theos*)[38] – quite a contradiction, as far as Greek religion is concerned. Hēraklēs is, therefore, the only Greek mortal who lives on Olumpos, and the only Greek god who is also a ghost.[39] His apotheosis is not an original part of his story, because in the *Iliad* he still appears as a mortal,[40] and the fact that he is a twin is quite irrelevant to his apotheosis. This development in the cult of Hēraklēs is quite similar to the cult of Asklēpios, who has a divine father and a human mother but is not a twin. Asklēpios is regarded as a hero until the fifth century, and then the Greeks start to worship him as a god of medicine. Even though Hēraklēs was born as one of two twins, this twinship is given very little importance. Homer and Hesiod do not mention his brother,[41] and when Iphiklēs finally appears in the Hesiodic *Shield of Hēraklēs* (*c*.600 BC), he plays no role in the adventures of his famous brother.[42] Hēraklēs may conform to the Dioscuric model, but he is so exceptional a twin that he contradicts the validity of Dioscurism for other Greek twins.

The other case of Dioscurism (the only real one), is that of the Dioskouroi themselves. According to the version of their story that would eventually become the most popular one, Lēdē gives birth to two sets of twins, each set consisting of one mortal and one immortal child. Of her daughters, Helenē was the immortal one, whereas Klutaimnēstra was very mortal indeed and ended up being murdered by her own son; the twin boys of Lēdē, the Dioskouroi, were the divine Poludeukēs and the mortal Kastōr. Some Greeks concluded that Poludeukēs must have been the son of Zeus, and Kastōr the son of Lēdē's earthly husband, Tundareos. This was, however, just one of the stories told about the birth and status of the Dioskouroi. From the earliest period of Greek literature, we find four versions:

1. In Homer's *Iliad*, both of the twins are human and quite dead. Their father is not mentioned.[43]
2. In Homer's *Odyssey*, both of them are the sons of the human father Tundareos, and both of them are part-time gods. They spend one day as dead corpses in the earth, and the next day as gods in the earth.[44] Such a complicated arrangement is unheard of anywhere else in Greek thought.
3. The early sixth-century *Homeric Hymn to the Dioskouroi* declares that both of them are the sons of Zeus,[45] and throughout the hymn regards both of them as gods, as does the contemporary Hesiodic *Catalogue of Women*.[46] The *Homeric Hymn* significantly

declares that they receive *white* sacrificial victims,[47] which means that they are Olympian gods, not gods of the earth.[48] Such white victims would not be offered at a tomb.

4. Finally, the later sixth-century *Cypria* makes Kastōr human and Poludeukēs divine, but (as in version 2) Zeus grants them part-time immortality.[49] Pindar later explains this arrangement by giving each of them a different father, and this became the standard version of their story. (For all we know, the *Cypria* may have provided the same explanation.)

So we have four different ways of describing the Dioskouroi: both twins are fully human; both twins are fully divine; both twins are half-divine; and finally, one twin is human, one twin is divine. The variety of the stories told about their birth and status will, I hope, be clearer from the following chart:

	father	Kastōr	Poludeukēs
Iliad	?	0	0
Odyssey	0	½	½
Homeric Hymn	1	1	1
Cypria (while alive)	?	0	1
Cypria (after death)	?	½	½
Pindar (Poludeukēs)	1		1
Pindar (Kastōr)	0	0	

0 = human, 1 = divine, ½ = part-time divine.

Obviously, the Dioskouroi were regarded as straddling the line between Olympian gods and chthonic heroes, and these stories were various attempts at defining their status. They share this ambiguous status with Asklēpios and Hēraklēs. Due to the great benefits they confer on the human race, the ambiguous Dioskouroi and the mortal Asklēpios and Hēraklēs are worshipped as gods after they die, but they are too human and too earthly to be acknowledged as proper gods while they are still alive.

As a doctor, Asklēpios has to associate with blood, disease and pollution, and this undermines his status as a god. In fact, it even makes him lower in status than the average Greek hero.[50] The very same objections are raised against the Aśvins in India for precisely the same reasons. Medicine is unsuitable not only for gods but even for Brahmins.[51]

Hēraklēs rids the world of monsters and is a great champion of the human race, but he performs these tasks as a slave under the orders of a human king, Eurustheus, and even spent a year living as a woman and working as a slave to a human queen, Omphalē. This miserable existence once again raises questions about his status as a human being, not to mention his divinity.[52]

Finally, the Dioskouroi are torn between their divine identity as Indo-European horse gods and their human identity as local Spartan heroes, who were simply the mortal sons of the mortal king Tundareos. By playing around with the contrast between sons of Zeus and sons of Tundareos, the Greeks explored the ambiguous divinity of the horse gods.[53] Their divinity is ambiguous because looking after horses is a lowly and servile task, unfit for a god or a hero, just as the practice of medicine or performing labours at the behest of another (including, significantly, the task of cleaning out a stable) is unworthy of a god or hero.

No such ambiguous divinity attaches to human twins. Greeks and Indians alike believed that human twins were of human origin alone; even in their myths, Indians never conceived of such a thing as 'Dioscuric' twins, and in Greek stories about mythical twins, we only hear of two cases. In the case of Hēraklēs, double paternity is acknowledged but the twinship is ignored; in the case of the Dioskouroi, the twinship is obvious but the paternity and status of the heavenly twins is anything but clear.

Twin Tabu

The second great principle of Dioscurism is that the twins, and sometimes their mother too, are invariably ostracized from society, if not put to death. In Vedic India, the birth of twins, whether human or animal, was certainly regarded as unusual. In the case of cattle, it is presumed that the mother of twin calves is violent,[54] and this angry cow is handed over to a Brahmin, whose holiness transforms her dangerous energy into a blessing.[55] If the wife (or cow!) of a Brahmin bears twins, he must make a special expiatory offering to the gods during the twice-daily gift of milk to the gods, the Agnihotra ritual.[56] Their birth is an anomaly in the world, but it is listed among a series of mishaps, such as losing a sacrificial implement or eating the wrong food in the middle of a sacrifice. Twins are unusual, but their birth is not an irreparable violation of the natural order, and there is certainly no notion that the twins should be banished or killed.

On the contrary, twins are regarded favourably in the *Ṛgveda*, and are used as a symbol of equality and harmony. Two offerings of the sacred drink, soma, are described as 'twin sisters of equal rank' (*RV* 10: 13, 2), and another hymn notes with surprise that twins are not always equally strong (*RV* 10: 117, 9). As we saw, the ancestors of the human race were a twin brother and sister (Yama and Yamī). This was not viewed as a problem until the anonymous poet of *RV* 10: 10 realized that the human race would thereby derive from an incestuous marriage between a brother and a sister.[57] The discomfort of the poet arises, of course, from the incest, not from their twinship. Finally, we have the Aśvins themselves, who are worshipped as gods, and have 54 hymns composed in their honour. They do indeed travel around the sky, not because they have been banished, as Zeller suggests,[58] but because they are saviour gods (*nāsatyā*), patrolling the heavens and looking for people to rescue, as is explicitly stated in the *Ṛgveda*.[59]

The Greeks are also quite indifferent to twins. They display no anxiety about the birth of human twins, neither fearing them nor worshipping them. As we have seen, Homer mentions three sets of human twins, two of which are born in the usual way from one mother and one father, and nobody thinks any the less of them for it. The third set is a pair of conjoined twins, the Moliones or Aktoriōnes, whose mother Molionē bore them to her divine lover Poseidōn, even though she had a human husband Aktoriōn. Since Homeric warfare requires close cooperation between the chariot-driver and the warrior, these conjoined twins are actually the perfect team.[60] The only criticism offered against them is that they have an unfair advantage in chariot-racing![61] Twins did create a problem in Sparta when the queen Argeia gave birth to two boys, but the Spartans solved it by establishing two royal families.[62] Obviously there was no tabu against twins, and neither of the boys was banished or prevented from inheriting his father's throne.

Divine twins are not banished either. Lētō was relegated to the island of Delos by Hēra, but she had not given birth to the twins Apollōn and Artemis yet, and Hēra behaved just as badly towards other goddesses and women who slept with her husband. Nor did anyone banish Lēdē or her sons. In fact, the only twins to be outlawed in the Greco-Roman world are Romulus and Remus, and as their myth makes perfectly clear, they are sentenced to death because they threaten the reigning king. The same fate is suffered by many founding heroes (Moses, Cyrus, Jesus Christ) and has nothing to do with twins.

Magic Powers

In Greek and Indian myth, the horse gods come to the rescue when people are in trouble. Even in the *Ṛgveda* itself, the statement that the Aśvins 'come most readily to misfortune' is already regarded as an old saying.[63] If somebody has been thrown into a pit or into the sea by their enemies and left to die, the Aśvins hear their cry and bring them to safety.[64] If people are dying of thirst, the Aśvins supply them with something to drink.[65] They rejuvenate men and find wives for them;[66] they make sure that women are married and have children.[67] Finally, they perform all kinds of miraculous cures,[68] even bringing the dead back to life.[69] They are the doctors of the gods, and for this reason are treated with some ambiguity by the other gods: the Aśvins are needed because they can heal any defects in a sacrifice, but at the same time the other gods do not want to drink soma with anyone who would practise medicine. As the gods complain, 'These two are impure; they wander among men and are doctors.'[70] Medicine was regarded as a polluting profession that was unworthy of a Brahmin,[71] and yet these twin gods condescend to practise it. The Aśvins are almost too nice to the human race, but they still receive the same respect and worship as any other god.

Although the Greek twins had once possessed quite different human characteristics (horse-trainer and boxer), the Dioskouroi in their capacity as gods always act as a pair and are worshipped as a pair. They are especially loved for joining their worshippers at banquets, and for rescuing sailors at sea. During a storm, they appear as lights flashing around the masts, and the sailors know from this miraculous sign that they will be saved from shipwreck by the Dioskouroi. Like all gods, they also help their worshippers to win battles and competitions. The range of their activities is more limited than that of the Indian horse gods, but we see once again the same intimacy with the human race, and the same concern for people in difficulty.

The twin horse gods possess these powers, not because they are twins, but simply because they are gods. Human twins have no special powers and are subjected to no special disabilities or penalties. They are born in the normal human way, and the only ancient work we have in which the mystery of twinship is explored is the comedy of Plautus, *The Menaechmus Brothers*.[72] The comedy rests on the fact that nobody can tell the difference between the two twins, not even their nurse or mother,[73] which leads to various embarrassing situations. The Ancient Greeks and Indians knew that twins look alike, but they knew nothing of the higher mysteries of Dioscurism. The notion that twins are the product of double paternity, or that they should be ostracized, or that they possess special powers, never entered their mind.

If we turn from the strange fantasies of Dioscurism to the sane and sensible world of Vedic India and Ancient Greece, we discover that although they had not yet discovered the scientific details of childbirth, they knew that one man and one woman could indeed produce twins, and they also knew that some twins were identical, and others were not. Their twin gods were not different in this respect from human twins. The Aśvins are identical twins. In fact, they do not even have separate names, so we do not have to worry which one is which! Both are called Nāsatyas, both are called Aśvins. When they get married they share one wife between them, Sūryā, the daughter of the Sun. In Vedic myth, the Aśvins always act as a pair, as a single unit. In Vedic ritual, they are worshipped first thing in the morning, along with Agni, the god of fire, and Uṣas, the goddess of dawn.[74] The sacred drink soma is offered to both of the twins from one single cup.[75] The Aśvins fit in perfectly with Turner's description of twins: 'what is physically double is structurally single and what is mystically one is empirically two.'[76]

Whereas their Indian counterparts were always called the Aśvins or Nāsatyas as a pair, the Greek horse gods have their own individual names, Kastōr and Poludeukēs; and they have their own special qualifications – Kastōr is a horse-tamer, Poludeukēs is a boxer. In the post-Homeric version of their story, we even find that they were of different status during their lives on earth: Kastōr had been human and mortal, whereas Poludeukēs had always been divine.[77] Since the Greek twin gods are recognized as separate individuals, they marry one woman each. These women conveniently happen to be twin sisters, which helps to ensure the unity of the brothers while acknowledging their individuality.

The remarkable thing about the horse gods is not that they are twins, but that they are horse gods. To see why this might make them gods of low and questionable status, we shall have to examine the relationship between men and horses in the ancient world.

Horses

Raising Horses

The long story of horses and humans started on the Eurasian steppes about 6,000 years ago, and it started off rather unpleasantly. Horses were the predominant animals on the great Eurasian plain, which was their natural habitat.[78] The early people who lived on the steppes hunted wild horses for their meat.[79] Even today, the Kazakhs, at the eastern end of the steppes, still breed horses mainly for their meat.[80] The first people to eat horses extensively were the Sredny Stog people (4200–3800 BC), who lived at the western end of the steppes in southern Ukraine.[81] It is not clear, however, whether these horses were domesticated or hunted. Since the Sredny Stog people ate so much horse meat, especially at the village of Dereivka, the American archaeologist, David Anthony, believes that they must have been raising herds of domesticated horses.[82] By studying the ages at which these horses were killed and eaten, however, the British archaeologist, Marsha Levine, concludes that they were wild horses and that the inhabitants of Dereivka had hunted them.[83] Unfortunately, this method has led to dubious results elsewhere,[84] but we can at least say that there is no undisputed evidence for domesticated horses before the fourth milleninium BC.

The first clear evidence for raising domesticated horses, as distinct from hunting wild horses, comes from Botai (3700–3000 BC), at the eastern end of the steppes in Kazakhstan.[85] Horses are an important source of meat on the steppes because unlike cows, sheep and goats, they can push snow aside with their hooves and eat the grass underneath, and they can also break through ice to get at the water below. They do not have to be provided with winter fodder. For these reasons, the people living on the steppes had a high incentive to domesticate horses.[86] It is almost impossible, however, to herd horses unless you are on horseback yourself, and this impossibility has been clearly stated both by Western scholars,[87] and by Mongolians for whom horse-raising is a way of life.[88] It is not very surprising, therefore, that the evidence from Botai reveals that the people living there both raised horses and rode them.[89] The pottery at Botai also shows that they drank mare's milk,[90] which is clear evidence that these people had domesticated horses.[91] The date of the village of Botai also agrees with the genetic evidence that horses were bred selectively for their colour from about 3000 BC.[92]

So, sometime around 3500 BC, the people of the steppes raised domesticated horses for meat and milk, and they also rode them. Riding was dangerous and uncomfortable, because although they did have reins with organic bits, they had no saddles[93] and no stirrups.[94] This is the way people rode horses for a long time, and almost 4,000 years later, the emperor Marcus Aurelius is still sitting on a horse blanket without saddle or stirrups. In the fourth millennium BC, there was no question of using horses as draught-animals, since there was no wheeled transport whatsoever until the ox-cart reached the steppes shortly before 3000 BC.[95] The ox-cart must have started off in a heavily forested region,[96] but it was used from the Rhine to the

Indus by 3000–2500 BC.[97] These ox-carts had solid wheels made of wood and moved at about 3 km/h.[98] Meanwhile, the Sumerians of Iraq tried using some other animals to pull these ox-carts. From 2500 BC, we find onagers and donkeys drawing carts and heavy battle wagons.[99] Interestingly, these animals had been treated like horses up until this time and had been raised only for their meat.[100] The west Asians realized that donkeys were more useful alive than dead, and eventually the people of the steppes and west Asia would discover that horses were also too valuable to eat.

Even after the introduction of the ox-cart, horses could not be used as draught-animals, because until the invention of the stiff collar in the third century AD[101] they could not draw a heavy vehicle without choking themselves. So throughout the third millennium BC, there was a division of labour: the ox was used as a draught-animal, the newly domesticated horse was used for riding alone.[102]

Horse Riders

The development of horse riding around 3500 BC did not produce any major changes in Bronze Age culture, and almost 3,000 years would pass before its significance for warfare was fully understood. Throughout those centuries, the status of riding was low and it was not practised by the Bronze Age elites. Horses were more or less ignored until the Sintashta culture (2100–1800 BC) of the southern Urals developed a very fast, light-weight vehicle that was specially designed for them: the chariot.[103]

Since Proto-Indo-European predates the twentieth century BC, the late invention of the chariot implies that the Indo-European horse gods must originally have been horse riders, not chariot drivers. The main function of horse riders on the steppes was herding and raiding, so the horse gods were first worshipped by people who visualized them as cowboys herding large numbers of sheep, cattle and horses, or making tribal raids on horseback to seize these animals from their neighbours.[104] Both of these were precarious tasks, and would naturally be assigned to reckless young men, whose lower status matched the lowly art of riding. This is why the youth and lowly status of the horse gods are constantly emphasized in the myths of India and

Greece. They are the sons of the sky-god, not independent adult males; they are young and unmarried; they do not deserve to join the soma-drinking gods in India; their divine status is dubious in Greece.

Cowboys and shepherds are always marginal figures in society, and horse riding did not improve their status. To quote an expert on the topic, 'Although [. . .] a venturesome young man was evidently "able" to ride a galloping horse, the act was both dangerous and uncomfortable'.[105] In India, the socially unacceptable young men known as *Vrātyas* continued to seek wealth through cattle raids, long after such raids had been abandoned by warlords, and these young men rode horses.[106] When they were on their raids, they imitated the violent behaviour of Rudra and his army; when they came back to the village, the better-behaved Maruts were their role-models.[107] The Maruts themselves are often called 'young men' (*maryas*) in the *Ṛgveda*,[108] and because of this parallel with the *Vrātyas*, the Maruts are the only Ṛgvedic gods depicted as horse riders.[109]

The first horse riders also served as scouts on the Eurasian steppes, searching for new sources of water and metal.[110] These were lonely and time-consuming tasks, but even if they were undervalued in the Bronze Age, they were essential both for maintaining its great wealth in cattle, and for the production of the metals that made this new age possible.

Given the Bronze Age function of riders as scouts, it is perfectly natural that the horse gods would be sent off on search and rescue missions, seeking out people who find themselves endangered in remote places where only the horse gods could find them. Their myth was constantly revised and updated, but the essential character of the horse gods as young scouts and cowboys was firmly established on the Bronze Age steppes and is recognizable behind all their later incarnations.

Chariot Drivers

The horse gods are young cowboys from the Bronze Age, but this age was changed forever by the invention of the chariot. This great innovation took place in the Sintashta culture (2100–1800 BC) of the southern Urals. The essential feature of the chariot was its new light, spoked wheel, which weighed only a tenth of what a solid, disk-wheel of the same size would have weighed. This new feature brought the weight of the entire chariot down to 30 kg,[111] so it was light enough to be drawn by horses. Their owners were proud of this new invention, so when they died, their horses and chariots were buried along with them.[112] These chariot-burials date from the twenty-first century BC.[113] Their chariots were very light vehicles, consisting of a wickerwork body big enough for one man only, and they had light wheels with eight to 12 spokes.[114] The chariot-burials reveal that by the twenty-first century BC, the chariot is already regarded as an important status symbol,[115] so important that no powerful person would want to leave this earth without one. With this new invention, humans had increased the maximum speed of their vehicles to 30 km/h.[116]

The impact of this new invention was enormous. It was similar in effect to the invention of the automobile, because it did not just increase the speed at which people travelled; it created an entirely new culture based on the ownership of chariots. The relatively late invention of the chariot also has implications for Indo-European myth and language. Since Hittite already existed as an independent language by the twentieth century BC, Proto-Indo-European must have been spoken before the invention of the chariot. This is why there is no common word for chariot among the Indo-European languages. Instead, they use words like 'roller' (Sanskrit *ratha*), 'runner' (Latin *currus*), 'framework' (Greek *harma*),[117] or 'carrier' (Mycenaean *wokhā*, Homeric *okhea*, German *Wagen*) to describe this new invention, which did not exist at the time of the original language from which they are all derived.

Since Sanskrit and Avestan have the same word for chariot (Sanskrit *ratha*, Avestan *raθa*) and charioteer (Sanskrit *rathastha*, Avestan *raθaešta*), Indo-Iranian must still have been one language when the chariot was invented.[118] The formulas for building a chariot were already embedded in the Indo-Iranian language, when its illiterate speakers carried this technique with them in their minds[119] and put it into practice in the new environments of Iraq (the kingdom of Mitanni), Iran, and India. These formulas would of course have been accompanied by memorized actions, but the verbal formulas themselves were vitally important, as can be seen from the horse-training manual of Kikkuli. When Kikkuli, the horse-trainer from Mitanni, wrote this work in the fourteenth century, he was still using Indic formulas, even though he must have written the work in Hurrian (the language of Mitanni). These Indic formulas were faithfully preserved once again when his work was translated into Hittite.[120] This memorized, oral art of making chariots and training horses was a rare skill, and the chariot was a luxury good, the prized possession of a great chieftain, on the Eurasian steppes, in Iran, and in India. In west Asia, the chariot became immensely popular and its use spread rapidly throughout the great kingdoms of that region. Its adoption was so rapid that it may in fact have been invented there independently,[121] though the presence of Indic-speaking 'horse-grooms and horse-trainers' in Mitanni[122] and the use of Indic formulas by Kikkuli suggests that these Indic-speaking immigrants influenced, if they did not actually create, the west Asian tradition of building chariots.[123]

What makes this tradition remarkable is its mass production of chariots. From 1950 to 1850 BC, we find depictions of horses and chariots in Anatolia.[124] A century later, King Zimri-Lim (1779–1761 BC) of Mari, a Mesopotamian city, had a fleet of chariots,[125] and by around 1750 BC, one Hittite city alone possessed 40 chariots.[126] By the sixteenth century, we have evidence that chariots were being used by the Kassite rulers of Babylon,[127] the kings of Mitanni,[128] the pharaohs of Egypt,[129] and the warlords of Mycenean Greece.[130] Within a few centuries the possession of a vast number of chariots had become obligatory for the great kingdoms of western Asia and for the neighbouring lands of Egypt and Greece. Each of the great kingdoms had 1,000 chariots at its disposal,[131] and a large class of chariot-owners emerged, who were called *maryannu* in Mitanni, Assyria, and Egypt, a term that some scholars relate to the Sanskrit *marya* ('young man').[132] These armies of chariots were very expensive to maintain, because in addition to the archer and his chariot-driver, they also required specialists to build and repair the chariot, and to train and look after the horses.[133]

In spite of its extraordinary popularity, many historians believe that the chariot was of little practical use in warfare. They argue that an archer could not have shot with any accuracy unless the ground was very smooth, and that a mass attack with chariots would have resulted in a disastrous pile of broken chariots and kicking horses.[134] The main function of the chariot would, therefore, have been to provide an exclusive taxi service to and from the battlefield, where the warrior would fight on foot.[135] This sceptical notion of the chariot is based on Homer, but he is not a reliable source for the chariot warfare of the Bronze Age, because he lived in an age of footsoldiers armed with spears. Even the older epic tradition, on which he was relying, cannot be trusted, because it originated in northern Greece, where there were no Bronze-Age palaces or chariot-armies. Neither Homer nor his tradition could have imagined a west Asian combat in which two armies of 1,000 archers would charge onto a battle-field in chariots.[136] In the epic tradition and in Homer's own day, the chariot was 'nothing more than a prestige vehicle'.[137] In the Bronze Age, on the other hand, the chariot had been a weapon of mass destruction, and surely no less accurate than the later Parthian technique of shooting from horseback.

Of course, it also served as 'a vehicle of prestige'[138] in the Bronze Age, demonstrating to the world that its owner was a member of the international elite of charioteers.[139] In Vedic India, its possession brought prestige and this was more important than its military function.[140] In Assyria, the possession of a chariot meant that its owner was a member of the warrior nobility,[141] and the king was constantly shown hunting from his chariot on the stone reliefs that decorated the walls of his palace.[142] In Israel, when one of David's wicked sons wanted to overthrow him, 'he procured a chariot and team with fifty guards to run ahead of him'.[143] In Ancient Egypt, the chariot was used very explicitly to show a man's social status[144] and, as in Sintashta, it was often entombed with its owner.[145] The pharaoh himself was shown in his chariot hunting wild animals or triumphing over his enemies.[146] In Mycenean Greece, the chariot-horse was an 'aristocratic' animal, and the chariot itself was used in 'ceremonial contexts'.[147]

Horse Riders in a World of Charioteers

Since the chariot was such a powerful symbol of social status, it was inevitable that it would become the only form of transport used by the gods in Vedic India,[148] and that the gods of classical Greece would travel in chariots.[149] Dyēus and the Indo-European horse gods, who had been worshipped long before the invention of chariots, had to get used to this new elitist technology. In India, the Aśvins could not ride, because 'this was not suitable for a soma-drinking god'.[150] In fact, the *Ṛgveda* clearly mentions riding only in two hymns. In a hymn celebrating a horse sacrifice, the poet apologizes for any rider who may have hurt the horse with his heels or whip (*RV* 1: 162, 17).[151] The only other reference to horse riders appears in a hymn to the Maruts. The poet clearly regards horse riding as an unsuitable activity for gods or heroes: 'the heroes spread their thighs, like women giving birth' (*RV* 5: 61, 3). Elsewhere in the *Ṛgveda*, every god, including the Aśvins and the Maruts, is visualized as a chariot driver.

As we have seen, the young Maruts make their appearance as horse riders in book five of the *Ṛgveda* only because their human counterparts, the impoverished young *Vrātyas*, were reduced to such disreputable practices as horse riding and small-scale cattle raiding.[152] The *Vrātyas* preserve the ancient connection between horse riding, cattle raiding, and young men who are not yet socially respectable.[153] A young *Vrātya* may have to content himself with horse riding for the time being, but his dream is to have 'a chariot, a servant (*marya*), cows, and the love of young women' (*RV* 1: 163, 8).[154] Instead of being a young man himself (*marya*), he will have a young servant (*marya*) of his own to boss around.[155] When a man acquires a chariot, he is no longer a young, dependent, student, living in his teacher's household; he has become an independent, adult sacrificer with a fireplace and household of his own.[156] Riding is a sign of youth, dependence, and low status. Falk sums up the status of riding in Vedic India in a manner that brings out its association with youth and poverty:

> This form of transport was associated with young men who were looked upon as dubious and who had their heavenly counterparts in the Maruts. Every settled householder or

> sacrificer made sure that he would not lower himself to their social status by riding, even though he had no doubt gone around on horseback himself when he was a young man.[157]

Hopkins points out that in the later epics of India, riders still act as mere assistants to the king:

> The horse-riders form a sort of aides-de-camp, and are dispatched with messages by the king, not being ordinary cavalrymen, but knights on horseback attending the monarch.[158]

In the Hittite Empire, riders likewise served as messengers, and the word *pithallu* meant both 'messenger' and 'rider'.[159] Tablets from Nuzi (modern Kirkuk) show that in the kingdom of Mitanni (northern Iraq), horse riders acted as 'messengers, courriers, and scouts'.[160] In Egypt, the main function of riders in wartime was to serve as 'mounted scouts',[161] and on reliefs commemorating the Battle of Kadesh (1274 BC), horsemen are specifically labelled as 'scouts'.[162] As elsewhere, riding was considered 'socially degrading' for an Egyptian prince.[163]

The same distaste for riding prevailed in Ancient Greece. In the Bronze Age, Mycenaean warriors drove chariots, and depictions of horsemen are very rare.[164] Later, we find that neither the Greek gods nor the Greek heroes permit themselves to ride, and Homer deliberately excludes riding from the narrative of his epics.[165] Riding only appears in two similes, which make it clear that his refusal to mention it elsewhere is deliberate. In *Iliad* 15: 676–686, Aias is jumping around on the beached ships, and Homer compares him to an acrobat leaping from one horse to another; in *Odyssey* 5: 371, Odusseus has been shipwrecked and is straddling a piece of wood, just like a rider on a horse. Both the similes have a touch of humour to them, and in each case the hero is in an awkard and slightly ridiculous situation. The mocking tone of these similes demonstrates the low status of riding. There is, however, one instance in which a hero does ride a horse. When Odusseus seizes some Thracian horses,

Diomēdēs wants to steal a chariot for them (*Iliad* 10: 503–506). Athēna appears and tells Diomēdēs to stop wasting time, so he jumps on the horses and rides them back to the Greek ships (*Iliad* 10: 512–514). The horses have been broken in to accept riders, and the two heroes are perfectly well able to ride.[166] They simply refuse to ride unless they are forced to by desperate circumstances. Homer accurately reflects the understandable preference of Bronze Age warriors for driving a chariot, even though the effective use of horsemen and footsoldiers, and the development of cavalry was making chariot warfare obsolete in Homer's day.[167]

A century later, Sappho (late seventh–early sixth century) could say that some people regard an army of horsemen as the finest thing on earth,[168] and the Greeks would eventually be quite happy to depict their heroes on horseback. They never felt comfortable, however, with the idea of gods riding horses. Poseidōn, who produced the first horse, is on a few rare occasions shown on horseback, and the only other exception to this tabu against gods riding is the Dioskouroi, the horse gods themselves.[169] Since the Dioskouroi were not part of the epic tradition,[170] they were never subjected to its rules, which derive from the late Bronze Age. Their image as horse riders was never brought up to date, and was preserved unchanged among later Greeks to whom chariot warfare was unknown.[171]

The contempt for horse riders was so strong in the Bronze Age that some of it was even directed against the driver of the chariot – he was a disposable servant. In one of the graves where a Sintashta chieftain was buried with his chariot, his driver and horses had been put to death and were buried in a separate chamber above the chieftain's body.[172] The same prejudice lives on in the *Mahābhārata*, where the Pāṇḍāva warriors refuse to associate with Karṇa, because he is merely the son of a charioteer. The chariot driver was inferior to the warrior, but horse riders were utterly disdained in the new world of chariot owners.

Horse gods who ride seem unusual and too modern in India and Greece, but they are behaving in a perfectly normal way. It is the chariot-driving gods who have changed and been updated. Ironically, the Greeks and the Indians view the radical idea of depicting gods in chariots as a timeless and unchangeable sacred tradition. Nobody dared to challenge this invented tradition later on when chariots became a thing of the past. The young horse gods ride and serve others not because their image is 'younger', in the sense of more recent, but because their image dates back to a time when the world was younger.

The Indo-European Horse Gods

There is a strong connection between youth, service, and riding horses, a connection that is not restricted to a particular society or language. It merely indicates that the image of these gods was formed in the early Bronze Age, when young men of low status rode horses. There is, however, a closer connection that ties together the horse gods of the Sanskrit, Greek and Baltic traditions. These horse gods are called the 'descendants of Dyaus' (*Divo napātā*) in India, the 'boys of Zeus' (*Dios kouroi*) in Greece, and the 'sons of Dievs' (*Dieva dēlī*) in Latvia. They are, therefore, related to the Indo-European sky-god Dyēus and are Indo-European gods themselves. Even the form of the ritual offerings made to them in Ancient Greece reveals their Indo-European origin.[173]

Before speaking of Indo-European gods, we must specify the meaning of this adjective. 'Indo-European' is a term that has been often misused, because it properly refers to languages alone, and should never be used for peoples or cultures. We can speak of 'Indo-European' languages, meaning those languages that are derived linguistically from a common 'Proto-Indo-European' language. This language may have disappeared before the advent of writing, but its basic vocabulary and grammar have been reconstructed with considerable accuracy by linguists over the past two centuries. We can speak of 'Indo-European' metre and poetry, because rhythmic speech is merely a specific form of a language, with its own special syntax and vocabulary.[174] And finally, we can speak of 'Indo-European' myths, or more accurately of Indo-European themes, that survive in the later myths of the Indo-European languages. When we learn a language, we do not just learn words and rhythms; we also learn certain formulas that help to describe reality. A formulaic expression found in several ancient languages refers to 'men and cattle', making it clear that slaves were regarded as possessions, as human cattle,[175] while the formulaic story of St George and the Dragon goes back to an old Indo-European theme of a hero killing a snake.[176] So there are shared Indo-European vocabularies, grammars, rhythms, and themes, but we cannot speak of the 'Indo-Europeans', because there never was such a thing as an 'Indo-European' race or culture.[177]

The simple mistake of confusing language with race was first made by Friedrich Schlegel in 1808.[178] Schlegel had learned that the various Indo-European *languages* derive *linguistically* from a common original language, and he incorrectly concluded that the *speakers* of these various languages must derive *racially* from a common Indo-European people. Schlegel gave the fatal name of 'Aryan' to this imaginary people in 1819.[179] Schlegel was not a racist himself; he was a German liberal who campaigned for Jewish emancipation (achieved in 1848 after his death), while his wife was the daughter of the German Jewish philosopher Moses Mendelssohn and the aunt of the great romantic composer Felix Mendelssohn.[180] Schlegel based the name of this imaginary race on the Sanskrit word *ārya*, but this harmless word simply means 'noble', and only in the moral and religious sense of the word 'noble'.[181] It was the term used by the Buddha when he spoke of his four *noble* truths (*ārya-satyāni*) and the *noble* path (*ārya-mārga*) of Buddhism. It does not refer to race, and before the nineteenth century, there was no such thing as an 'Aryan' or 'Indo-European' people. This people exists only in the paranoid world of race-madness.[182] So if we think of the Aśvins as Indo-European gods, we must not imagine that they have blond hair and blue eyes, or that they speak Sanskrit with a distinctly English or German accent.[183] It simply implies that horse gods like the Aśvins are found in the myths of several Indo-European languages, and since these myths share enough common features, they must have existed in the story-telling vocabulary of the original Proto-Indo-European language. Just as the words in a sentence will be organized by the rules of Indo-European syntax, so the structure of a story will be based on the themes of Indo-European myth. The ethnic identity of the people who spoke this language and told such stories is both unknowable and irrelevant.

Stories behave more as waves than as particles, and they spread like the bubonic plague rather than like an invading horde of heroes, or a tragic chorus of migrants. We can only observe the waves they cause and the symptoms they produce in a given society; we cannot identify the carriers. If we try to name the carriers, we cease to analyse an ancient myth and start to invent a new myth of our own.[184] This is the source of the great nineteenth-century myth of the Aryan invaders and their wandering tribes. We are left, therefore, with the mobile and moving stories themselves, but that should be quite enough for us; they have managed to entertain people for thousands of years.

If we discover some common Indo-European themes in the story of the horse gods, what can we do with this knowledge? In the nineteenth century, the answer was obvious. The first scholars of Indo-European myths were romantics, and they were frustrated by the reactionary politics of Christianity, by its indifference to the natural environment, and by its repression of human sexuality. They believed that Indo-European myths must have celebrated the wonders of nature,[185] including human sexuality,[186] so they went hunting for the 'Natural Substrate' that lay hidden beneath the surface of every myth. Every battle between two heroes, every defeat of a monster by a hero, was really a representation of the conflict between day and night, between summer and winter. Every hero was the sun, every heroine was the moon. Indo-European myths were boiled down until they had all been turned into the same, tasteless mush.[187]

The school of Nature Mythology became so distasteful that it led people to abandon comparative mythology throughout the first half of the twentieth century. It was brought back to life by Georges Dumézil, who followed Durkheim in believing that religion is a symbolic way of thinking about society. The mythic themes shared by Indo-European languages belonged to the Proto-Indo-European language, and these themes would therefore be based on the society of the speakers of Proto-Indo-European. This society, he believed, was organized into three classes: the priestly rulers; the warriors; and the producers. Indo-European myths would, therefore, reflect and explain this social structure.

If Schlegel was wrong to argue from a shared family of languages to the existence of an 'Aryan' race, it is equally wrong 'to extend that reality into the social sphere'.[188] Dumézil is arguing from a shared linguistic heritage to a common society.[189] There may be shared myths that show an interest in bishops, knights, and pawns, but we cannot conclude that there was an Indo-European society based on these three classes. In fact, Dumézil's three social functions seem to be based on the three Indian classes, which did not develop until the *end* of the Ṛgvedic period,[190] and on the three feudal estates, which emerged considerably later. Their absence from Ṛgvedic India, their dubious survival and rapid disappearance in the Greco-Roman world of the farming citizen-soldier, and their abolition in Dumézil's homeland during the summer of 1789, make it quite clear that the three classes are not inherently Indian or European.[191]

Dumézil's approach is ultimately as reductive as nature mythology, but society is a more interesting topic than the weather, and it does tend to have a greater impact on what we say and do. It would take some effort to show that Cinderella is rather like the moon (unseen by day, brilliant at night), but it is impossible not to notice that there is a bit of a social gap between her and the prince. Fortunately, Dumézil was not reductive by nature, and what makes his work stand out is his love and respect for the unique details of every myth he analyses. Although his three classes were consigned to the dustbin of history in 1789, and do not merit apotheosis in reconstructed myths, it is hard not to admire Dumézil's retelling of the *Mahabhārata*.[192] It brings clarity to an epic that seems overwhelming and unmanageable, and it inspired the work of Hiltebeitel.[193] Dumézil's analysis of the early Roman kings is superior to the tedious details of Livy or Dionysius, and he makes these legends sound intelligent and interesting.[194] There was indeed a risk that Dumézil's approach might turn mythology into conservative sociology, but he succeeded in evading it. His love for the imaginative freedom of myth overcame his belief in the rigid structures of its thought, his scholarship overcame his odious politics.[195]

Dumézil has indirectly shown us what we could do with Indo-European themes. We can point them out and acknowledge their existence, but the life of myth is based on its variety, and we must always respect the variations more than the theme that lies behind them. Bruce Lincoln's work, *Priests, Warriors, and Cattle*,[196] provides a model for such an approach, and he represents a third generation of comparative mythologists, by his effective use of anthropology. His comparison between East Africans and Indo-Iranians has disinfected his work from any taint of racism, which has always been a ghost haunting Indo-European studies, ever since its playing-field was invaded by a gang of right-wing hooligans and racist scholars in the late nineteenth century.[197] Lincoln's work explains why Indo-European myths would focus on the cooperation and rivalry between priests and warriors in the endless pursuit of cattle. There is an interesting ideological war being fought between the warrior culture of the Nuer and the priestly traditions of the Dinka, between the warrior-kings of India and the priests who obey no king but Soma, between the violent cattle raiders of Iran and the reformist Zoroastrians, and these culture wars are reflected in their religions and their myths.

Myth cannot, however, be the story of warrior-kings and priests alone. A chess-game may ultimately be decided by the knights and the bishops, and every myth may seem to tell their story,[198] but we must not forget the pawns, because there are always more of them.[199] I would, therefore, like to focus on the cowboys rather than on their sacred and noble employers, and I am encouraged by some ancient poets who did the same thing. The great Iranian god, Ahura Mazdā, may have saved the ox from the meat-eating warrior and placed this animal under the protection of the great priest and prophet Zarathushtra, but the hymns (*Gāthās*) of the prophet also tell us that the god did not forget the humble men who did the daily work of looking after cattle. When the ox asked the god for help and protection, Ahura Mazdā replied:

> The creator shaped you for the herdsman and the pastoralist.[200]

Homer may have celebrated the epic achievements of warrior-kings and priests, but even though the Muses despise the 'shepherds living in the fields' as 'low-class disgraces, mere bellies',[201] they still granted their favours to one of those peasants, Hesiod. They inspired him to denounce the 'gift-eating kings' (*dōrophagoi basilēs*),[202] and to celebrate the hard life of the Greek peasant. They transformed him from a poor local poet to a Panhellenic spokesman.[203] We all know and love the wonderful stories told by priests and warriors in which they themselves appear as magicians and heroes, but we must not forget the third estate. These 'People of No Importance' have their own stories too, stories about horse-riding gods who take care of them and understand the life they lead.

CHAPTER 2

THE FAMILY OF THE AŚVINS

The horse gods appear for the first time in the earliest Sanskrit work known to us, the hymns of the *Ṛgveda*. In these hymns, which were composed somewhere between 1500 and 1200 BC, the twin gods are called the Aśvins, which means 'horse gods'. They are also called the Nāsatyas, which means 'saviours',[1] and this is what they are called both in the *Ṛgveda* itself and also in a document from west Asia, the fourteenth-century Treaty of Mitanni. In this document, the Nāsatyas and the other major Vedic gods (Indra, Mitra, and Varuṇa) are called upon to witness the treaty.[2] So 'Nāsatya' is not just a fanciful or poetic way of referring to the horse gods, it is their official, sacred title no less than the name Aśvins. As Bergaigne remarks, 'the Aśvins are essentially saviour gods'.[3]

If we are to judge by the number of hymns addressed to them in the *Ṛgveda*, the Aśvins must have been very popular gods. The main god of the Vedic Indians is Indra, a heroic and rowdy god; he tops the list with about 250 hymns composed in his honour.[4] Next come Agni, the god of fire (200 hymns), and Soma, the divine drink of the gods (120 hymns).[5] This is only natural, because the Vedic Indians honoured the gods by making offerings into a sacred fire, and Agni is both this fire itself and the fire god who transports their offerings to the other gods. Soma is likewise both a god and a real plant, and the greatest sacrifice that can be made to the gods is an offering of soma juice, poured into the sacred fire. After the chief god, Indra, and these two gods who are physically present in the everyday world and act as intermediaries between gods and men, come the Aśvins with 50 hymns.[6]

The Aśvins are very close to human beings and just as helpful as Indra, but in a somewhat quieter way. Indra is the mighty god who kills monsters with his thunderbolt, he is 'the lord of power' (*śacipati*); the Aśvins, in contrast, are 'the lords of splendour' (*śubaspatī*), pleasant, wonder-working gods (*dasrā*) who help people in trouble. The poet Viśvāmitra celebrates the 'gentle friendship' (*sakhiyaṃ śivam*)[7] of the Aśvins, and even in his time it was already an ancient tradition that the Aśvins 'come most readily to deal with misfortune'.[8] As Bergaigne pointed out a century ago, Indra is warlike, the Aśvins are peaceful; he helps fighters, they help victims; he defeats the enemy, they protect the oppressed; he is an ally, they are saviours.[9] We shall see later that there is some tension between Indra and the Aśvins; Indra does not quite approve of them, he considers them low-class. But even Indra himself sometimes needs their services, and the friendly Aśvins gently come to his assistance.

Morning Gods

From the hymns of the *Ṛgveda*, one thing is obvious about the Aśvins – they are up and about early in the morning.[10] The priests, of course, are awake before anyone else. They have to get up every morning while it is still dark, and make their offerings to the fire god Agni and the sun god Sūrya. This libation to Agni (the *agnihotra*) kindles the fire and energizes the sun every day.[11] Such a Vedic sunrise is described by a poet of the Vasiṣṭha family in a hymn (RV 7: 67, 2–3) that honours all three morning gods: Agni the fire god, Uṣas the dawn goddess, and the Aśvins.

Agni shines out, lit up by us,
the end of the darkness is seen.
The banner of Uṣas is conspicuous in the east,
made for the splendour of Heaven's daughter.

Now the eloquent Hotar priest, o Aśvins,
honours you with hymns, o Nāsatyas.
Come here to us by many paths,
with your chariot of light and treasure.

A hymn from the Atri family (*RV* 5: 76, 1) begins in the same way:

Agni lights up the face of Uṣas,
the god-loving voices of the inspired priests rise up.
Come here now on your chariots,
o Aśvins, to the overflowing hot milk (*gharma*).

In each hymn, we see how the priests bring the sacred fire back to life, the fire god awakens the dawn goddess, and the priests invite the horse gods to enjoy their hymns and join them in a cup of hot milk.

On the main day of a soma sacrifice, the invitation is more elaborate. On this day, the soma stalks will be crushed to make soma juice, and this juice will be offered to the gods. The priests start the day off with a hymn called the Morning Recitation (*prātaranuvāka*). This long hymn, consisting of selected verses from the *Ṛgveda*, is recited just before daybreak, and it honours the three morning gods, Agni, Uṣas, and the Aśvins. The priests will crush the soma and honour the other gods only after this Morning Recitation has been performed. If the soma sacrifice is a long overnight ritual (*Atirātra*), one that lasts throughout the first day and the following night up until the morning after, then the entire sacrifice will end on the second morning with a second recitation to the same gods called the Aśvin Hymn (*Aśvinaśastra*).[12]

The relationship between the Aśvins and Uṣas is especially close. When the priests sing their chant of praise to her, the Aśvins wake up too (*RV* 3: 58, 1):

The goddess with the shining chariot brings the bright light.
The chant of praise for Uṣas has awoken the Aśvins.

In one hymn, Uṣas is even asked to wake them up (*RV* 8: 9, 17):

> Wake up the Aśvins, o Uṣas,
> up, o great kind goddess.

She goes first, and the Aśvins follow her path (*RV* 1: 180, 1; *RV* 1: 183, 2; *RV* 8: 5, 2). In one case (*RV* 1: 180, 2), she is even called their sister, which would mean that all three are the children of the sky god, Dyaus.[13] This family relationship is really just a way of explaining that the Aśvins are morning gods and must therefore be born from the daylight. The real relationship between them is that of colleagues who are up and about early in the morning; Uṣas is 'the friend of the two Aśvins' (*sakhā aśvinor*, *RV* 4: 52, 2 and 3).

Yaska's Theory about the Aśvins

This close connection between the Aśvins and Uṣas led early Indian scholars to make some curious speculations about the true nature of the Aśvins. The first to discuss the Aśvins in some detail was Yaska, who composed his *Nirukta* (*Interpretation*) in the fifth century BC. Previous Indian thinkers had separated the twin gods, and since the Aśvins appear at twilight, they had placed each of the gods on either side of the line dividing the powers of light from the powers of darkness.

> So what are the Aśvins? Some people say Heaven and Earth. Others say Day and Night. Others say Sun and Moon.
> (*Nirukta* 12, 1)

Nineteenth-century scholars in Europe continued to make such identifications with cosmic phenomena,[14] but some thinkers in Vedic India were more down-to-earth:

> The historically-minded say that they were two kings who did good deeds.
> (*Nirukta* 12, 1)

In spite of its secularist reductionism, this Euhemerist view presents us with a more accurate image of the Aśvins. Yaska himself rejects all of his predecessors, both the nature school of mythology and the historical interpretation. Instead, he pursues a structuralist approach, based on his reading of several Vedic hymns. Here are the main stages of his analysis:[15]

> Stage 1: Moist Darkness and Hot Light.
> They pervade the universe, one with moisture (*rasena*), the other with light (*jyotiṣā*).
>
> (*Nirukta* 12, 1)

> Transition from Stage 1 to Stage 2.
> The part sharing in darkness (*anutamobhāga*) is the atmosphere (*madhyama*), the part sharing in light (*jyotirbhāga*) is the sun (*āditya*).
>
> (*Nirukta* 12, 1)

> Stage 2: Dark Atmosphere and Heavenly Sun.
> One is the promoter of great strength (*sumahato balasyerayitā*) and is the atmosphere (*madhyama*), the other is called the blessed son of heaven (*divo 'nyaḥ subhagaḥ putra*) and is the sun (*āditya*).
>
> (*Nirukta* 12, 3)

> Stage 3: Night and Dawn.
> One is the son of Night (*vāsātya*),[16] the other is the son of Dawn (*uṣaḥ putra*).
>
> (*Nirukta* 12, 2)

These compressed statements refer to the origin of the universe, and they give the Aśvins a major role in its development.

Stage 1 – Moist Darkness and Hot Light

Rasa usually means juice, but in Yaska's Stage 1, it is a dark cosmic liquid that pervades the entire universe along with hot cosmic light (*jyotis*). In the transition to Stage 2, Yaska makes it clear that this liquid is identical with darkness, because although the universal light is again called *jyotis*, he now speaks of the other primal element as darkness (*tamas*) rather than liquid (*rasa*). By darkness and liquid, Yaska means the inert dark waters of Not-Being (*asat*) at the beginning of the world, from which the active bright heat (*tapas*) of desire emerges to produce Being (*sat*).[17] For Yaska the Aśvins represent these two primal elements of Moist Darkness and Hot Light.

Transition from Stage 1 to Stage 2

When Moist Darkness and Hot Light emerge as separate forces, they interact to produce our universe. The Atmosphere (*madhyama*) emerges from Darkness, the Sun (*āditya*) emerges from Light.

Stage 2 – Dark Atmosphere and Heavenly Sun

At this second stage, the visible Atmosphere below (*rajas*, *madhyama*) has separated from the invisible Heaven above (*dyaus*, *vyoman*). This distinction between Atmosphere and Heaven is so important that when the creation hymn wishes to describe the situation before our universe emerged, it does so in the following way:

> There was no Being at that time, there was no Not-Being, there was no Atmosphere (*rajas*), there was no Heaven (*vyoman*) beyond.[18]

This separation of the Atmosphere from Heaven marks the real beginning of our universe, but since the Aśvins are going to operate in our part of the universe, Yaska cannot identify them as Dark Atmosphere and Bright Heaven. One Aśvin is equated with the Atmosphere itself (*madhyama*), but the other cannot be Heaven, he can only be the son of Heaven (*divo. . .putra*). He is therefore equated with the Sun (*āditya*), which is the only part of Heaven that we can actually see.

Stage 3 – Night and Dawn

The third great division of the universe is the distinction between Day and Night, which emerges naturally from the previous division between Dark Atmosphere and Heavenly Sun. Once again, Yaska relates this development to the Aśvins. Each of the Aśvins has a different mother, the sister-goddesses Night (Vasāti) and Dawn (Uṣas), so each Aśvin is identified with the opposite side of this cosmic division through his mother.

The equation of the Atmosphere (Stage 2) with Darkness (Stage 1) and Night (Stage 3) may seem a little strange at first, but it is taken for granted in Vedic thought. In the hymn to the Sun (*RV* 10: 37), the god turns his bright side (*jyotis*, light) to the world during the day, but when he turns his dark side to humans during the night, the word used to describe this darkness is *rajas*, atmosphere.[19] The connection between Moist Darkness, Atmosphere and Night in the middle world is just as natural as the association between Hot Light, Heaven, and Day in the world above.

The fundamental elements of our world are Watery Darkness and Fiery Brightness, Dark Atmosphere and Bright Heaven, Atmospheric Night and Heavenly Day. These elements did not exist originally, they had to be produced, and every morning they have to be recreated by Vedic ritual. When the Aśvins arrive in the morning, they both embody and reproduce these divisions on which the universe is based.

As with most structuralist analyses, this one will be a lot clearer from a chart:

Stage 1	
Water (*rasa*, *ambhas*, *salila*) Darkness (*tamas*)	Heat (*tapas*) Light (*jyotis*)
Stage 2	
Atmosphere (*madhyama*) Atmospheric darkness (*rajas*)	Heaven (*dyaus*, *vyoman*) Heavenly sun (*āditya*)
Stage 3	
Night (*vasāti*)	Dawn (*uṣas*)

Yaska's interpretation of the Aśvins is brilliant and exciting, because it makes them play a major part in the birth of the universe, but it is an intellectual house of cards, and it is based on very slim evidence. The divisions that he mentions are, of course, vitally important ones in Vedic thought, but in order to equate them with the Aśvins, he must first analyse the twin gods as if they were radically different from each other, and then make a further leap of faith, and identify these contradictory Aśvins with the polar oppositions of Vedic cosmogony. There is little evidence, however, for such a polarization of the Aśvins. The only Vedic passages that separate the two Aśvins are the following:

> Born here and there, they are in harmony,
> flawless in their body and their names,
> one of you is called a victorious patron of Sumakha,
> the other is called the fortunate son of Heaven (Dyaus).
> (*RV* 1: 181, 4)

> Born separately and flawless,
> you have entered a friendship with us.
> (*RV* 5: 73, 4cd)

> One is called the son of Night,
> the other is the son of Dawn.
> (*Nirukta* 12, 2)

Yaska himself cites the first lines, which come from the *Ṛgveda* (*RV* 1: 181, 4 = *Nirukta* 12, 3), and the last lines, which come from an unknown source. He admits, however, with disarming honesty, that these passages present us with a highly unusual depiction of the Aśvins.

> In general, they are praised together, appear at the same time, and perform the same activities. (*Nirukta* 12, 2)

Yaska is telling us, in effect, that his wonderful interpretation is based on a very selective use of his sources, and that it distorts the general picture of the Aśvins. Yaska had done his research well, and 25 centuries later, Dumézil, who also hoped to find two opposite horse gods, had to admit that there was no further evidence for such a distinction. He makes this confession with regret: 'Not only the Vedic hymns, but also the ritual treatises and their commentaries hardly allow us to observe any distinction between the two divine twins.'[20]

The Dioscuric Theory about the Aśvins

In their discussions of twin gods, Harris and Zeller take the two Ṛgvedic passages cited above as evidence for the 'Dioscuric' theory that the Aśvins are the product of one mother and two fathers, and that one of these fathers is divine, the other is human.[21] Neither of these conclusions is warranted.

Two Fathers. There are indeed two fathers in *RV* 1: 181, 4; Dyaus is the father of one of the Aśvins, and the other Aśvin has a different father, but the identity of this second father is unclear. The words *sumakhasya sūrir* would most naturally mean that this Aśvin is 'a patron of *sumakha*'. *Makha* means 'sacrifice',[22] and 'patron (*sūri*) of the good (*su*) sacrifice (*makha*)' would make perfect sense, as would Yaska's paraphrase *sumahato balasya īrayitā*, 'promoter of great strength'.

Geldner takes the word 'son' (*putra*) from the next line, applies it to this one too, and translates it as 'the victorious patron, *the son* of Sumakha', but who is Sumakha?[23] Since it means 'good sacrifice,' Zeller plausibly identifies him as Vivasvant, the first sacrificer.[24] That would help to reconcile this story about the birth of the Aśvins with the more usual story that both of them were the sons of Vivasvant and the goddess Saraṇyū (*RV* 10: 17).

These lines do not, however, say anything about the mother or mothers of the Aśvins. The mention of Dyaus in the fourth line suggests that the second Aśvin's mother was Uṣas,[25] and we have the unidentified line quoted by Yaska (*Nirukta* 12, 2) to show that when Uṣas is regarded as the mother of one Aśvin, Night is the mother of the other.[26] Their parents would therefore be Dyaus and Uṣas for one Aśvin, Vivasvant and Night for the other. So one Aśvin is associated with Dawn and Heaven, the other with Night and

Vivasvant, who is usually a mortal in the *Ṛgveda*, but might here be the later Vivasvant the sun god. We do have two fathers here, but we cannot jump to the conclusion that there is only one mother shared by these two fathers, and this version of the story strongly suggests that the Aśvins are neither twins nor brothers.

One Mother. Harris and Zeller make much of the phrase 'born here and there' in the first line of *RV* 1: 181, 4. This phrase clearly refers to a mother or mothers giving birth in two different places, but Harris wants it to mean something very different and much more complicated. He wants it to say that *one* mother gives birth in *one* place to twins begotten by *two* different fathers. Harris starts by interpreting 'here and there' as 'earth-born and sky-born'. He then reinterprets his own paraphrases to mean 'child of the sky-god' and 'child of an earthly father'.[27] Zeller tries to save Dioscurism by translating *jātā* as 'begotten' (*erzeugt*).[28] She argues that we must interpret the phrase *iheha jātā* in terms of the next lines, and since these lines make it clear that the Aśvins had different fathers, she takes *iheha jātā* to mean 'begotten by different fathers'. 'Begotten' is not the most obvious way to translate *jātā*, but even if we accept that it means 'begotten' in this line, *iheha* would mean not that two fathers from different places slept with one mother (Zeller, out of loyalty to Harris, assumes that there can only be one mother), but that the fathers slept with the mothers in two different places.

When we turn to the only other place in the *Ṛgveda* where the expression *iheha jātā* is used, we shall discover that it has nothing to do with one mother sleeping with two different fathers. In the Atri family book, we find the following statement: 'born here and there, they are twin sisters and related' (*RV* 5: 47, 5d). The twin sisters here are either Heaven and Earth (*Dyāvāpṛthivī*), both of whom are regarded as feminine when coupled like this, or Night and Dawn (*Naktoṣāsā*), who are always regarded as sisters, though not always as twins. Heaven and Earth are the first gods, and obviously could not have had two fathers; Night and Dawn have only one father, Dyaus. 'Born here and there' simply means that Heaven and Earth emerged at opposite ends of the world, with the Atmosphere in-between. Night and Dawn belong to different worlds, so that when Dawn appears Night must leave (*RV* 7: 71, 1). The remainder of the verse states that in spite of being opposites, they are nevertheless twin sisters.

Returning now to the Aśvins, the phrase 'born here and there' simply means that for this poet, Agastya, the Aśvins were born into different worlds (the earth and the sky). As a matter of fact, Agastya believes that they are not identical twins. This is an unusual view, as Yaska correctly points out and Zeller acknowledges.[29] The remainder of the verse reveals that in spite of being different, the two gods are nevertheless in harmony; they are very good-looking, and both of them have the same name. Significantly, Agastya does *not* state, as did *RV* 5: 47, that the gods in question are twins.

Having established that the Aśvins themselves, though a team, are quite different from each other, the poet Agastya then goes on to make the further and more radical claim that the Aśvins have different fathers. Zeller makes the following comment on this claim:

> So the Aśvins have two fathers, and can, therefore, be distinguished as a human and a divine partner. This very fact, however, proves their identity as twins beyond a doubt.[30]

Once again, she is assuming that we have two fathers sleeping with one woman, that one is human and one is divine, and that their children are twins. Everywhere else, the Aśvins are twins, and have one father and one mother. When Agastya gives them two fathers, we cannot automatically assume that he has anticipated Harris by giving the Aśvins two fathers but only one mother. There is no evidence for such a notion in Vedic India, and the archetypal twins, Yama and Yamī (whose names simply mean 'twin boy' and 'twin girl') have one father and one mother, Vivasvant and Saraṇyū (*RV* 10: 17, 1–2).[31]

The Vedic View of the Aśvins

Like Agastya in *RV* 1: 181, Yaska played with the idea that the Aśvins were not identical twins, but he was too honest to conceal that his elaborate interpretation went against the general picture of the Aśvins presented in the Vedas. It is not, however, his last word on the subject, because he frames his polarizing interpretation of the Aśvins inside a very different view of the gods. Before he embarks on his structuralist analysis, he quotes a stanza that he does not bother discussing, because its meaning is self-evident – 'it is explained by reciting it' (*Nirukta* 12, 2):

> You go around in the night,
> like two black rams.
> When, o you Aśvins,
> did you go to the gods?

This stanza, from an unknown Vedic source, assumes that the Aśvins are identical twins. It is as hard to tell the difference between them as it is to distinguish between two black rams in the dark! Right after this statement, Yaska makes the remark we saw above, which once again assumes that they are identical: 'in general, they are praised together, appear at the same time, and peform the same activities' (*Nirukta* 12, 2). Instead of pointlessly trying to differentiate between the two Aśvins, Yaska focuses instead on the very obvious and enormous difference that separates both of them from all the other gods. This is a very significant aspect of the Aśvins in Vedic thought, and will lead to a wide range of speculations in the later interpretations of Vedic ritual. In the *Ṛgveda*, we learn that the Aśvins were not allowed to join the other soma-drinking gods: 'the Embryo of Truth (soma) was hidden from the twins' (*RV* 9: 68, 5b).

Yaska ends his discussion of the Aśvins with a similar contrast between the Aśvins and the other gods:

> The time of these two gods is up until the rising of the sun. At that point, the other gods receive libations.
>
> (*Nirukta* 12, 5)

Yaska does not develop this thought, but he is aware that the contrast between the Aśvins and the other gods belongs to the mainstream of Vedic thought and ritual, unlike his own subtle attempts to make distinctions between the two Aśvins. This strange gap that separates the Aśvins from the other gods is, as we shall see later, one of their most striking features and posed an intellectual problem that quite literally gave splitting headaches to many scholars in Vedic India.[32]

The Birth of the Aśvins

The Aśvins are normally regarded as the twin sons of one mother and one father. In one hymn, their father is Dyaus: they are 'born of Dyaus' (*RV* 4: 43, 3c); in another, their mother is almost certainly Uṣas, though neither she nor they are mentioned by name in this riddle-hymn (*brahmodya)*:

> The mother of the twins gave birth to the twins. . .
> . . . born as a pair, they pursue beauty,
> destroying darkness, at the base of the fire (*tapus*).[33]
>
> (*RV* 3: 39, 3)

The presence of the twins, the destruction of darkness, and the power of the fire leave us with little doubt that the mother mentioned here is the third morning deity, Uṣas. The Aśvins are the children of the incestuous relationship between Dyaus and his daughter Uṣas. On five other occasions, they are referred to as 'the descendants of Dyaus' (*divo napātā*), an ambiguous expression that could mean son or grandson of Dyaus.[34] This genealogy from Dyaus and Uṣas is based on the fact that the Aśvins are morning gods, but a different story was to become the standard Vedic version of their birth, and would inspire close analysis in the *Brāhmaṇas*. This story focuses on the close bond between the Aśvins and the human race, and on the corresponding gap that separates the Aśvins from the other gods. It appears for the first time in the funeral hymn attributed to Devaśravas:

> Tvaṣṭar is making a marriage for his daughter!
> So every living being comes together there.
> The mother of Yama, being married,
> the wife of great Vivasvant disappeared.

They hid the immortal woman from the mortals,
and creating a woman of the same type (*savarṇā*),
they gave her to Vivasvant.
She gave birth to the Aśvins when this happened.
Saraṇyū abandoned her two twin children.

(*RV* 10: 17, 1–2)

In this hymn, the marriage that Tvaṣṭar is organizing sounds like a *svayaṃvara* ('her own choice'), a marriage where suitors assemble and the young woman herself is free to choose her husband.[35] The male guests who attend ('every living being') may, therefore, be suitors as well as guests. The important point is that these living beings include both gods and men,[36] so it is not too surprising when Saraṇyū marries the somewhat mortal Vivasvant. In books 1–9 of the *Ṛgveda*, he is always regarded as a mortal,[37] and he is renowned as the first man to offer sacrifice to the gods, both in the Iranian Avesta and in the Indian Vedas.[38]

Vivasvant and Saraṇyū get married,[39] and she gives birth to Yama, the first man to die and later lord of the dead, and to his twin sister Yamī. At this point, Saraṇyū disappears and abandons her twin children. The hymn only names Yama, but Yamī is included later in the phrase 'her two twin children'.

We now learn that her disappearance has been planned by the gods, who hide this immortal goddess from 'the mortals'. This word is in the plural form (*martiyebhyaḥ*), and it reveals that Vivasvant is regarded as a mortal in this hymn. The plural must refer to *three* people at least, and since there are no other eligible mortals around apart from Yama and Yamī, it must include Vivasvant as one of them. The gods seem to feel sorry for Saraṇyū, and they decide to rescue her from her unequal marriage. They cannot, however, mistreat Vivasvant either, so they provide him with a 'woman of the same type'. The word *savarṇā* is ambiguous,[40] because it could mean a woman just like Saraṇyū herself, or a woman just like Vivasvant, in other words a mortal being like himself. Vivasvant seems to be quite happy with this consolation prize from the gods, or perhaps she resembles Saraṇyū so closely that he has not even noticed that she is not the same woman.

When Saraṇyū 'abandons her two twin children', she is already pregnant with the Aśvins and then gives birth to them among the gods, which probably explains why the Aśvins are divine, unlike their twin siblings. In this hymn, Yama and Yamī are the first human beings, just as Yima is the first man in Iran.[41] This is the Indo-Iranian version of human origins accepted by the newly arrived Vasiṣṭha family (*RV* 7: 33, 9), but the more usual Indian story traces the human race back to the eponymous Manu.[42] Naturally, our hymn does not mention Manu, but other passages from the *Ṛgveda* make it clear that the *ṛṣis* knew the alternative story that Manu was the son of Vivasvant and his new substitute wife (the *savarṇā*).[43] In this version of the story, the Aśvins would be divine because their mother was the goddess Saraṇyū, and Manu would be a mortal because his mother was a created being, the *savarṇā*.

The Aśvins are not very important in this Ṛgvedic funeral hymn,[44] and the main point of these stanzas is to tell us how Yama, the king of the dead, was born from a mortal man and a goddess. This is why his sister Yamī is ignored and the Aśvins are barely mentioned.

Almost a millennium later, the story was retold in greater detail by Yaska in his *Nirukta*.

> A story is told about this. Saraṇyū the daughter of Tvaṣṭar bore a pair of twins (*yamau*) to Vivasvant the Āditya. She placed another woman of the same type (*savarṇām anyām*) there instead. Taking on the form of a mare she ran away. Vivasvant the Āditya took on the form of a horse, went after her, and mated with her. From this the Aśvins were born. From the surrogate woman, Manu (was born).
>
> (*Nirukta* 12, 10)

Yaska's version of the story starts in the usual way with Saraṇyū giving birth to Yama and Yamī, but then it becomes quite different. This time Saraṇyū does not need any help from the other gods. She runs away herself and it is she who creates the substitute wife for Vivasvant. Yaska's phrase '*another* woman of the same type' makes it clear that the substitute was a woman who looked just like Saraṇyū herself, rather than a woman who was a mortal just like Vivasvant.[45]

This trick is quite enough to conceal her disappearance, but Yaska adds a new episode to the story. He tells us that Saraṇyū turned herself into a mare and then ran away from her family. Vivasvant is deceived neither by the substitute nor by the metamorphosis. He changes into a horse himself, and in this form he mates with her, and she gives birth to the Aśvins. Yaska seems to have used this story about the metamorphosis to explain why her sons are horse gods and bear the name Aśvins. Bloomfield makes the very Ovidian suggestion that Saraṇyū changed into a mare because she could only be satisfied by a stallion![46] He believes that the story was taken for granted in the Ṛgvedic hymn: the metamorphosis can be 'inferred from the designation of her second pair of twins as "the horsemen (*açvin*)"'.[47] This is precisely the sort of reasoning followed by Yaska and by the Brahmins, who use this story of her metamorphosis to provide a folk-etymology for the name of the Aśvins. The Greek parallels to this story suggest that it was not invented by Yaska,[48] and that he was probably drawing on an old myth. This does not mean, however, that we can read Saraṇyū's transformation back into the *Ṛgveda*, because there is no case of metamorphosis in the *Ṛgveda*. The Vedic parallels cited by Bloomfield refer to the transformations of Prajāpati and derive from later cosmological speculation.[49] Prajāpati is barely mentioned, even in book 10 of the *Ṛgveda*, and nowhere does he appear as a cosmogonic god, except in the very last stanza of *RV* 10: 121 (which was probably inserted later).[50] Perhaps the notion of gods in animal-form was regarded as a 'primitive' one that had to be excluded from the *Ṛgveda*.[51] Its late appearance in the Vedic tradition suggests a squeamishness about metamorphosis that Plato would have strongly endorsed.[52]

Yaska makes a final addition to the story as we saw it in *RV* 10: 17. He tells us that Manu was the son of Vivasvant and the substitute wife. Here he is once again using an old story, but this time it is one that has been accepted by the Ṛgvedic *ṛṣis*.[53] The story about Manu was omitted from *RV* 10: 17 only because it was not relevant to a hymn about Yama. In his interpretation of the Ṛgvedic hymn, Yaska is simply drawing on all the old traditional material he can find, but the application of the horse metamorphosis to the story of Saraṇyū is probably his own contribution.

Later again, during the Puranic age,[54] Śaunaka's *Bṛhaddevatā* tells the story of Saraṇyū in even greater detail:

6: 162. Tvaṣṭar had twin children,
Saraṇyū along with Triśiras.
He himself gave Saraṇyū
to Vivasvant in marriage.

6: 163. Then Yama and Yamī were born
to Saraṇyū by Vivasvant.
And both of them were also twins,
but the older of them was Yama.

7: 1. Without her husband's knowledge,
Saraṇyū created a woman of the same appearance (*sadṛśī*);
she entrusted her two children to this woman,
turned herself into a mare, and departed.

7: 2. Not realizing this, Vivasvant
begat Manu in this woman;
he too became a royal sage,
just like Vivasvant in splendour.

7: 3. When, however, Vivasvant became aware
that Saraṇyū had departed in the shape of a mare,
he quickly went after the daughter of Tvaṣṭar,
having turned himself into a horse of the same type (*salakṣaṇaḥ*).

7: 4. When Saraṇyū recognized Vivasvant
in the form of a stallion,

she approached him for sexual intercourse,
and he mounted her there.

7: 5. Then in their agitation
the semen fell on the ground,
and the mare sniffed up that semen
in her desire for offspring.

7: 6. Now from the semen which had just been sniffed up,
two young men were born,
Nāsatya and Dasra,
who are renowned as the Aśvins.

(*Bṛhaddevatā*, 6: 162–7: 6)

Śaunaka closely follows Yaska's version of the story, but he adds some details of his own. The *Ṛgveda* seems to have regarded Saraṇyū's marriage as a *svayaṃvara*, but the *Bṛhaddevatā* makes it quite clear that she did not choose her own husband; Tvaṣṭar married her off to Vivasvant (6: 162).[55]

As in Yaska's version, it is Saraṇyū herself who creates the substitute, but Śaunaka makes it very clear that the substitute looks exactly like Saraṇyū (*sadṛśī*, 7: 1), that Saraṇyū intends to deceive her husband with this substitute, since she cleverly created it while her husband was not around (7: 1), and that her trick succeeds (7: 2). Śaunaka adds a nice detail in telling us that Saraṇyū entrusted the twins Yama and Yamī to the substitute. Neither the poet Devaśravas nor the scholar Yaska had thought about finding a baby-sitter for the twins. Saraṇyū's trick works so well that Vivasvant has a baby (Manu) with the substitute before he realizes that he has been fooled. In order to produce this effect, Śaunaka must alter the normal birth order. In the *Bṛhaddevatā*, her children appear in the sequence Yama–Yamī, Manu, and Aśvins, rather than in the traditional order, Yama–Yamī, Aśvins, and Manu, that we saw in the *Ṛgveda* and *Nirukta*. Śaunaka also has to present us with the implausible scenario of Saraṇyū wandering around as a mare for over nine months, while the substitute (*sadṛśī strī*) produces Manu, before Vivasvant decides to pursue her as a stallion.

When they meet again, Śaunaka once again gives agency to Saraṇyū, since it is she who approaches Vivasvant for intercourse. The most extraordinary innovation that Śaunaka makes to her story is the grotesque deatil of her insemination through the nose (7: 5–6). Just as the metamorphosis of Saraṇyū and Vivasvant into horses had been used by Yaska to provide a folk-etymology for the name Aśvins, this new detail was created to explain their other name, Nāsatyas, which Śaunaka must have interpreted as Nose Gods, deriving this name from the word *nas*, 'nose'.[56] As Bergaigne pointed out long ago, Yaska and Śaunaka are drawing on old myths to create new stories of their own that will explain obscure lines in the *Ṛgveda*.[57]

The story of Saraṇyū raises some doubt about the divinity of the Aśvins. How can the sons of a mortal man and a goddess be real gods? It also emphasises the close relationship between the Aśvins and the human race. They are the sons of Vivasvant, the first man to offer sacrifice; the brothers of Yama, the first man to die, and of his twin sister Yamī; and the half-brothers of Manu, the eponymous ancestor of the human race (*manuṣya*). As the gods themselves say in the *Taittirīya Saṃhitā*, 'These two are impure, they associate with human beings (*manuṣyacarau*).'[58]

The Aśvins and the Daughter of the Sun

A Chariot Built for Three

Even though they were originally gods of horse riding, the Aśvins, like all the other gods, drive a chariot, but theirs is unique because it has three wheels and three seats. The third seat is for their shared wife, the Sun Goddess, the Daughter of the Sun (Sūryā, *Duhitā Sūryasya*). This *ménage à trois* is such an important characteristic of the Aśvins that a riddle can simply refer to them as 'the two men who travel by bird with one woman' (*RV* 8: 29, 8). No embarrassment is expressed over the sharing of one woman by two men; in fact, the number three is given a favourable, mystical significance. Just as the first two steps of Viṣṇu can be seen by mortals, but his third step goes beyond the visible world and cannot even be seen by birds (*RV* 1: 155, 5), so two wheels of the chariot in which Sūryā rides with her husbands are visible, but the third wheel requires supernatural insight (*RV* 10: 85, 16):

> O Sūryā, the brahmins (*brahmānaḥ*) know two of your wheels correctly,
> but that one wheel which is hidden, only seers (*addhātayaḥ*) know it.

The three-wheeled chariot belongs to the Aśvins ('Aśvins in their three-wheeler', *RV* 10: 85, 14ab), but now Sūryā owns it too ('your wheels, Sūryā', *RV* 10: 85, 16a). This hymn does not dwell on her relationship with the Aśvins. It appears only as a brief interlude (*RV* 10: 85, 14–16), since it interferes with the main theme of the hymn, Sūryā's marriage with Soma. Other hymns describe the beginning of her affair with the Aśvins. It all starts off when she goes away with them in their chariot:

> When Sūryā mounted your chariot...
>
> (*RV* 5: 73, 5a)

The phrase 'mount a chariot' (*ratham ā-sthā*) is a formula for elopement,[59] so she is not just asking the Aśvins to drive her somewhere. She has decided that she will be a permanent feature of their chariot. We find a variant of the same formula (*ratham ā-gam*) when the goddess Rodasī decides to run away with the Maruts, and her misbehaviour is explicitly compared with Sūryā's: 'she mounted the chariot, just like Sūryā' (*RV* 1: 167, 5c).[60] In one hymn that mentions Sūryā's elopement, there is an interesting feminist reversal of the normal formula: 'the wonderful chariot that the Aśvins mounted (*ratham ā-sthā*) for Sūryā' (*RV* 8: 22, 1).[61] The same reversal is expressed in another hymn (*RV* 4: 43, 6), where the poet celebrates 'the journey by which you became the husbands of Sūryā'.[62] In effect, Sūryā is abducting them, they are mounting the chariot for her.

This irregular sort of elopement, based on mutual desire and aiming at sexual pleasure alone, would later be classified by the law-books as a *gāndharva* marriage.[63] In the *Ṛgveda*, however, Sūryā is not motivated by any desire to obey law-books. She does as she pleases, and the poet Paura is surely criticizing her irresponsibility when he expresses pity for the winged horses of the Aśvins. Suddenly faced with the unexpected task of transporting the hot and dazzling Daughter of the Sun, the horses have to 'keep away the heat from burning them' (*pari* [. . .] *ghr̥ṇā varanta ātapaḥ*, *RV* 5: 73, 5d).[64] In the *Ṛgveda*, Sūryā is presented as an independent and impetuous goddess, who is a bad influence on an impressionable young goddess like Rodasī, and if the Aśvins themselves are overjoyed that she has decided to run off with them, their horses find her a little overwhelming. It is not surprising that Sūryā and Rodasī run away with young gods of dubious social status who ride horses, because in Vedic India an independent heiress was quite likely to pursue one of the penniless *Vrātyas*, who are the human counterparts to the horse-riding Maruts.[65] At least the Aśvins are respectable enough to possess a chariot, even if it is an unusual three-wheeled chariot.

Sūryā's Wedding

Sūryā's behaviour would be more socially acceptable if her relationship with the Aśvins had arisen from a proper *svayaṃvara* marriage, as Geldner and Jamison suggest.[66] In that case, the Aśvins would have come as formal suitors along with other hopeful men, she would have chosen them as her husbands, and they would be properly and legally married, if it were not for the annoying prohibition of bigamy. A *svayaṃvara* obliges a woman to choose just one man from among her suitors; unfortunately, she is not allowed to keep all of them, she is not even allowed to keep two of them, not even if they happen to be twins, like the Aśvins.[67] Sūryā did indeed choose the Aśvins, but she chose to run away with them instead of marrying anyone.

According to Geldner, however, there are some hints in the *Ṛgveda* that the Aśvins came to the wedding of Soma and Sūryā not as friends of the groom, but as rival suitors for her hand, that there was a general competition with Sūryā as the prize. The main evidence for this is the presence of yet another rival, Pūṣan. Three times in the book of the Bharadvāja family, he is described by the formula *kāmena kṛta*, 'overcome by desire' (*RV* 6: 49, 8b and *RV* 6: 58, 3d and 4d). In *RV* 6: 49, 8b, 'he is overcome with desire and wins praise (*arka*)'; in *RV* 6: 58, 3d, 'you go on a mission to Sūrya (the sun god), overcome with desire, longing for glory (*śravas*)'. It is possible that Pūṣan longs for the praise and glory of marrying Sūryā, but when the *Ṛgveda* speaks of the Aśvins marrying her, they do it for 'splendour' or 'beauty' (*śrī*), not for praise (*arka*) and glory (*śravas*).[68] And if Pūṣan were really presenting himself as a suitor for Sūryā's hand, it would be strange to describe this as a 'mission' or 'embassy' (*dūtyā*) to her father, because a 'messenger' or 'envoy' (*dūta*) always acts on someone else's behalf.

The only place where Pūṣan's desire is clearly directed towards Sūryā herself is in *RV* 6: 58, 4d, where 'the gods gave him, overcome with desire, to Sūryā'. This cannot mean that they allowed him to marry her, because no version of her story says so, and this expression would be a very unusual way of describing a marriage, because usually a daughter is 'given' to a husband, not the other way round. We can understand this puzzling verse by looking at two other strange statements made about Pūṣan. When the Aśvins run away with Sūryā, we are told that 'the son Pūṣan chose them as his fathers' (*RV* 10: 85, 14d); in another hymn, we are told that Pūṣan is 'the suitor (*didhiṣu*) of his mother' (*RV* 6: 55, 5a). The term *didhiṣu* does normally mean 'suitor' or 'husband', but its literal meaning is 'wishing to obtain,' 'striving after', and in this case *mātur didhiṣu* could mean 'longing for a mother'. Geldner is surely right in concluding that when the gods give Pūṣan to Sūryā, he becomes her son.[69] This would explain why he chooses and receives the Aśvins as his fathers rather than competing against them as his rivals, and why he longs for and receives Sūryā as his mother, rather than suing for her hand in marriage. Pūṣan wants praise and glory and a mother like Sūryā and a father. He succeeds in all his goals; he even manages to find two fathers. There is no evidence that Pūṣan ever attended a *svayaṃvara* and presented himself as a future husband for Sūryā.[70]

The same theme of a competition for her hand might also be deduced from the account in the *Taittirīya Saṃhitā*: 'you came to the wedding (*vahatu*) of Sūryā on your three-wheeler, wishing to sit together' (*TS* 4: 7, 15⁴). There is nothing unusual about sitting together (*saṃsadam*) on a chariot, because a chariot always carries a team of warrior and driver working closely together. So there would be no point in mentioning it unless something strange were going on here. The three wheels may reveal an ulterior motive. There will be more than the usual pair 'sitting together' on this chariot; it will have an extra stowaway passenger when they go home from the wedding. Whatever ulterior motives the Aśvins may hold, however, they are going to someone else's marriage ceremony, not their own. We find a similar statement in *RV* 10: 85, 14: 'you Aśvins came to the wedding (*vahatu*) of Sūryā on your three-wheeler, asking (for her).'[71] Since they are attending the wedding of Sūryā and Soma, their official role is merely to act as best men or friends of the groom. They may secretly want to wreck the wedding and run away with Soma's bride, but that does not transform her wedding with Soma into a *svayaṃvara*.

The First Part of the Wedding Hymn

Fortunately, we do not have to speculate about these matters, because Sūryā's wedding is described in great detail in the Marriage Hymn (*RV* 10: 85).

> Soma was the groom (*vadhūyur*),
> the two Aśvins were friends of the groom (*varā*),
> when Savitar gave Sūryā to her husband (*patye*),
> and she approved in her mind.
>
> (*RV* 10: 85, 9)

Since Savitar gives her in marriage to Soma, this cannot be a *svayaṃvara*, but luckily for everyone, Sūryā approves of her father's decision.[72] The Aśvins are described as the *varā*, which must mean 'friends of the groom' here.[73] It is too late for them to turn up as rival suitors, since the sun god has already given his daughter to one husband (*patye*, singular), and Soma is already described as the bridegroom (*vadhūyu*).[74] The ceremony proceeds in the proper way, and in the end Sūryā mounts the traditional matrimonial wagon (*anas*)[75] and sets off for her new home:

> Sūryā mounted the wagon (*anas*) of the mind,
> going to her husband.
>
> The wedding procession of Sūryā proceeded,
> Savitar had sent it on its way . . .
>
> (*RV* 10: 85, 12–13)

A Brief Interruption

At this point, when it seems that the wedding has come to an end, the Aśvins suddenly intervene and ruin everything for Soma.

> . . . when you two Aśvins came to the wedding of Sūryā
> on your three-wheeler, asking for her.
> All the gods agreed to it,
> and Pūṣan chose you to be his fathers.
>
> When you two lords of splendour came
> to choose (*vareyam*) Sūryā.
>
> (*RV* 10: 85, 14–15)

This hymn treats the marriage of Sūryā and Soma as the model for everyone to follow, so it is quite shocking that the gods would approve of the outrageous behaviour of the Aśvins. The gods have retroactively recognized the elopement as a legal marriage, just as the law books will one day declare that an elopement is a legitimate *gāndharva* marriage. We have two very different stories here: a wedding between Soma and Sūryā, and in stanzas 14–16 a polyandrous elopment with the Aśvins. The story of her relationship with the Aśvins was was too well established to be ignored, so it is dutifully inserted into the wedding hymn. It is, of course, completely incompatible with the story of her marriage to Soma, so it has to be ignored throughout the rest of the wedding hymn.[76]

The Final Part of the Wedding Hymn

After telling us the story about Sūryā and the Aśvins, the wedding continues as if we had heard nothing. Soma and Sūryā are once again portrayed as a happy couple, and she has decided to make do with one husband alone (*patye*, singular again in stanza 20 as in stanza 9).

> Decorated with Butea flowers, made of cotton-tree wood,
> multi-coloured,
> golden-coloured, nicely-turning, with good wheels,
> mount this place of immortality, Sūryā,
> make this a nice wedding for your husband (*patye*).
> (*RV* 10: 85, 20)

From this point on, the hymn ignores the divine couple. It leaves the paradigmatic marriage of Soma and Sūryā behind, and focuses instead on normal human weddings. When the gods appear again, they play their proper divine roles in a wedding between mortals.

> Pūṣan must hold your hand and lead you away from here,
> the Aśvins must bring you on their chariot,
> go to the house so that you may be its mistress,
> as its mistress you may give orders.
> (*RV* 10: 85, 26)

The human bride is identified with her heavenly role-model, Sūryā,[77] but Pūṣan has no designs on her (neither as a wife nor as a mother), and the Aśvins are well-behaved friends of the groom, who bring the bride to her new home. Soma is still regarded as the model divine husband of every bride. He passes her on to the Gandharva, who in turn passes her on to Agni, who finally hands her over to her human husband (*RV* 10: 85, 40-41). The *Brāhmaṇas* likewise regards Soma as the real husband of Sūryā, and the Aśvins merely provide entertainment at the wedding by competing in a chariot-race.[78] This procedure is typical of the tendency in book 10 to censor ancient myths. The old story of an incestuous union between the twins Yama and Yamī lies behind *RV* 10: 10, but it is rejected as impossibile; the traditional polyandrous union of Sūryā and the Aśvins makes a sudden appearance in the middle of the marriage hymn, but it is rejected as an impossibility in the rest of the hymn; the wedding goes on as if nothing had happened. The Kuru kings may be happy to include all sorts of ancient hymns and stories in their definitive edition of the *Ṛgveda*, but book 10 is their own addition and it reflects their concern with order and discipline.

Sūryā's Other Relationship

The earlier books of the *Ṛgveda* do not attempt to reconcile ancient myths with proper ritual behaviour, and they are quite happy to record such stories without censorship. In this less complicated world, the Daughter of the Sun chooses both of the Aśvins because they will make good husbands and good friends:

> She came to marry you for friendship,
> the noble young woman chose you as her husbands (*patī*).[79]
> (*RV* 1: 119, 5)

Sūryā is delighted with her choice, which she regards as a personal victory:

> The Daughter of the Sun went onto your chariot,
> as if reaching the finishing-line first with a race-horse.
> All the gods agreed in their hearts.
> (*RV* 1: 116, 17)

The reaction of the gods to her polyandrous relationship is significant. It is the same one we found awkwardly included in the marriage hymn, when the Aśvins eloped with her and the gods granted their approval to the relationship.[80] Sūryā has made her choice on inscrutable, personal grounds – she likes the look of them[81] – and nobody questions her decision. She does not care too much for traditional marriage; on the contrary, as we saw from the story of Rodasī and the Maruts (*RV* 1: 167, 5), she is a role-model for other free-thinking goddesses.

We have, therefore, two traditions about Sūryā. In book 10 of the *Ṛgveda*, she marries Soma to please her father. In the earlier books of the *Ṛgveda*, she runs off with the the Aśvins to please herself. Her marriage with Soma in book 10 is the only one that is called a marriage (*vahatu*),[82] but her elopement with the Aśvins is the only relationship recognized in the rest of the *Ṛgveda*. The Aśvins are the gods 'who possess Sūryā as their treasure' (*sūryāvasū*, *RV* 7: 68, 3d), their chariot is 'the one that carries Sūryā' (*yaḥ sūriyāṃ vahati*, *RV* 4: 44, 1c). It is, in fact, one of their most famous achievements, and it is celebrated in no less than 13 of the 54 hymns dedicated to the Aśvins.[83] It is not too surprising that Vedic myth would have brought together a goddess who does as she pleases and two young gods who do not worry too much about the conventions of society. It is anachronistic to view them as rebels, however, because they really belong to a world that preceded the invention of these new traditions. We hear about the radically innovative notion of traditional marriage for the first time in the last book of the *Ṛgveda*. It is only in this book that we find a rigid form of marriage imposed on all; it is only here that we see the first hints of a class system. The Aśvins and Sūryā belong to an age that was more primitive but enjoyed greater freedom and simplicity.

CHAPTER 3

NĀSATYAS – SAVIOUR GODS

The birth and marriage of the Aśvins are personal events that take place in the world of the gods alone. The Aśvins are, however, deeply involved in the adventures of humanity, and they are actually criticized by the other gods for associating too much with humans.[1] Their fame and popularity rest on their readiness to come and help people in trouble. In *RV* 8: 9, 13, we hear that 'the help of the Aśvins is the best', and elsewhere we learn that this is already regarded as an ancient tradition about the two gods:

> Why do the inspired poets born long ago say, o Aśvins,
> that you come the most readily (*gamiṣṭhā*) to any misfortune?
> (*RV* 1: 118, 3)

The formula 'coming most readily with help' (*avasā āgamiṣṭhā*) is used of the Aśvins and the great hero-god, Indra.[2] The Aśvins are especially famous for helping those who have been trapped by enemies, for providing people with emergency food-supplies, and for solving marital problems. Some of the hymns give rapid lists of all their rescue missions (*RV* 1: 112, *RV* 1: 116, and *RV* 1: 117), but we shall look closely at four adventure stories that were very famous and inspired a lot of commentary from later Vedic interpreters.

The Sea-Rescue of Bhujyu

The rescue mentioned most frequently is the story of Bhujyu, which appears in 17 of the Aśvin hymns.[3] Bhujyu was lost at sea, and an account of his plight is found in *RV* 1: 116, 3–5:

[3] Tugra left Bhujyu behind, o Aśvins, in a cloud of water,
just as a man leaves his wealth behind when he is dead.
You brought him back with your living ships
that float in the atmosphere, waterproof.

[4] For three nights and for three days, o Nāsatyas,
you carried Bhujyu with your fliers that pass by
to the shore of the ocean, to the far side of the water,
in three chariots with a hundred feet and six horses.

[5] You did that heroic deed in the ocean that cannot
be held on to, cannot be stood upon, cannot be grasped,
when you brought Bhujyu home, o Aśvins,
after he boarded your ship with its hundred oars.

Bhujyu is the son of Tugra, and his father abandoned him in the middle of the ocean. Most versions of the story leave it at that, and go on to describe his rescue by the Aśvins, but this hymn by Kakṣīvant focuses on the abandonment. It exonerates Tugra by telling us that he abandoned his son unwillingly, just as a man does not willingly let go of his life and everything he holds dear to him.

In another of his hymns, Kakṣīvant says that the Aśvins saved Bhujyu as a favour to Tugra, who was an old friend of theirs.

With your old ways (*pūrviyebhir evaiḥ*),
you remembered Tugra once again, o young gods,
you carried Bhujyu out of the waves of the ocean
with your grey bird-horses.

(*RV* 1: 117, 14)

For Kakṣīvant, both Bhujyu and his father are victims to be pitied. Other versions are more critical of Tugra:

> You went to the man who was weeping far away,
> distressed at his abandonment (*tyajas*) by his own father.
>
> (*RV* 1: 119, 8ab)

The word for abandonment, *tyajas*, is a very negative one, and could also be translated as 'hostility' or 'hatred,' so the abandonment of Bhujyu is presented here as criminal negligence, if not deliberate murder. An interesting compromise is found in a hymn from the Vasiṣṭha family.

> And his friends with their evil ways (*durevāsaḥ*) abandoned, o Aśvins,
> Bhujyu in the middle of the ocean,
> but the malicious man (*arāvā*) who was your devotee rescued him.
>
> (*RV* 7: 68, 7)

Tugra is, of course, the 'malicious' man who goes along with the 'evil ways' of the treacherous friends who try to murder his own son.[4] He must, as Geldner suggests, have repented at the last minute,[5] and since he was a devotee of the Aśvins, they enable him to rescue Bhujyu. The Aśvins remain loyal to the old ways (*pūrvya eva*, *RV* 1: 117, 14a) and to their old friends, unlike Tugra who adopts evil ways and bad company (*dur-eva*, *RV* 7: 68, 7a), and abandons his own son. In spite of Tugra's misbehaviour,[6] the Aśvins remember once again (*punar-manya*, *RV* 1: 117, 14b) how things used to be, instead of dismissing Tugra and his son. The Aśvins are good and loyal friends, and they are even closer to Bhujyu than his own father. This is not the only story in which they intervene to save a son from the consequences of his father's anger. When Ṛjāśva is blinded by his 'cruel father' (*RV* 1: 117, 17), the Aśvins intervene to restore his sight. This intimacy with humans, which allows them to intervene in private family quarrels, is an important feature of the Aśvins, but the story of Bhujyu focuses on the surreal plight of the hero and the spectacular manner in which he is rescued.

In most of the hymns, the story is briefly mentioned in four lines or less, and the Aśvins come to the rescue in their usual chariot (*ratha*)[7] which is drawn by their 'bird-horses' (*vibhir aśvaiḥ*, *RV* 1: 117, 14d).[8] There are, however, two hymns that give a fuller account of this rescue (*RV* 1: 116, 3–5 and *RV* 1: 182, 5–7), and they state that the Aśvins used magic ships to reach him and bring him home.[9] These ships are 'living ships',[10] they have a soul (*ātman*), and they are also flying ships. They sail through the atmosphere (*antarikṣaprudbhir*, *RV* 1: 116, 3d), they have wings (*pakṣiṇam*, *RV* 1: 182, 5b), and they enable the Aśvins to fly properly (*supaptanī petathuḥ*, *RV* 1: 182, 5d).

In some hymns, we discover that Bhujyu is not merely lost at sea; he is floundering in a cosmic ocean that includes both the earthly sea and the atmosphere itself. When the Aśvins arrive by flying chariot, their bird-horses carry Bhujyu through the *atmosphere* (*rajobhiḥ*, *RV* 6: 62, 6b); in another chariot-rescue hymn, Bhujyu has been 'tossed about in the ocean, at the far side of the *atmosphere*' (*rájasaḥ*, *RV* 10: 143, 5b).[11]

These hymns conflate the ocean with the atmosphere, and they emphasize the vastness and instability of the undefined space in which Bhujyu has lost himself. In *RV* 1: 182, 6b, the waters (*apsu*) are called 'the darkness (*tamasi*) that cannot be held onto (*anārambhaṇe*)'. The terms used here for water (*ap*) and darkness (*tamas*) are the same ones that describe the cosmic water and darkness at the beginning of the universe. It is unclear whether he is lost in the ocean or in outer space, whether the Aśvins are flying (*petatuḥ*, 5d) or sailing (*nāvaḥ*, 6c) to the rescue. The same adjective, 'that cannot be held onto' (*anārambhaṇe*), is used to describe the ocean (*samudra*) in *RV* 1: 116, 5a, but once again, it is unclear whether we are dealing with the normal ocean or an atmospheric one, whether the Aśvins are travelling through the atmosphere (*antarikṣaprudbhir*, 3d) or by ship across the sea (*naubhiḥ*, 3c; *nāvam*, 5b). The ocean is described by a series of adjectives that similarly emphasise the fundamental instability of the region into which Bhujyu has disappeared: 'it cannot be held onto, it cannot be stood on, it cannot be grasped' (*anārambhaṇe anāsthāne agrabhaṇe*, *RV* 1: 116, 5ab). By way of contrast, Agastya in *RV* 1: 182, 7 wonders whether there was any tree in the middle of the ocean for Bhujyu 'to hold on to,' and the word he uses is *ārabhe*, the exact opposite of *anārambhaṇe*, 'that which cannot be held onto'. The indefinable nature of this confusing space is admirably captured in the word that Kakṣīvant chose to describe it: *udamegha*, 'the cloud of water' (*RV* 1: 116, 3a), a term that combines and confounds the sea and the sky. We find a close parallel to this conception of the sea in the Greek word *pontos*, described as follows by Détienne and Vernant:

> Pontos, the Salty Deep, is a primordial power of the open sea, the vast expanse bounded only by sky and water [. . .]. In this chaotic expanse where every crossing resembles breaking through a region unknown and ever unrecognizable, pure movement reigns forever.[12]

Such was the view of the sea-faring Greeks. For the land-loving Vedic Indians, the open sea must have been even more terrifying and bewildering. To be lost and alone at the opposite end of the atmosphere, the other side of the darkness, in a chaotic region where sky and sea can no longer be distinguished, where one must fly or sail, but cannot drive a chariot or ride a horse – this Vedic nightmare was the fate of Bhujyu.

Nine times the poets say 'you two carried him away' (*ūhathuḥ*) – a verbal form that appears frequently when the Aśvins are helping people in trouble;[13] twice we hear that the Aśvins 'bring him across' (*pāraya*)[14] safely. The sense of relief echoes the emotions of the poet when night is finally over, when morning has come and men can pray to the Aśvins once again: 'we have crossed over to the far side (*pāram*) of this darkness (*tamasas*),'[15] 'the end of the darkness (*tamasas*) is now visible'.[16] In the vastness of the night, the poets recognize the same chaotic darkness that they see in the ocean and in the atmosphere, they see the primeval disorder from which our universe emerged. The Aśvins have the power to rescue men from this terrifying and unbounded chaos.

Atri in the Cooking Pot

Mortals rarely have to face such cosmic forces alone, and most of their troubles are on a smaller scale. Their human enemies cause them quite enough difficulties and often require divine intervention. A very popular rescue story, which has important implications for the cult of the Aśvins, is the adventure of Atri, which turns up in 14 of the Aśvin hymns.[17] Atri was thrown by unidentified enemies into a burning trench, which is referred to as a pit (*ṛbīsa*), a fire (*agni*), or *gharma*, which could mean 'heat,' but is more plausibly identified as a cooking pot by Jamison.[18] The Aśvins rescue him from the burning pit,[19] from distress,[20] and from darkness.[21] Oddly enough, this 'rescue' does not involve removing him from the pit itself; instead, they make it bearable for him. They 'keep away the burning fire with snow' (*RV* 1: 116, 8a), they (keep away?) 'the heated pot from Atri with snow' (*RV* 1: 119, 6b); they 'sprinkle the pot with snow for Atri' (*RV* 8: 73, 3). The last hymn cited explains that they 'created a helpful (*avantam*) house for Atri' (*RV* 8: 73, 7), so they have made a safe and cool space within the burning trench for Atri, which will enable him to survive the ordeal. As a result, they 'keep the fire away so that it won't burn him' (*varethe agnim ātapo*, *RV* 8: 73, 8).

This notion of a 'helpful house' within the fire explains a strange expression we find in other hymns: 'you made the heated pot helpful (*omiyāvantam*) for Atri' (*RV* 1: 112, 7b); 'you made the heated pit helpful (*omanvantam*) for Atri, for Saptavadhri' (*RV* 10: 39, 9cd). It is not very helpful to be tossed into a burning pit or boiled alive in a pot, but the word 'helpful' refers here to the imaginary igloo that the Aśvins have created around him. As another hymn puts it, 'his life evaded the burning (fire) with your help (*omanā*)' (*RV* 7: 69, 4d). This case makes it clear that 'with your help' (*omanā*) means the same thing as saving him 'with snow' (*himena*), or creating a 'helpful house' for him.[22] Jamison suggests that Atri is being compared to an embryo that is in danger of being burnt to death in its mother's womb, and needs to be protected by a surrounding 'membrane of snow' (*himasya jarāyuṇā*), a fear mentioned in several Vedic texts that she cites.[23] We must visualise Atri being saved by some such fireproof membrane.

The Aśvins also help out by providing Atri with refreshment which is, suprisingly, a hot drink of milk, that is confusingly called *gharma*. So we have a play on the heated pot (*gharma*) that burns Atri and the heated milk (*gharma*) that revives him.[24] This word-play works well in Sanskrit because the *gharma* pot is used for heating milk in the *Pravargya* ritual,[25] and this ritual offering of hot milk was presented to the Aśvins. In the myth behind this ritual, they present the hot milk to Atri instead. The Aśvins 'choose the honeyed drink of hot milk (*gharmam madhumantam*) for Atri' (*RV* 1: 180, 4a).[26] The hot milk is called 'nourishing strength' (*pitumatim ūrjam*, *RV* 1: 116, 8b) or simply 'strength' (*ūrjam*, *RV* 1: 118, 7b), or 'the wonderful food (*citram bhojanam*) that is yours' (*RV* 7: 68, 5a). In the last case, this 'wonderful food' is equated with the 'help' (*omānam*, *RV* 7: 68, 5c) given to Atri by the Aśvins. Geldner suggests that this food may be some form of ambrosia,[27] but it is surely the hot milk of the Aśvins. The equation of their milk with their help shows that these terms are simply different ways of describing the same action. They provide him with a magic, cooling protection from the fire by giving him a magic, hot drink in the fire. The *gharma* milk saves Atri from being boiled alive, just as it prevents the *gharma* pot from cracking in the *Pravargya* ritual. So Atri is being equated with the *gharma* milk itself, because he is being boiled in a pot over the fire but is also protected from the fire by that snowy, helpful pot; and he is also being identified with the *gharma* pot itself, because he is filled with hot milk by the Aśvins which saves his life while he is being heated over the fire.

The Atri family created the *Pravargya* ritual, and one of their hymns commemorates its origin. The trauma of the original ordeal is forgotten, and the Atri family remembers only the life-saving drink of hot milk that the Aśvins presented to their ancestor, and that they now present to the Aśvins:

> Atri thinks about the two of you
> with kind thoughts, o heroes,

when he eagerly sips with his mouth
your flawless hot milk (*gharma*), o Nāsatyas.

(*RV* 5: 73, 6)

Whether Atri refers to the original hero of the story, or one of his contemporary descendants, he recalls and repays the kindness of the Aśvins to the famous Atri whenever he offers hot milk to them and drinks some himself during the *Pravargya* ritual.[28]

The gratitude of Atri's family to the Aśvins is also expressed in *RV* 1: 180, 3–4, but in this hymn his descendants thank the Aśvins not just for the original offering of hot milk to their founder, but for the creation of milk itself:

You two (gods) placed the milk (*payas*) in the red cow,
the cooked (milk) in the raw cow, the ancient (milk) of the cow,
which the libation-bearer, like a shining bird,
offers to you in a wooden bowl, o gods whose appearance is true.

You chose the honeyed hot milk (*gharma*) for Atri,
to come to him like a flood of water.
That was a cattle-raid for you, o heroes, o Aśvins:
like chariot-wheels, (your gifts) of the sweet drink return to you.

The Aśvins are well rewarded for their generosity: they have given one drink of hot milk to Atri, and it is as if they had won an entire herd of cows in a cattle-raid, because they are guaranteed a supply of hot milk offerings in perpetuity. Atri was the first person to receive this drink, so he was under a special obligation to repay the Aśvins by performing the *Pravargya* ritual in their honour. It is not, however, a ritual duty that is confined to the Atri family alone, because this cycle (or 'chariot-wheel,' *RV* 1: 180, 4d) of gift and counter-gift has a cosmic origin that binds all human beings. Everyone should offer hot milk in a bowl to the Aśvins because everyone has benefitted from their creation of milk inside cows.

The *Pravargya* ritual was performed in honour of the Aśvins, but Indra also received these offerings of hot milk.[29] There is no particular myth to explain why Indra deserves this hot milk, so the poets have to resort to the more general kind of explanation that we find in *RV* 1: 180.

> You placed the cooked (milk) inside the raw (cows),
> you raised the sun into the sky.
> Heat it up like a cooking-pot (*gharma*) with chants of praise,[30]
> great and pleasant for the one who loves songs.
> (*RV* 8: 89, 7)

As in *RV* 1: 180, the original gift of milk to the human race is repaid with offerings of hot milk to the god Indra, who created milk in the first place.

Indra does not, however, play any role in the story of Atri. In fact, the only other god mentioned in connection with Atri is the fire god, Agni. At first sight, this is surprising, because Agni would seem to be the villain of the story, the one from whom Atri must be rescued by the Aśvins. In a hymn to Agni we find the following explanation: 'Agni saved Atri inside the cooking-pot (*gharma*)' (*RV* 10: 80, 3c). Here, as with the Aśvins, we find the fire-god himself trying to make the ordeal in the fire bearable for Atri. He is not saved from the fire; he is saved in the fire and by the fire god. He is being treated very much like the pot of hot milk in the *Pravargya* ritual, which could not, of course, take place without the fire to heat the milk. The goal of the *Pravargya* ritual is not to cremate the milk, but to turn it into a hot nourishing drink, and in the same way, the purpose of Atri's ordeal is not to burn him alive, but to nourish and strengthen him, and his entire family through him.[31]

Atri's ordeal is a dangerous one, but the *Pravargya* ritual itself is not without its risks: the cooking pot must be handled with tongs, and flames burst out from the heated pot when the milk is poured into it.[32] After all this dangerous playing with fire, however, the priests and the gods can quietly enjoy a drink of hot milk. Van Buitenen wonders whether the Aśvins saved Atri from a *Pravargya* ritual that went badly wrong and started a conflagration,[33] but the story seems rather to celebrate the danger and excitement inherent in every *Pravargya* performance. The Atris start off with a very ordinary adventure story about a man thrown into a pit by his enemies;[34] but they change it into a bewildering and exciting story about a man who is being boiled alive in a cooking pot over a fire. He is saved in the fire by the external protection of that same cooking pot; he is saved in that cooking pot by the internal protection of a hot drink from the Aśvins. The Atris invented this aetiological myth by thinking hard about the origins of the first hot milk drunk by a man, and about the first hot milk offered by that man to the Aśvins.

Atri and Saptavadhri

A strange twist is given to the story of Atri in three hymns. His story melts into that of Saptavadhri, another member of the Atri family, who is mentioned only in connection with the ordeal of Atri in the burning pit. The name Saptavadhri means '(tied by) seven straps', so his function in the story is to be trapped and tied up, though not with 'seven straps'. The first two of these hymns (*RV* 5: 78 and *RV* 8: 73) are in fact attributed to Saptavadhri Atreya himself, though this is probably because his words are quoted in the first and he is directly addressed in the second. In *RV* 5: 78 Atri is down in the burning pit, as usual, so he cries out to the Aśvins for help, and they respond immediately. Without any transition, we suddenly hear the words of Saptavadhri, who is trapped inside a tree.

[4] When Atri went down into the pit,
he called on you like a young woman in distress,
you came with the fresh and benevolent
speed of a hawk, o Aśvins.

[5] 'Open up, lord of the forest,
like the womb of a woman giving birth,
hear my cry, o Aśvins,
and free Saptavadhri.'

[6] For the terrified man in distress,
for the seer Saptavadhri,

you Aśvins with your magic powers
closed and opened up the tree.

The hymn ends with a prayer that a pregnant woman may safely give birth to her child, 'a living boy from a living mother' (*RV* 5: 78, 9d).

This poet of the Atri family makes several bold leaps of the imagination in this hymn that honours two of his ancestors. He throws a series of images at us: Atri, trapped in the burning pit; Saptavadhri, enclosed in the tree trunk; and an embryo, enclosed in the womb. Atri's cries for help are compared with those of a young woman crying 'in distress' (*nādhamānā*, 4b); Saptavadhri is likewise 'in distress' (*nādhamānāya*, 6a), and his release from the tree-prison is equated with the release of a child from the womb. Birth is equally distressing for the mother and the child, for the cooking pot or the tree trunk as well as for Atri and Saptavadhri. The hymn moves without transition to a prayer for the trouble-free birth of a child (*RV* 5: 78, 7–9).

These comparisons, explicit and implicit, support Jamison's view that Atri's revival in the pit is regarded as a new birth, and that the cooking pot and burning pit are viewed as incubators.[35] Jamison's approach would also explain why Atri has to stay in the cooking pot until the burning pit has cooked him properly and he is ready to face the world. The hymn we are looking at right now presents us with the very end of that process, when Atri, Saptavadhri, and the embryo are already fully 'cooked' and may at last emerge from their incubators. The connection between Atri and Saptavadhri in these hymns is that both men are seers from the same family, they have been trapped in a pot-womb and a tree-womb, and their stories are metaphors for childbirth, and spiritual rebirth.

We get a similar jump from Atri to Saptavadhri in *RV* 8: 73, 7–9, but this time there is no explicit connection with birth. The poet (again from the Atri family) has altered the stories considerably.

[7] You two Aśvins made
a helpful house for Atri.
Let your help truly be near.

[8] You prevented the fire from burning
on behalf of Atri who spoke beautifully.
Let your help truly be near.

[9] Saptavadhri by his trust
put to rest the cutting blade of the fire.
Let your help truly be near.

Here we do not make a sudden transition from the burning pit of Atri to the hollow tree of Saptavadhri, as in *RV* 5: 78; instead, Saptavadhri intervenes in the story of Atri, quenches the fire, and almost makes the assistance of the Aśvins superfluous. At the end of the hymn, however, we have a reference to the usual story of Saptavadhri and the tree, but here again he takes the initiative and destroys the tree through his own efforts.

[17] Looking at the Aśvins,
as a man with an axe looks at a tree –
let your help truly be near –

[18] smash it like a fort, you brave man,
you are harassed by the black tribe.
Let your help truly be near.

The 'black tribe' of pagan demons, or demonic pagans, has harassed him, but it is not clear what they have done to him, or what the target of his anger will be. Both the tree and the fort seem to be metaphorical. Saptavadhri's trust in the Aśvins has freed him from the power of his enemies, and now he can attack them from the outside. He is not a prisoner escaping from inside a tree; he is like a man getting ready to fell a tree or demolish a hill-fort, both of which are doomed to destruction.

The stories of Atri and Saptavadhri are once again combined, in a brief reference in *RV* 10: 39, 9cd:

and you made the hot pit helpful
for Atri, for Saptavadhri.

The composer of this hymn may have regarded Atri and Saptavadhri as one and the same person,[36] so the second line could be translated as 'for Atri Saptavadhri'. The two *ṛṣis* cannot, however, be conflated in the other two hymns, even though Saptavadhri intrudes into the Atri story in all three hymns.[37] Śaunaka's unconvincing attempt to reconcile the two stories is a strong argument against such an identification: he ingeniously suggests that Saptavadhri–Atri was placed in a wooden vat (*vṛkṣadroṇī*) in a pit (*ṛbīsa*), thereby combining the ordeals of the tree and the pit (*Bṛhaddevatā*, 5: 82).

It is not very surprising that the story of Saptavadhri Atreya might be confused with that of the famous Atri, but the two stories are really quite different. Both the name and the story of Saptavadhri focus on his entrapment, from which he must be released immediately; Atri, in contrast, must be nourished so that he will stay in the cooking pot and survive there. If we see these stories as metaphors for pregnancy and birth, then the story of Saptavadhri is about the delivery of the baby, whereas Atri's story is about its nourishment in the womb. Atri must not try to escape from the cooking pot; he must go through his ordeal right to the very end. As a result of his rebirth after this experience, he creates a new ritual relationship between all men and the Aśvins, the *Pravargya* ritual that honours the horse gods.

The Rejuvenation of Cyavana

The Aśvins saved Bhujyu from the atmospheric ocean, and they enabled Atri to endure the burning fire of a Vedic ritual. They are also famous as doctors (*bhiṣajā*),[38] and the other two stories we shall look at celebrate their medical achievements. One of their greatest miracles fulfils the eternal human fantasy that old age might be curable. Knowing that this is within their power, the poet Atri Sāṃkhya asks the Aśvins to make him young again in *RV* 10: 143. He reminds them that by their power, his own ancestor Atri became 'like a horse reaching the winning-post', and that they made Kakṣīvant, from the Aṅgiras family of poets, 'new again like a chariot' (*RV* 10: 143, 1cd). Kutsa, another Aṅgiras poet, and Ghoṣā, the daughter of Kakṣīvant, celebrate how the Aśvins changed Kali into a young man and found him a wife (*RV* 1: 112, 15b and *RV* 10: 39, 8ab).

The most famous of all these rejuvenations was the case of Cyavana, and it was destined to have a long and complicated history. His story is told eight times in the *Ṛgveda*.[39] The name Cyavana derives from the present participle of the verb *cyu* and means 'moving',[40] or 'shaking',[41] and in four of the eight accounts we have the formulaic expression 'make young again' (*punar yuvan kṛ*).[42] The experiences of Cyavana are presented as the archetypal story of a 'mover and a shaker' who has 'grown old' (the verb *jṛ* crops up in five accounts[43]), but is 'made young again'. The short account in *RV* 5: 74, 5 includes all the details of the story:

From Cyavana who had grown old,
you removed his skin like a garment.
When he was made a young man again,
he satisfied his wife's desire.

The reason why the Aśvins help him out is quite obvious in the *Ṛgveda*. Cyavana offers libations to them (*havirde*, *RV* 7: 68, 6b), he is 'a man without duplicity' (*advayāvinam*, *RV* 5: 75, 5d), and several hymns assure us that the gods protect such people. Addressing the ancient gods Earth and Sky, one hymn proclaims, 'you two protect (*pāthaḥ*) the step of any son who is without duplicity' (*advayāvinaḥ*, *RV* 1: 159, 3d). The goddess Aditi is herself 'without duplicity' (*advayāḥ*, *RV* 8: 18, 6b) and therefore 'must protect' (*pātu*, *RV* 8: 18, 6c) the cattle of her worshippers.

The gods will, of course, be especially protective of anyone who is both 'without duplicity' and also their priest. The Hotar priest who prays to the Maruts is 'without duplicity' (*advayāvī*, *RV* 7: 56, 18d), and all such Hotar priests are ultimately basing their behaviour on the great divine Hotar, Agni himself. Agni is praised as 'the Hotar priest without duplicty' (*hotāraṃ advayāvinaṃ*, *RV* 3: 2, 15a) and 'the Seer without duplicity' (*kavim advayantam*, *RV* 3: 29, 5a). This simple-hearted worship from the priest-seer Cyavana is the only reason for the intervention of the Aśvins on his behalf, but later elaborations of Cyavana's story will come up with much more complicated explanations.

The manner in which the Aśvins cure him is likewise clear. They 'strip away his outer body (*vavri*) as if it were a garment',[44] and they give him a new 'form' (*varpa*, *RV* 7: 68, 6c) to use from then on. The notion of the body as a garment that can be disposed of has a long and famous history in Indian thought,[45] but here we are simply dealing with plastic surgery – it is merely the skin that is replaced, the outer appearance that is changed. The same image of the outer form as garment appears in *RV* 1: 164, 7d, where the rain-clouds 'dress themselves up in the outer body (*vavri*)' of cows. The Aśvins are well qualified to change the outer appearance of Cyavana, because they themselves 'take on many forms' (*varpāṃsi*, *RV* 1: 117, 9a), leading one exasperated poet to wonder when they will 'put on their own outer body' (*svaṃ vavriṃ*, *RV* 1: 46, 9c).

The closest parallel to the story of Cyavana appears in *RV* 9: 71, 2c. When the soma plant has been crushed, it must then be purified in a strainer. As a result of this straining, 'it leaves its outer body (*vavri*) behind and goes to its dinner appointment as juice'. Its old body, the pulpy mixture, has been left in the sieve; it now has a new body, soma juice. In the same way, as Jamison has demonstrated from her analysis of Vedic texts, a man removes the external coverings of hair, beard and dead skin;[46] the outer caul is removed from a newborn child;[47] infected skin is removed from a woman;[48] and dark spots are stripped from the sun.[49] So the Aśvins literally strip off Cyavana's aging skin, and the young skin that is exposed beneath is, in and of itself, the new form that he receives from the Aśvins (*RV* 7: 68, 6c). Judging by Jamison's parallels, it is not necessary to replace the old skin with a new one; removing the old one is quite enough. The end result is that he satisfies the wife he already has (*RV* 5: 74, 5d), or marries several young girls (*RV* 1: 116, 10d).

This short and simple story of a good man who is made young again may hardly seem worth the telling, but it was a popular one and it became very important later on. The Vedic ritualists will turn Cyavana into the priest who had first introduced the Aśvins to the delights of soma.

The Head of Dadhyañc

Later Indian thinkers associated the stories of Cyavana and Dadhyañc,[50] and since the healing of Dadhyañc is the most spectacular cure performed by the Aśvins, we shall now turn to his story. Throughout the *Ṛgveda*, the Aśvins receive soma like all the other gods, but this was not always so. A hymn to Soma tells of their exclusion:

> The seer is born with an intelligent mind.
> The embryo of the divine order is hidden away from the twins.
> They were young men when they discovered him for the first time.
> One birth is placed in secret, the other is offered.
>
> (*RV* 9: 68, 5)

The 'embryo of the divine order' (*ṛtasya garbho*, 5b) is soma, and 'the twins' are the Aśvins. They are frequently referred to as 'young men' (*yuvānā*) throughout the *Ṛgveda*, and they are already young men when they are allowed to drink soma. This sacred drink exists in two forms: the divine soma of Tvaṣṭar, which is kept in a secret place, and the soma here on earth, which is offered by humans to the gods.

The divine soma is hidden from the Aśvins and they must use trickery to discover its secret, but even Indra, the greatest soma-drinker of all, was originally compelled to obtain soma by stealth. He stole it directly from his father, Tvaṣṭar (*RV* 3: 48, 4cd), or he received it from an eagle who had snatched it (*RV* 4: 18, 13d). In Indra's case, being deprived of soma is quite a serious matter, because he needs it to to perform his mighty deeds (*RV* 6: 47, 1–2). Soma is Indra's very being, his *ātman* according to *RV* 9: 85, 3b, and he is quite helpless until he drinks it (*RV* 4: 18, 13a–c). Indra must have soma or dwindle away, so these myths explain how he acquired it and eventually handed it on to his worshippers.[51] The Aśvins, in contrast, seem to manage quite well without soma, so in their case, the myth explains why they receive soma in addition to their normal offering of hot milk (*gharma*) from the priests of the Atri family.

The Aśvins eventually discover the secret of Tvaṣṭar's heavenly soma, and the story of this revelation is told three times in the *Ṛgveda*. The divine soma is called 'honey' (*madhu*) in each of these tellings (*RV* 1: 116, 12c; *RV* 1: 117, 22c; *RV* 1: 119, 9a).[52] Originally, the Aśvins had not even known what they had been missing, but a bee told them about the existence of this special 'honey' called soma:

> That bee whispered to you about the honey.
>
> (*RV* 1: 119, 9a)

> With her mouth, the bee told you Aśvins about the honey,
> just as a girl arranges a rendezvous.
>
> (*RV* 10: 40, 6cd)

Soma is often equated with honey, and the expression *somyam madhu*, 'the honey of soma,' or 'soma-honey' occurs 18 times in the *Ṛgveda*. This explains why the bee knows all about soma and why she describes it as 'honey'. The Aśvins were already young men at the time they learned of its existence (*RV* 9: 68, 5c), whereas Indra had demanded soma on the very day he was born (*RV* 3: 48, 1–3), and then became the great lord of soma in the *Ṛgveda*.[53]

Once the Aśvins have discovered that soma actually exists, they want to acquire this wonderful drink. Luckily, they manage to win the friendship of Dadhyañc, a priest who knows all about the production of soma and is also a close ally of Indra's. Dadhyañc is the son of Atharvan, who produced the first sacrificial fire (*RV* 6: 16, 13), and Dadhyañc assisted his father by stoking this fire (*RV* 6: 16, 14). Atharvan also taught him about soma, and through its power Dadhyañc helped Indra to break open the fortress of the demon Vala

(*RV* 9: 108, 4a). Indra repays the family by giving support to the father Atharvan (*RV* 10: 48, 2a) and by presenting the son Dadhyañc with cattle (*RV* 10: 48, 2d). In a hymn to Indra, we learn that Manu, Atharvan, and Dadhyañc were among the earliest men to sing the praises of Indra (*RV* 1: 80, 16). Dadhyañc was therefore one of the first men to offer soma, and he was an especially favoured protégé of Indra. In spite of this, the Aśvins 'win over the mind of Dadhyañc' (*RV* 1: 119, 9c) and persuade him to betray Indra by revealing the secret of soma to them.

Before Dadhyañc can explain it to them, the twin gods have to behead him and replace his own head with a horse's head.

> On Dadhyañc son of Atharvan, o Aśvins,
> you placed the head of a horse,
> upholding the divine order, he taught you about the honey
> of Tvaṣṭar, an intimate secret for you, o wonder-workers.
> (*RV* 1: 117, 22)

The strangest part of this story is the detail about the horse's head, and the unusual exchange of heads that takes place. Dadhyañc replaces his own head with a horse's head; using this head, he tells the secret of soma to the Aśvins; Indra punishes this betrayal by cutting off his horse-head; the Aśvins bring Dadhyañc back to life by putting his human head back on his shoulders. These details were later explained in the *Śatapatha Brāhmaṇa* (*ŚB* 14: 1, 1^{18-24}) as a legal fiction that would enable Dadhyañc to avoid betraying the secret (it did not escape from *his* lips) but to communicate it nonetheless. In *RV* 1: 119, 9d we hear that 'the horse's head spoke,' so the poet Kakṣīvant was probably aware of this legal trick. Unfortunately, Indra beheaded Dadhyañc anyway, so the legal subterfuge obviously did not work; and in any case it is not the real reason for the exchange of heads.

Dadhyañc before the Ṛgveda

The story of Dadhyañc and the horse's head is an extremely ancient one. It originates in northern Asia, and from there it eventually came down to the poets of the *Ṛgveda*. Archaeologists have found the body of a decapitated man with the head of a horse in a north Asian tomb dating from around 2100–1700 BC.[54] Both were presumably sacrificial victims, and this gruesome ritual is remembered in the Ṛgvedic story of Dadhyañc.[55] The story has, however, been revised by the addition of some Central Asian elements. The hero, Dadhyañc, is called the son of Atharvan, and **atharwan* is a Central Asian term meaning 'priest,' which survives in both Sanskrit and Avestan;[56] Dadhyañc knows about soma, and the soma plant likewise comes from Central Asia and once again retains its Central Asian name (**anću*) in India and Iran.[57]

In the new Central Asian version of the story, the priests (who must be Indo-Iranian) learn the secret of soma from the local **atharwan* priests.[58] In Vedic times, however, the Adhvaryu priests were beginning to challenge the management of Vedic ritual by the Hotar priests.[59] So the story about Indo-Iranian priests acquiring soma from Central Asian priests is reinterpreted as a story about Adhvaryu priests taking over the soma ritual from the Hotar priests. Indra and the other gods represent the ancient Hotar priests, and the Aśvins represent the upstart Adhvaryu priests. In order to overrule the Hotar priests, the Adhvaryus naturally appeal to the ancient authority of the Atharvans, which is represented by Dadhyañc in their reinterpretation of the Central Asian story. The revised myth of Dadhyañc proclaims that the Atharvans are siding with the Adhvaryu priests against the Hotar priests; they are sharing their ancient knowledge with the modern Adhvaryus.

By the time the story of the horse's head on the man's body has reached South Asia, it has acquired yet another new significance. Although the South Asian story of Dadhyañc still includes the north Asian beheading of a horse and a man, and the substitution of their heads, it does not accept this double decapitation as a ritual practice. On the contrary, the Indian story-tellers use this exchange of heads to guarantee that there will not be any human sacrifices; that there will be just one animal victim, which will replace the double sacrifice of a horse and a human. So the horse becomes a substitute for the human victim, Dadhyañc, and this story becomes a justification for the practice of ritual substitution. The gruesome exchange of heads is now seen as the first step on a long march to non-violence in ritual, and when the Adhvaryus take over the sacrificial space from the Hotars in the Middle Vedic period, they will completely eliminate decapitation from Vedic ritual. They will insist on suffocating the victim rather than beheading it.[60] Ultimately the killing of an animal will also be considered improper, and the victim will be replaced by bread or rice.[61] Through the Ṛgvedic story of Dadhyañc, the Adhvaryus are asserting their status as important players in Vedic sacrifice, and are setting up a precedent for their practice of ritual substitution.[62]

The Skull of Dadhyañc

The story of the horse-head does not end here, because another hymn tells us that Indra defeated his enemies with 'the bones of Dadhyañc' (*dadhīco asthabhir*, *RV* 1: 84, 13), and that the horse's skull was hidden in Lake Śaryaṇāvant (*RV* 1: 84, 14). Śaryaṇāvant is celebrated as one of the places where the best soma grows,[63] and the horse's skull has special powers because it is associated with Dadhyañc, soma, and Śaryaṇāvant. There is even an obscure story that Indra used the horse's skull to extract the secret of soma from its guardian.

> One man had an internal vision of soma,
> but the guardian revealed it to the other one because of the bone (*asthā*),
> he wanted to fight against the bull with the sharp horns,
> but he stood caught in the thick (noose) of his treachery.
> (*RV* 10: 48, 10)

The man who had the 'internal vision' is Dadhyañc, the 'other one' who uses 'the bone' is Indra with the horse's skull. The soma-guardian wanted to resist Indra ('the bull with the sharp horns'), but such 'treachery' did him no good, and he finally revealed the secret to Indra.[64]

This unusual story is a variation on the story of Dadhyañc and the Aśvins. In each version, Dadhyañc knows how to produce soma juice; his secret knowledge is hidden from the Aśvins by Indra, or from

Indra by the guardian; but the secret is discovered by means of a horse's head, which is used as a microphone by the Aśvins, and a threatening weapon by Indra. These similarities suggest that the connections between the Atharvan priest, soma, and the horse's head are ancient, and were not simply invented at a later stage by the Adhvaryus to liven up their story about the Aśvins. These associated themes were part of a shared Vedic tradition. It was probably the Hotar priests who combined a northern Asian story about the beheading of a man and a horse with a Central Asian story about learning the secret of the **ancu* plant from an **atharwan* priest. Dadhyañc was the teacher, and Indra was the student. Later, the Adhvaryus declare that they are the true heirs of the Atharvan tradition, so Dadhyañc teaches the secret of soma to their patron gods, the Aśvins, and the Ṛgvedic Hotars acknowledge this claim in their own collection of hymns.

The story of Dadhyañc and the Aśvins represents the adoption of the Adhvaryus into the community of soma-drinkers. This late adoption will radically alter the nature of the soma sacrifice, as the Adhvaryus refine the ritual by gradually eliminating its more blatant elements of bloodshed and violence. The story of Dadhyañc and the horse's head will go through some interesting developments in the Middle Vedic period, when the Adhvaryus reinterpret it from a very different point of view, and the original role of Dadhyañc as the man who introduced the Aśvins to soma will be completely forgotten.[65] For the Early Vedic period, however, Dadhyañc is the great innovator who placed soma at the centre of correct ritual practice.

Low-Class Gods

The story of Dadhyañc reveals that there is some discord between Indra, the lord of power (*śacīpati*), and the Aśvins, the lords of beauty (*śubhaspatī*). Indra and the twins are helpful and powerful gods, but there is a contrast in their mode of operation, between demonstrating one's divine power (*śacī*) and offering one's assistance (*ūti*), between defeating the enemies of a favourite, and rescuing a friend from danger.[66] The Aśvins, as we have seen, 'go most readily towards misfortune' (*praty avartiṃ gamiṣṭā*, twice in the *Ṛgveda*), 'come most readily with their help' (*avasā āgamiṣṭhā*, five times in the *Ṛgveda*). Their only rivals in this respect are Indra (*avasā āgamiṣṭhaḥ*, twice in *RV* 6: 52) and the ancestors (*āgamiṣṭhāḥ*, *RV* 10: 15, 3d). Since Indra is the most powerful god, it is not surprising that people would call on him, and it is reassuring to learn that he responds, but the case of the ancestors (*pitaraḥ*) is more interesting. They cannot help much (the word *avasā* has disappeared from the formula), but they do, of course, come most readily to the calls of mortals because they are former humans themselves.

The Aśvins are also very close to the human race because they, like the ancestors, are related to us, being brothers of the first human couple, Yama and Yamī, and half-brothers of Manu, who is the ancestor of the human race according to a different story.[67] Some hymns draw attention to this relationship between the human race and the Aśvins.

> You have an ancestral friendship with us,
> the same relationship (*bandhur*), remember this.
>
> (*RV* 7: 72, 2cd)

> You have the same family (*sajātiyaṃ*),
> you have the same relationship (*bandhur*), o Aśvins.
>
> (*RV* 8: 73, 12ab)

> The Nāsatyas are my ancestors (*pitarā*), they care for their relatives (*bandhupṛchā*),
> (to have) the same family (*sajātiyaṃ*) as the Aśvins is a beautiful honour.
>
> (*RV* 3: 54, 16ab)

The term used in two of these hymns to describe the relationship between the Aśvins and humans, 'belonging to the same family' (*sajātyam*, *RV* 3: 54, 16b and *RV* 8: 73, 12a), is a very strong one,[68] but it would be unwise to read too much into one word.[69] As Geldner reminds us in this context, 'relationship and friendship are almost equivalent expressions'.[70] Nevertheless, the accumulation of striking terms in *RV* 3: 54, 16ab – ancestors, concerned relatives, family members (*pitarā*, *bandhupṛchā*, and *sajātiyaṃ*) – must surely refer to the real, biological relationship between Manu and the Aśvins.

This blood relationship explains why poets will have little hesitation in appealing to the Aśvins, and why the Aśvins will respond so readily, but it also explains why the other gods, especially Indra, might not be so willing to share their heavenly soma with them. After all, the other offspring of Vivasvant and Saraṇyu were mortal, so the Aśvins are a little too close to humanity. The *ṛṣis* are perhaps protesting a little too loudly when they proclaim that the Aśvins are 'most like Indra and the Maruts' (*indratamā* [...] *maruttamā*, *RV* 1: 182, 2a), that they come 'to exercise their power (*śaktim*) at the critical moment, like Indra' (*RV* 4: 43, 3b). This second comparison with Indra is no small honour, because Indra and the Aśvins are the only gods who intervene 'at the criticial moment' (*paritakmiyāyām*).[71] Indra might not, however, have been too flattered by the comparison.

In the Middle Vedic period, the Aśvins are regarded as inferior gods because they are doctors and move among humans too much (*Taittirīya Saṃhitā*, 6: 4, 9). The significance of the second objection is that humans are unhealthy creatures who are constantly sick or dying, and therefore expose the Aśvins to the pollution of sickness and death. The *Ṛgveda*, in contrast, acknowledges that the Aśvins are doctors and perform menial tasks, but does not think any the less of them for that. Their right to receive offerings of soma is unquestioned, and even if the secret of the soma ritual was hidden from them in the past, there is no hint that they were too 'impure' to drink soma. It was, after all, Dadhyañc,[72] a member of the ancient priestly family of the Atharvans, who introduced the Aśvins to the secrets of the ancient soma sacrifice. Doctors are mentioned in the *Ṛgveda*, but never regarded as unsuitable. This reflects the less rigid class divisions of the *Ṛgveda*; later, in the Middle Vedic period, medicine will be denounced as unsuitable for a Brahmin.

The Aśvins are called 'doctors' (*bhiṣajā*) throughout the *Ṛgveda*,[73] and are expected to 'heal' (*bhiṣajaya*) human afflictions.[74] Many of the stories about the Aśvins involve miraculous healings. They restore youth and male fertility to Cyavana (*RV* 5: 74, 5) and to Kakṣīvant (*RV* 10: 143, 1cd); they enable Puraṃdhi (*RV* 10: 39, 7d) and Vadhrimatī (*RV* 1: 117, 24ab) to get pregnant; they restore his eyesight to Ṛjrāśva (*RV* 1: 116, 16), and provide Viśpalā with an artificial leg (*RV* 1: 116, 15cd); they perform a head-transplant for Dadhyañc (*RV* 1: 117, 22ab); and they even bring Rebha (*RV* 10: 39, 9ab) and Śyāva (*RV* 1: 117, 24cd) back to life. In short, they are 'the healers of the blind, the weak, and the broken' (*RV* 10: 39, 3cd).

It is true that Rudra (*RV* 2: 33, 4d) and Varuṇa (*RV* 1: 24, 9a) are also called doctors in the *Ṛgveda*, but their case is somewhat different. They are more famous as gods who inflict illness on mortals as a punishment, and they are doctors only in the sense that they can remove this affliction. The stanzas where Rudra is praised as a healer begin with an expression of fear that improper worship or praise might arouse his anger.[75] The appeal to the 'gentle healing hand' of Rudra (*RV* 2: 33, 7ab) is wishful thinking, as is his later name Śiva, 'the gentle one'. Varuṇa punishes sinners by tying them in the 'bonds without ropes' (*RV* 7: 84, 2b) of illness. His worshippers ask him to 'heal' them only in the sense of begging him not to kill them (*RV* 7: 89)!

The Aśvins, in contrast, are healing gods alone. Nobody expresses any fear that the Aśvins might kill them or harm them. There is only one strange case where they use their medical knowledge to kill an enemy,[76] but otherwise they are characterized throughout the *Ṛgveda* as helpers and healers alone. This in itself will be a source of criticism later, but there is no such prejudice against medicine in the *Ṛgveda*.

One hymn may seem to poke fun at doctors: 'the carpenter wants something to break, the doctor wants someone to be injured...' (*RV* 9: 112, 1c). It regards doctors and carpenters as craftsmen and mocks both of them for their love of money, but then the poet continues with the self-mocking words, '... and the brahmin wants someone to press soma' (*RV* 9: 112, 1d). Brahmins are no better than carpenters or doctors, and this hymn does not exhibit the later Vedic contempt for craftsmen.[77] The same *ṛṣi* remarks later in this hymn, 'I am a poet, daddy is a doctor, mammy grinds grain, everyone has different ideas for getting rich' (*RV* 9: 112, 3), once again making it clear that priest-poets, doctors, and millers are all alike. The lack of any prejudice against medicine is also obvious from a hymn to the herbs used in healing: 'when the herbs have been gathered, like kings at an assembly, the inspired poet-priest is proclaimed as a doctor, a killer of demons, an expeller of illnesses' (*RV* 10: 97, 6cd). It is perfectly acceptable, therefore, and indeed something of an honour, for a poet-priest to practise medicine. The hymn itself is actually attributed to 'the Atharvan doctor,' which makes it clear that even the most ancient family of priests had no objections to medicine.[78] So the fact that they are doctors is not something that could be held against the Aśvins.

The Aśvins are also described as Adhvaryu priests (*adhvaryantā*, *RV* 1: 181, 1b), and in one hymn where Agni takes on his traditional role of Hotar priest (*RV* 10: 52, 2a),[79] he assigns the task of acting as Adhvaryu priests (*adhvarayaṃ*, *RV* 10: 52, 2c) to the Aśvins.[80] Such close cooperation between the Hotar and Adhvaryu priests is taken for granted in the *Ṛgveda*. In *RV* 1: 83, 3ab we hear that Indra has 'assigned the song of praise to the two of them, the pair (*mithunā*) who worship (*saparyataḥ*) while holding the ladle'. This intimate pair of priests (the word *mithunā* really implies a 'married couple' or 'a set of twins') are the Hotar and the Adhvaryu. Strictly speaking, the Hotar priest alone recites the hymn and the Adhvaryu priest alone works with the ladle, but they are treated in these verses as almost indistinguishable, and therefore the poet attributes both tasks to both priests.[81] The same expressions, 'the pair' (*mithunā*) and 'worship' (*saparyataḥ*), occur again in a hymn to Agni: 'whom the two men of equal age worship (*saparyataḥ*), the pair (*mithunā*) who live together in the same womb' (*RV* 1: 144, 4ab). The similarity in the vocabulary of these two hymns supports Sāyaṇa's interpretation that the pair from the same womb are, once again, the Hotar and Adhvaryu priests.[82] The Hotar is the highest-ranking priest, so by pairing him with the Adhvaryu, these hymns make it clear that the Hotar needs the Adhvaryu, and that the Aśvins as Adhvaryus are as essential as Agni the Hotar.

There is, however, a contrast between the activities of the Hotar and the Adhvaryu. The Hotar has a more dignified role: he addresses the gods themselves, he recites the verses from the *Ṛgveda*. The Adhvaryu is his acolyte: he does the physical work of the sacrifice, he mutters formulas as he goes through his tasks, he has 'fine hands'.[83] A description of the Aśvins working as Adhvaryu priests brings out this point: 'O Aśvins with your auspicious hands (*bhadrahastā*), with your good hands (*supāṇī*), hurry here and mix (the soma) with honey in the waters' (*RV* 1: 109, 4cd). The focus on their hands emphasises that the Aśvins, as Adhvaryu priests, have to do manual labour. *Supāṇi*, used here of the Aśvins, is elsewhere used mainly of Tvaṣṭar, the craftsman of the gods.[84] Its equivalents, *suhasta* and *suhastya*, describe the Adhvaryu priests and also the Ṛbhus, who were once again craftsmen working for the gods.[85] This association of the Adhvaryus with craftsmen and manual labour may explain why the helpful but low-class Aśvins are regarded as Adhvaryus, but these features are not problematic in the Early Vedic period.

In examining the status of the Aśvins in the *Ṛgveda*, we discover that the Aśvins are close to human beings, both by birth and by choice. They are hard-working gods, who intervene physically to save mortals from embarassing predicaments, but they intervene rather as rescuers than as conquering heroes, and they never threaten anyone. They are doctors, healing people from all sorts of personal maladies, and even providing remedies for old age and death. Finally, they are Adhvaryu priests, the men who did most of the actual work in a Vedic sacrifice, while the Hotar recited, the Udgātar chanted, and the Brahmin looked on in silence. Even though they are rescuers who work among mortals, and doctors, and Adhvaryu priests, the Aśvins are treated with the same respect that is given to the other gods, because the early society depicted in the *Ṛgveda* regards doctors as proper Brahmins, and the Adhvaryu priest as a respected acolyte of the Hotar priest.

The Aśvins may have been unusual gods who were exceptionally close to human beings, they may have received offerings of hot milk and remained blissfully ignorant for some time about the delights of soma, but such diversity was well accepted in the Early Vedic age.

During this period, people who spoke different languages were welcomed inside the fold of Vedic culture, the class system had not yet been formed, different tribes and priestly families held onto their own version of the hymns, and ritual had not yet been standardized for all of northern India.[86] This situation would change in the age of the Kuru-Pañcāla monarchy, and it is to the era of these kings that we must turn to discover the role of the Aśvins in Vedic ritual.

CHAPTER 4

THE AŚVINS IN VEDIC RITUAL

The *Ṛgveda* presents us with a very open-minded world, where gods like the Aśvins could freely associate with human beings; where the Hotar and Adhvaryu priests collaborate in fraternal unity to perform Vedic rituals; where the parents of a seer might be a doctor and a woman who grinds flour (*RV* 9: 112, 3). It is also, of course, a rather brutal world where sacrificial victims are beheaded at the stake. As soon as we leave the *Ṛgveda* and the Early Vedic period behind, we find ourselves in a very different world. The new kingdom of the Kuru-Pañcālas was a confederation of formerly independent tribes, and it was the first real state in Vedic India. The old melting-pot of ethnic and social groups was replaced by a division of society into respectable people who go to heaven (*āryas*) and the unredeemable people of the under-class who do not (*śūdras*).[1] The good people were divided into three social classes: the elite classes of the priests (*brāhmaṇas*) and the warriors (*kṣatriyas*), and the exploited *vaiśyas* who supported the *brāhmaṇa-kṣatriya* elite with their produce.[2] The *śūdras* were added as a fourth under-class at the bottom.

The Kuru kings also developed and imposed a nationwide standard of correct ritual ('orthopraxy') in the Middle Vedic period.[3] This new, reformed ritual was paradoxically called the 'traditional' (*śrauta*) system,[4] and the Kuru kings entrusted its development to the lowly Adhvaryu priests. The elevation of the Adhvaryus to this new position of control helped to diminish the power of the Hotar families whose inherited collections of hymns (the 'Family Books' of the *Ṛgveda*) were now nationalized. In the *Ṛgveda*, the Adhvaryus had been accepted as partners of the Hotars, but in the new texts composed by the Adhvaryus themselves (the texts of the *Yajurveda*), there is a sense that they are recent intruders, and the same prejudice is expressed against their divine role-models, the Aśvins.[5] The great change is not the presence of the Adhvaryus, but rather their new domination over the field of ritual knowledge. These stories reflect the resentment of the old Hotar establishment against the new *śrauta* regime of the upstart Adhvaryus, but of course the Aśvins always prevail.

The old-fashioned gods may accuse the Aśvins of being impure, but it was their Hotars and their Early Vedic ritual that permitted the bloody and violent beheading of the sacrificial victim, and it was the Hotars who were currently adopting as their own the impure, medicinal magic compiled in the 'Veda of the Bhṛgu and Aṅgiras Families' (*bhṛgvaṅgirasaveda*).[6] The reason for this paradox is that the Hotars had never been obsessed with purity. They had controlled ritual in the Early Vedic period, but they had never looked down on the Adhvaryus as being impure. The new criterion of impurity is established by the Adhvaryus themselves, and they use it to explain both their own former subordination (they were failing to live up to the standard that they had not yet invented) and their new intellectual predominance (they have now reached a standard that they themselves have set).

In this cultural war, both the Hotars and the Adhvaryus appeal to the ancient, pre-Vedic tradition of the Central Asian **atharwan* priests and to the sage Atharvan, who is regarded as the representative of this tradition. The Adhvaryus claim that their new *śrauta* system derives from the ancient teachings of Atharvan's son Dadhyañc, who first passed this secret knowledge on to the Aśvins.[7] The old Hotar families likewise claim that their new collection of ancient magic mantras comes from the Atharvan tradition, so the new, fourth 'Veda of the Bhṛgu and Aṅgiras Families' was called the *Atharvaveda*.[8] The alliance between the reciters of hymns and the practitioners of magic is new, and the compilation of everday magic into an official text is new, but much of its content is genuinely ancient. By calling it the 'Veda of the Bhṛgu and Aṅgiras Families', the Hotars, who belong to these families, are taking over this material and granting the approval of the oldest Veda, their own *Ṛgveda*, to the newest one.[9] By calling it the 'Veda of the Atharvans', the Hotars are asserting, with some truth, that the newest Veda contains the oldest material.[10] Meanwhile, the Adhvaryus place their rules of orthopraxy and purity in the mouths of the old-fashioned gods and the great sage Atharvan, but these rules are really a very new obsession of the modernizing Adhvaryus.[11] They are using the voice of the Atharvan tradition to legitimize the new *śrauta* system.

The Adhvaryus want to justify their new position of power, and this concern is reflected in the stories they tell about the Aśvins. The horse gods are associated with several Vedic rites, and all of these connections had to be examined and explained by the scholars of the Middle Vedic era. In this chapter, we shall look at these rituals and the stories told about them:

- The *Āśvinagraha* (Aśvin Cup) – a cup of soma juice offered to the Aśvins during the soma sacrifice.
- The *Pravargya* (Heating Ritual) – an offering of boiled milk to the Aśvins, which takes place on the preparatory days of a soma sacrifice.
- The *Prātaranuvāka* (Morning Prayer) – a long hymn to the Aśvins and other morning-gods that is recited early on the day that the soma plant is crushed.
- The *Saṃdhistotra* (Twilight Chant) and the *Āśvinaśastra* (Aśvin Hymn) – a long chant and hymn that are recited on the following morning if the soma sacrifice lasts through the night and on to a second day (this longer version of the soma sacrifice is called the Overnight Sacrifice, *Atirātri*).
- The *Sautrāmaṇī* (Good Saviour Ritual) – a separate ritual in which alcoholic *surā* is offered rather than soma. It honours Indra the Good Saviour (*indra sutrāman*).

The *Āśvinagraha* (Aśvin Cup)

The Aśvin Cup was that part of the soma sacrifice in which the Aśvins received their offering of soma juice, so any doubts about their status as soma-drinking gods would naturally focus on this ritual event. As we have seen, the *Ṛgveda* says that the Aśvins had known nothing about soma until a bee told them of its existence, and the Atharvan priest Dadhyañc revealed the secret of its preparation to them. The Early Vedic period is quite content with gods who prefer hot milk to soma, but in the Middle Vedic period such anomalies are an embarrassment. On the main day of the soma sacrifice, the 'pressing day' (*savanāha*), the soma stalks are crushed at morning, noon and evening, and their juice is offered to the gods. These offerings of soma follow a particular pattern called a Soma Sequence:

- the cups are filled with soma;
- the Samavedic priests sing a chant (*stoma*) from the *Sāmaveda*;
- the cups of soma are offered to the gods and drunk by the participants;
- the Hotar recites a hymn (*śastra*) from the *Ṛgveda*.

After the first pressing of the soma juice in the morning, soma is offered to the 'pairs of gods' (*dvidevatya*): Indra and Vayu, Mitra and Varuṇa, and the two Aśvins. There is, however, a strange anomaly in the case of the Aśvins. After the soma juice has been extracted from the soma stalks, cups are filled for various gods: one for Indra and Vayu, one for Mitra and Varuṇa,[12] but none for the Aśvins. They are completely ignored.

The sacrificer and all the priests then form a procession and march to the north-west corner of the Great Soma Hall (*mahāvedi*), where the Samavedic priests sing their first chant, the Outdoor Purifying Chant (*bahiṣpavamānastotra*).[13] It is only *after* this chant has taken place that the Adhvaryu fills the cup of the Aśvins,[14] so the normal sequence is deliberately disrupted. The Aśvins are segregated from the other divine pairs, because their cup is conspicuously filled *after* the Outdoor Chant rather than before it.

After this insult to the Aśvins, the soma sequence continues in the normal way. Now that all three cups are filled, they can be offered to the three pairs of gods, and this time the Aśvins are included with the other gods. The first cup is offered to Indra and Vayu, the second to Mitra and Varuṇa, the third to the Aśvins. From this point on, nothing distinguishes the Aśvins from the other gods and nothing disturbs the soma sequence. The participants drink soma, and finally the Hotar recites his first hymn of the day, the Butter Hymn (*ājyaśastra*).

The Headless Sacrifice in the Taittirīya Saṃhitā

The strange way in which the cup for the Aśvins is prepared only at the last minute strongly suggests that their offering was an afterthought, and that originally they did not receive a cup of soma at all. This sense that the Aśvins do not really belong to the soma sacrifice comes out clearly in the *Taittirīya Saṃhitā*, the sacred text of those Adhvaryu priests who studied in the Taittirīya school. These scholars associate the late inclusion of the Aśvins in the soma sacrifice with their own late assumption of control over Vedic ritual. The arrival of the Aśvins marks the end of the old, violent, and polluted form of sacrifice that had been practised in the bad old days, before the Adhvaryus purified the ritual and made it whole.

They explain the odd timing of the Aśvin Cup with the following story, one that emphasizes the violence and mutilation involved in an old-fashioned sacrifice. The gods announce that they wish to kill King Soma and offer him up as a sacrifice. In exchange for their collaboration, Indra–Vayu and Mitra–Varuṇa demand that the first cups of soma be offered to them.[15] By the time that the Aśvins arrive on the scene, the victim has already been beheaded.

Decapitation was the original way of killing a sacrificial victim,[16] and in the *Ṛgveda* Indra, the great soma god, brutally beheads Makha, the sacrifice.[17] Such explicit violence was not allowed in the correct ritual practice that was developed by the Adhvaryus in the Middle Vedic period; instead the victim was suffocated in order to preserve its wholeness.[18] The purpose of this change is not to avoid death and violence, but rather to kill the victim in a polite and elegant manner.[19] The story in the *Taittirīya Saṃhitā* will go on to explain the change-over from the old practice of beheading the victim to the new practice of offering a whole victim with no parts missing and no messy blood. The new 'medical' practice of bloodless killing will be introduced by the Aśvins, who are the doctors and Adhvaryus of the gods, whereas the old-fashioned priests, represented by Indra and the other gods, had no qualms about decapitating victims at the stake.

In the *Taittirīya Saṃhitā*, the gods have beheaded their victim in the Early Vedic way, and then it suddenly occurs to them that they now have only three-quarters of a mutilated victim to work with, whereas they need a whole one for their ritual. Luckily for them, the Aśvins arrive on the scene.

> The head of the sacrifice was cut off. The gods said to the Aśvins, 'You are doctors; put this head back on the sacrifice.'
> Those two said, 'Let us choose a favour. A cup must be poured here for us also (*api*).'
> The gods filled this Aśvin Cup for the two of them.
> Then the two of them placed the head back on the sacrifice.
> The Aśvin Cup is filled so that the sacrifice may be healed.
> (*TS* 6: 4, 9^{1})

The narrative points out that the Aśvins arrive *after* the victim has been sacrificed, and that they receive a cup *also* (*api*) – in other words, as late-comers, as an afterthought, and only because the gods had killed the victim in an inappropriate way. The gods make it quite clear that they are allowing the Aśvins to participate in the soma sacrifice only under duress. Ironically, their medical skill, which is necessary if the sacrifice is to be healed, is the very characteristic that would have disqualified them from participating in the sacrifice.

> The gods said about the two of them, 'they are impure (*apūtau*) because they associate with humans and they are doctors.'
> That is why a Brahmin should not practice medicine, because he would be impure (*apūto*) and unsuitable at a sacrifice (*amedhyo*).
> (*TS* 6: 4, $9^{1\text{-}2}$)

Throughout the *Taittirīya Saṃhitā*, the Aśvins are called 'the doctors of the gods' (*devānām bhiṣajau*),[20] but in spite of this, medicine is inappropriate not only for gods but even for Brahmins. The qualities of the Aśvins that were especially praised in the *Ṛgveda* – their healing powers and their helpfulness to humans – are now a source of impurity.

This impurity should make them ritually unsuitable (*amedhya*) as participants in the soma sacrifice, but the scholars of the Taittirīya school create a clever way out of this dilemma:

> They (the gods) purified the two of them with the Outdoor Purifying Chant, and filled the Aśvin Cup for them.
> That is why the Aśvin Cup is filled after the Outdoor Purifying Chant has been sung.
> And that is why somebody who understands this should perform the Outdoor Purifying Chant.
> For the Outdoor Purifying Chant is a means of purification (*pavitra*).
> He (the performer) purifies himself.
>
> (*TS* 6: 4, 9^2)

The Outdoor Purifying Chant was, of course, sung to celebrate the purification of the soma juice, as it was being poured from the main vat through a filter (*pavitra*) into the Container of the Purified (Soma) (*pūtabhṛt*). The Taittirīya scholars ingeniously reinterpret the purifying (*pavamāna*) and filtration (*pavitra*) of soma to mean the purification of a person. This was how the gods managed to purify the Aśvins of their unsavoury features, and thereby allowed them to participate in the soma sacrifice. This clever interpretation also explains why it is precisely at this point in the ritual, *after* the Outdoor Purifying Chant, *after* the Aśvins have been purified, that the Aśvin Cup is filled.

Even though the Aśvins have been rehabilitated, their late arrival at the soma sacrifice implies that they are *ānujāvara*, a term that means 'born later', and therefore 'inferior', 'of lower rank'.[21]

> A man of lower rank should fill the Aśvin cups first (*agrān*).
> The Aśvins are of lower rank (*ānujāvara*) among the gods,

so they came to the forefront (*agram*) somewhat later (*paśceva*).
The Aśvins are the gods of the man who is of lower rank (*ānujāvara*).
They lead him to the forefront (*agram*).

(*TS* 7: 2, 7^2)

These lines come from a passage that interprets the sequence of the cups to the double gods, the very part of a soma sacrifice that includes the Aśvins among the soma-drinking gods, even though it also relegates them to an inferior position among those gods. The sacrificer of low rank overcomes his own low status and the inferiority of the Aśvins by reversing the normal order of the soma cups.[22]

Surprisingly, we find elsewhere in the *Taittirīya Saṃhitā* that even the king of the gods, the great soma-drinker Indra himself, is described as being 'of lower rank among the gods' (*TS* 2: 3, 4^2):

Indra was (*āsīt*) of lower rank (*ānujāvara*) among the gods.
He ran to Prajāpati for help.
He offered him this Indra-offering of rice-shoots on eleven potsherds.
Because of that offering, Prajāpati led Indra to the forefront (*agram*) of the gods.

(*TS* 2: 3, 4^2)

Indra's low rank is regarded as a strange anomaly that is relegated to the past (*āsīt*), whereas the inferiority of the Aśvins was expressed as their normal status. As in the case of the Aśvins, this myth about Indra explains why a warlord (*rājanya*) who is of lower rank must make an offering to Indra.

Whatever warlord (*rājanya*) might be of lower rank (*ānujāvara*) should offer him (Indra) this Indra-offering of rice-shoots on eleven potsherds.
Thus, he runs to Indra for help, (offering him) his proper share.
He (Indra) leads him to the forefront (*agra*) of his colleagues.

(*TS* 2: 3, 4^3)

Once again there is a difference between the 'lower rank' of a warlord, who naturally belongs to the higher ranks of society, and the perfectly normal inferiority of the man who alters the order of the soma cups to benefit the Aśvins. The follower of the Aśvins arrives at the forefront of society (*agram*); the follower of Indra comes to the forefront *of his colleagues* (*agraṃ samānānām*) who are already at the forefront of society.

The inferiority of Indra was a thing of the past, a temporary anomaly, whereas that of the Aśvins seems present and permanent. They may join the other gods at the forefront, but they are like latecomers (*paśceva*), they seem anomalous. For Indra, inferiority is not just a temporary aberration, it is a violation of his very essence. Being at the forefront is his real nature: Indra is not Indra unless he is at the forefront. His essential superiority comes out in another passage from the *Taittirīya Saṃhitā*, which discusses the long 12-day soma sacrifice.

> Prajāpati made Indra sacrifice with that (the twelve-day soma sacrifice)
> Then Indra became Indra.
> This is why they say:
> 'It is the sacrifice of the inferior (*ānujāvarasya*).'
> In the beginning (*agre*) he sacrificed with this.
>
> (*TS* 7: 2, 10^2)

In Indra's case, the 12-day soma sacrifice belongs to the past, it is something he used to do 'in the beginning', but at that time he was not yet Indra. The Aśvins, in contrast, are very much themselves when they are denounced as inferior and impure. It is, paradoxically, that same inferiority and impurity that enables them to force their way into the soma sacrifice. So their inferiority is an essential and necessary part of their divinity, and also of their participation in the soma sacrifice.

Their human protégés also bring out the difference between the Aśvins and the other gods. The Aśvins take care of people who are naturally inferior, Indra takes care of 'inferior' warlords, and Bṛhaspati takes care of 'inferior' Brahmins.[23] In the myths that explain this patronage, Bṛhaspati was never inferior; Indra was briefly so, but that was before he was really himself; and the Aśvins only emerged from their inferiority at a 'somewhat later' stage (*paśceva*, *TS* 7: 2, 7[2]). Finally, Bṛhaspati takes care of low-ranking Brahmins, and Indra looks after similar warlords, in so far as Brahmins and warlords can be considered 'low-ranking'.[24] This leaves the Aśvins as the patrons of the third class, the *naturally* low-ranking Vaiśyas.[25]

In a discussion of animal sacrifices, there is yet another reminder of the ambiguous status of the Aśvins.

> A man who is a bad Brahmin (*durbrāhmaṇaḥ*) and wants to drink soma should offer a victim with grey spots to the Aśvins.
> Of (all) the gods, the Aśvins did not drink soma.
> Later (*paścā*) they gained the right to drink soma. (So) the Aśvins are the gods of that man who is a bad Brahmin and wants to drink soma.
> He runs to the Aśvins for help, offering them their proper share.
> They grant him the right to drink soma; the right to drink soma comes to him.
>
> (*TS* 2: 1, 10[1])

This is rather harsh criticism of the Aśvins, because they are being associated with bad Brahmins. Just as their medical skills equated them with Brahmins who disgraced themselves by practising medicine, so their initial exclusion from soma makes them similar to bad Brahmins who are not entitled to drink it. In effect, the bad Brahmin has fallen so low that he is too ashamed to address Bṛhaspati; he must humiliate himself by appealing to the gods of the inferior Vaiśyas.

It is surprising to find the Aśvins described as gods of low status in the *Taittirīya Saṃhitā*, because they play an important role in the rituals analysed by this text. A large number of ritual actions are accompanied by the Savitar-formula, which is repeated twelve times in the *Taittirīya Saṃhitā*, and the Aśvins are an essential part of that formula.

> At the instigation of Savitar, with the arms of the Aśvins, with the hands of Pūṣan.
>
> (*TS* 2: 1, 10[1])

What makes this even stranger is that on four occasions, the expression 'with the arms of the Aśvins' is explained by pointing out that the Aśvins are 'the Adhvaryu priests of the gods'.[26]

> 'With the arms of the Aśvins', he says. The Aśvins were the Adhvaryu priests of the gods.
>
> (*TS* 2: 6, 4[1] and elsewhere)

So the Adhvaryu scholars who composed the *Taittirīya Saṃhitā* are identifying themselves with a pair of gods whom they themselves declare to be impure, inferior, and all-too-human. Since the four Vedas are parallel to the four social classes,[27] and the Aśvins are regarded as Vaiśya gods,[28] the Adhvaryus and their *Yajurveda* are being equated with the Vaiśyas. And yet, the Adhvaryus have taken over all the tasks of the Hotar priest, leaving him with little more than the honour of reciting Vedic hymns.[29] Their false modesty makes their rise to supremacy all the more splendid. They are not, after all, humbly requesting the right to help out at a soma sacrifice, for they had always possessed this dubious privilege. What they are asserting is their right to be at the forefront (*agra*), to control the sacrifice, and to determine who has access to it. In spite of their hints that they are being treated as if they were not much better than *Vaiśyas*, it must not be forgotten that their struggle for power against the Hotars is taking place inside the Brahmin elite. The Adhvaryus may be Brahmins 'of inferior rank', but they are still Brahmins, and they are pushing their way forward to the forefront of their colleagues. And the Aśvins, however late and impure they may be, are still soma-drinking gods who can tell their colleagues how to perform a sacrifice properly.

The Aśvin Cup in the Śatapatha Brāhmaṇa

In the *Ṛgveda*, a honey-bee told the Aśvins that they alone among the gods were being deprived of soma (*RV* 1: 119, 9a and 10: 40, 6cd), but in the later *Brāhmaṇas* this role is played by Cyavana. He had nothing whatsoever to do with the secret of soma in the *Ṛgveda*. In those hymns, Cyavana was simply a man whom the Aśvins had rejuvenated so that he could make a woman happy. The *Śatapatha Brāhmaṇa* does allude to the Early Vedic story where Dadhyañc teaches the Aśvins how to produce soma: 'Dadhyañc, son of Atharvan, told them the secret called honey (*madhu*),' which means soma in this part of the *Śatapatha Brāhmaṇa* (*ŚB* 4: 1, 5^{18}).[30] This allusion is something of an afterthought, and in its explanation of the Aśvin Cup, the *Śatapatha Brāhmaṇa* gives us the new version where Cyavana tells them about the existence of the soma sacrifice, and Dadhyañc is ignored.[31] Nobody has to teach the Aśvins how to produce soma, they demand soma as their right. The main points of the story are as follows (*ŚB* 4: 1, $5^{8\text{-}13}$):

Sukanyā ('beautiful young woman'), the daughter of a chieftain, is given in marriage to the elderly Cyavana. The Aśvins find her very attractive, but she rejects their advances. They are surprised that she would choose Cyavana over them, but Sukanyā tells them that they are just as defective as her husband. They make her husband young again, and in exchange Cyavana reveals to them how they are defective: the other gods are offering a soma sacrifice at Kurukṣetra and they have excluded the Aśvins. The story continues much as it did in the *Taittirīya Saṃhitā*. The Aśvins tell the gods that the sacrifice is defective because it is headless, and then the Aśvins heal the sacrifice in exchange for the Aśvin Cup.

We are not told how they heal the sacrifice, but the authors of the text promise us that this will be explained later, a promise that is fulfilled when the text discusses the *Pravargya* ritual.[32] There we will be told that the secret honey of Dadhyañc was not soma after all, but rather the *Pravargya* ritual (compare *ŚB* 4: 1, 5^{18} and *ŚB* 14: 1, 1^{25}), and that the missing head of the sacrifice was the *Pravargya* ritual; the Aśvins restore the head of the sacrifice by adding this ritual to it.

In the section on the Aśvin Cup, however, the answer lies in the healing powers of the Aśvins themselves and in their status as Adhvaryus. The Aśvins and the Adhvaryus are the missing ingredient in the soma sacrifice; they are the head of the sacrifice. This approach suggests a strong sense of self-confidence among the Adhvaryu priesthood. It is true that in the *Śatapatha Brāhmaṇa*, as in the earlier

Taittirīya Saṃhitā, we once again hear the gods complaining that the Aśvins 'have wandered and mingled a lot with men, healing them' (*ŚB* 4: 1, 5[15]). This time, however, the Aśvins boldly declare, 'We are the heads of the sacrifice because we are Adhvaryus' (*ŚB* 4: 1, 5[16]). Even the shape of their soma-cup reveals their supremacy. 'The Aśvins are the head gods (*mukhyau*), and the head (*mukham*) has lips; this is why the Aśvin cup has lips' (*ŚB* 4: 1, 5[19]). The Adhvaryus have lost their humility; and their mythical prototypes, the Aśvins, demand their rights as the chief gods (*mukhyau*) of the sacrifice.

The *Taittirīya Saṃhitā* had presented us with a world where the Aśvins were called in to the rescue only because the gods had made a mess of the sacrifice, but the Aśvins themselves were not wanted. In the *Śatapatha Brāhmaṇa*, the Aśvins are incomplete only because they have not attended the soma sacrifice, but the soma sacrifice is likewise incomplete because the Aśvins are missing. In this new world, the Aśvins may be late-comers without a proper invitation, but such ill-treatment is a great injustice; the Aśvins should rightly be the chief guests at the sacrifice.

In the *Ṛgveda* itself, the only reason the Aśvins do not drink soma is that nobody told them about it. The bee tells them that soma exists, and Dadhyañc tells them the secret of its production, but he does this simply because the Aśvins ask him nicely. Once they know the secret, there is no question of their not being allowed to drink soma. By the time of the *Taittirīya Saṃhitā*, the Aśvins are regarded as impure and they have no right to participate in the soma sacrifice. The gods are reluctantly forced to admit them only because they need the help of the Aśvins in healing the headless sacrifice. Finally, in the *Śatapatha Brāhmaṇa*, the gods are once again obliged to call in the Aśvins, who always had a natural right to participate in the sacrifice,[33] but are now asserting their right to attend the sacrifice, and demanding the privilege of controlling it. All the stories about the Aśvin Cup explain why the Aśvins receive this honour, and supply different answers – a personal favour from Dadhyañc, a concession extorted from the gods, and a right that is naturally theirs as soon as they decide to exercise it.

The *Pravargya* (Heating Ritual)

The Aśvins were unusual in being offered boiled milk, whereas all the other gods received offerings of soma. This did not prevent them from participating in the soma sacrifice too, but hot milk was always the special offering to the Aśvins. In the Middle Vedic period this offering is called the *Pravargya* (Heating Ritual), but in the *Ṛgveda* it was simply called the *Gharma* (Hot Milk) offering.[34] In the Early Vedic period, a simple version of this ritual was performed by the Atri family alone. As we saw in the last chapter, the Atris told how the Aśvins had rescued their ancestor Atri and given him hot milk; ever since then, Atri and his descendants had offered hot milk to the Aśvins (*RV* 5: 73, 6). The Atris heated milk in a metal pot (*gharmaś cit taptaḥ* [. . .] *ayasmayas*, *RV* 5: 30, 15cd) and offered it to the Aśvins.[35] Their ritual is described in four lines that were always recited during the later *Pravargya* rite,[36] but it had originally been composed for the simple *Gharma* offering by the Atri family:

> The inspired priests anoint it, as if they were spreading (sacred grass);[37]
> they heat it on the fire, as if it were a victim's omentum;[38]
> the *gharma*-pot is ritually placed on the fire,
> as if it were a beloved son on his father's lap.
>
> (*RV* 5: 43, 7)

This simple *Gharma* ritual is then adopted by the other families of Vedic priests, and by the end of the Early Vedic period, the hymns and rituals of the Atri family have become the common property of all the priestly families in the Pūru-Bharata tribal confederation.[39] By this time, the ritual is more elaborate: it may perhaps have included the ritual construction of a clay pot,[40] and it already has the ritual milking of the cow:

> I call this easily milked cow,
> may the skilful-handed milkman milk her.
> May Savitar give the best stimulation.

The *gharma*-pot has been inflamed. I proclaim that well.
The lowing mistress of wealth
has come here, longing in her heart for her calf.
May this cow give her milk for the Aśvins,
and may she grow big for our great fortune.

(*RV* 1: 164, 26–27)

These milking mantras were composed especially for the *Gharma* ritual of the Pūru-Bharata chieftains, and this milking ritual will later become a standard event in the fully developed *Pravargya* rite of the Kuru-Pañcāla kingdom.[41] The Ṛgvedic ritual ends with the traditional offering of this hot milk to the Aśvins.

The more elaborate *Pravargya* ritual was incorporated into the soma sacrifice around the time that the *Ṛgveda* was compiled under the Kuru-Pañcāla kings. Scholars argue about when exactly this incorporation took place,[42] but the Pravargya is definitely a part of the soma sacrifice by the Middle Vedic period.[43] It was always, however, an optional element in the soma sacrifice,[44] which reveals that it originally did not belong there. Just as the inclusion of the Aśvins themselves in the soma sacrifice required interpretation, so the role of the *Pravargya* in the soma sacrifice gave rise to all kinds of creative explanations throughout the Middle Vedic period.

There are two ways in which the *Pravargya* could be incorporated into a soma sacrifice. Normally, it is performed twice daily on the three *Upasad* days that precede the main day of the sacrifice, the Pressing Day on which the soma is crushed to produce soma juice. There is, however, an alternative way of including the *Pravargya*, and in this version it plays a very minor role.

Instead of being repeated twice daily throughout the three *Upasad* days, it is performed just once on the Pressing Day itself.[45] The hot milk (*gharma*) is offered to the Aśvins after the Midday Chant of Purification (*mādhyaṃdinaṃ pavamānam*), and this offering takes place at the Hut of the Fire Priest (*āgnīdhrīya*) in the Great Altar Hall (*mahāvedi*). Immediately afterwards, an offering of heated yogurt (*Dadhigharma*) is made to Indra in the hut of the same priest.[46]

The yogurt offering is, as van Buitenen remarked, 'a balancing rite', because every soma sacrifice must have both the *Pravargya* of the Aśvins and the *Dadhigharma* of Indra on the Pressing Day, or neither of them; and Indra's offering comes after the hot milk for the Aśvins 'in order to top it'.[47] This midday offering of yogurt to Indra was already a part of the soma sacrifice in the Early Vedic period, because it is mentioned in the *Ṛgveda*: 'Drink the yogurt at the mid-day pressing, Indra!' (*RV* 10: 179, 3cd). It would, therefore, be better to say that the *Pravargya* was brought in to balance the *Dadhigharma*, or rather that the similarity between the two offerings suggested that this might be a suitable point at which the priests might sneak the *Pravargya* into the soma sacrifice. Both the *Dadhigharma* and the later *Pravargya* are minor offerings and do not distract attention from the soma sacrifice. As van Buitenen points out, this discreet intrusion on the Pressing Day was probably the original manner in which the *Pravargya* was incorporated into the soma sacrifice.[48]

Normally, however, the *Pravargya* played a much more prominent role in the soma sacrifice, and was perfomed (as we mentioned above) twice on each of the *Upasad* days. Instead of viewing it as a discreet element within the soma sacrifice, brahminical interpretations compare and contrast the *Pravargya*, which belongs to the Aśvins, with the entire soma sacrifice, which belongs to Indra.[49] This balance between the two rituals is built into the procedure of the soma sacrifice itself. The *Pravargya* rite takes place in the smaller Bamboo Hut (*Prāgvaṃśa*) to the west, the soma sacrifice is in the Great Altar Hall (*mahāvedi*) to the east. This contrast is repeated inside the Bamboo Hut itself, where the soma stalks (King Soma) are placed on the Royal Throne (*Rājāsandī*),[50] whereas the *Pravargya* pot ('the Emperor Mahāvīra') is placed on the Imperial Throne (*Saṃrāḍāsandī*). All of the *Pravargya* equipment is cleared away on the last Day of Preparation (*Upasad*);[51] it is only after this happens that the sacred fire is brought forward from the Bamboo Hut to its new home in the Great Altar Hall in a solemn procession that is called the Advancement of Agni (*Agnipraṇayana*).[52]

Somewhat later another solemn procession leads both Agni and Soma to the Great Altar Hall, the Advancement of Agni and Soma (*Agniṣomapravayaṇa*).[53] The Bamboo Hut may be good enough for the *Pravargya*, but Agni and Soma must attend to the more important soma sacrifice in the Great Altar Hall. The contrast between the two rites is very visible, and it is only natural that the Brahmins would appeal to it in analysing them. In fact, they even took over mantras from the soma sacrifice and used them in the *Pravargya*, believing that the two rites were parallel and perhaps hoping to endow the *Pravargya* with the power of the soma ritual.[54]

The Pravargya *in the* Aitareya Brāhmaṇa

The usual way of performing the *Pravargya* as a major ritual throughout the three *Upasad* days makes it a parallel and almost rival event to the soma sacrifice, and it is treated in interpretative works as an essential prerequisite for the success of a soma sacrifice. The significance of the *Pravargya* comes out in the analysis made of the ritual by the Ṛgvedic scholars of the Aitareya school:

> The sacrifice went away from the gods: 'I will not be your food,' he said.
> 'No,' said the gods, 'you definitely will be our food.'
> The gods chopped him up, but when he was chopped up, he was no use to them.
> The gods said, 'Now that he is chopped up like this, he will not be enough for us. Come on, let's put the sacrifice together!'
> 'All right.'
> They put him together.
>
> After they put him together, they said to the Aśvins,
> 'Heal this (sacrifice).'
> The Aśvins are the doctors of the gods, the Aśvins are Adhvaryu priests.
> This is why the two Adhvaryu priests put the *Gharma* (equipment) together. When the two (Adhvaryu priests) have put it together, they say,

'Brahmin priest, we shall proceed with the Pravargya ritual.
Hotar priest, recite the hymn.'

(*Aitareya Brāhmaṇa* 1: 18)

In explaining the soma-cup of the Aśvins, the interpreters of the Taittirīya school had said that it was a medical fee extorted by the Aśvins from the other gods; in exchange for this fee, the Aśvins had replaced the head of the sacrifice. Now the Ṛgvedic scholars provide a similar explanation for the hot milk offering of the Aśvins. This time, the gods chop the sacrifice to pieces rather than beheading it, but as usual they discover that they have made a dreadful mistake and that such a sacrifice will never serve their purposes. Once again, the Aśvins come to the rescue as doctors and Adhvaryu priests. The gods assembled the pieces (*saṃjabhrus*), just as the human Adhvaryu priests get the equipment ready for the *Pravargya* in an earthly soma sacrifice (*sambharatas*).[55] This procedure of putting things together again (*sambhṛ*) did not work in heaven when the other gods tried it, for they still needed the Aśvins to come along and heal the sacrifice for them. It did, however, work for the Aśvins and it does work on earth for the Adhvaryus. This story also demonstrates that control over the *Pravargya* provides the sacrificer with power over the entire soma sacrifice. When the human Adhvaryus gather the *Pravargya* equipment, this action automatically puts the sacrifice together again and heals it.

At the end of their discussion of the ritual, the Aitareya scholars provide the *Pravargya* with a metaphysical significance that is normally reserved for the soma sacrifice itself. At first this interpretation sounds rather Freudian, for it equates the hot milk with semen and the fire into which it is offered with a womb, but its real focus is on rebirth rather than sexual activity.

This semen is poured into the fire, the womb of the gods, in the procreative act.
The fire is the womb of the gods.
With the libations, he is born from the fire, the womb of the gods.

> ... the person who understands this goes to the gods, and also the person who understands this and performs a sacrifice with this ritual.
>
> (*Aitareya Brāhmaṇa* 1: 22)

The *Pravargya* is a divine marriage that results in the birth of a new being; the sacrificial body of the man who performs it. As in the soma ritual, the sacrificer is born again with a new body, and can fly with his new body to the gods.[56] This interpretation does not mention the Aśvins, but it shows that the offering of hot milk to the Aśvins possesses the mystical powers of a soma sacrifice, so the *Pravargya* rivals the soma sacrifice, and the Aśvins are challenging Indra in his own sacred ritual.

The Headless Sacrifice in the Kauṣītaki Brāhmaṇa

The Ṛgvedic scholars of the Kauṣītaki school came up with a different explanation for the *Pravargya*, one that brings us back to the beheading of sacrificial victims and the realization that such a mutilated victim will be inadequate:

> This head of the sacrifice is the *Mahāvīra* pot. He should not perform the *Pravargya* rite with it at his first soma sacrifice. The second sacrifice yields to the man who does not perform the *Pravargya* at his first sacrifice.
> ... It is the self (*ātmā*) of the sacrifice. With the self (*ātmanā*) he makes the sacrifice successful.
>
> (*Kauṣītaki Brāhmaṇa* 8: 3)

The *Mahāvīra* ('Great Hero') pot is the name given to the earthenware pot used in the *Pravargya* ritual. The Atri family had originally used a metal pot, but when the standard version of the *Pravargya* developed in the Middle Vedic period, the Adhvaryu priests used a tall pot in three sections called the *Mahāvīra* pot. This pot was made by hand in a deliberately archaic ritual that ignored the invention of the potter's wheel. Such radically modern efforts to appear ancient and traditional were typical of cultural life in the Kuru-Pañcāla kingdom.[57]

In the standard *Pravargya* ritual, the construction of this pot is an elaborate ritual in its own right, and it takes place before the Preparatory Days (*Upasad* Days) of the soma sacrifice.[58] The *Mahāvīra* pot is treated with as much respect as Soma himself; both Soma and the *Mahāvīra* pot are placed on thrones and worshipped as gods; but if Soma is a king (*rājā*), *Mahāvīra* is an emperor (*saṃrāj*). This almost makes the *Pravargya* more important than the soma sacrifice, and ritual experts argued about which of the two thrones should be the higher, the consensus being that the Emperor Pot's throne was indeed higher than King Soma's.[59]

In the *Kauṣītaki Brāhmaṇa*, this imperial pot is explicitly equated with the missing head of the royal soma sacrifice, which explains how it is that the *Pravargya* can heal the sacrifice, something that was merely hinted at in the *Aitareya Brāhmaṇa*. The Aśvins are, in effect, supplying the sacrifice with a new head to replace the one that the gods unwisely removed. This surgical transplant is a repeat of the operation they performed on Dadhyañc, and because of this parallel, the later *Śatapatha Brāhmaṇa* will draw him into its explanation of the *Pravargya*. This head transplant is, however, too complicated for a beginner, so a first soma sacrifice should not include the *Pravargya*. The real reason for this tabu is probably that the *Pravargya* did not originally belong to the soma sacrifice, and even though it became customary, it was never an obligatory element of the soma sacrifice.[60] The *Kauṣītaki Brāhmaṇa* does not wish to diminish its importance, however, and boldly states that the *Pravargya* is absolutely essential: it is the self, or soul (*ātmā*), of the sacrifice.

The Beheading of the Sacrifice in the Taittirīya Āraṇyaka

The *Aitareya Brāhmaṇa* and the *Kauṣītaki Brāhmaṇa* explain how the Aśvins heal the mutilated soma sacrifice by adding the *Pravargya* rite to it. The *Taittirīya Āraṇyaka* explains why the sacrifice was beheaded in the first place.

The gods are sacrificing at Kurukṣetra, the religious center of the Vedic world in the days of the Kuru-Pañcālas. Their soma sacrifice is a *sattra*, one in which the priests both participate and benefit (as distinct from a normal sacrifice where the priests perform and the patron benefits). The gods explain how their *sattra* works: all of them will share its glory.[61] Makha, however, does not obey this rule. He happens to be the son of the powerful god Viṣṇu, and his name means 'sacrifice', so he greedily takes all the glory for himself, rather than sharing it with the whole group.

> The gods, desiring glory, were performing a *sattra* soma sacrifice ending in success. They said:
> 'Whichever one of us glory comes to first, let that glory be shared by all of us.'
> Their altar was at Kurukṣetra.
> Among them (the gods), the glory came to Makha, the son of Viṣṇu; he desired it; he went away with it....
>
> (*Taittirīya Āraṇyaka* 5: 1, 1–2)

In order to win back some glory from the sacrifice, the gods are reduced to making a bargain with the lowly ants. The gods will grant them a constant supply of water, and the ants will deal with Makha. Using his own bow against him, they behead Makha.

> He stood leaning on his bow.
> The ants said (to the gods), 'Let us choose a favour, and we will make this man subject to you. Wherever we dig, let us dig up water.' This is why ants dig up water wherever they dig, that was what they chose.
> The ants ate the string of his bow. Splitting apart, the bow ripped off his head....
>
> (*Taittirīya Āraṇyaka* 5: 1, 4–5)

By dying in this way, Makha has become both the soma sacrifice and the sacrificial victim, soma itself. The gods make his sacrifice last all day long by dividing him into three pressings, as in a normal soma sacrifice. In spite of all their efforts, they still do not get any of the blessings they pray for, because their sacrifice does not have a head.

When he was streched out, the gods took him in three parts. Agni took the morning pressing; Indra took the midday pressing; All the Gods took the third pressing. When they sacrificed with that headless sacrifice, they did not get their wishes, they did not win the world of heaven.

(*Taittirīya Āraṇyaka* 5: 1, 6)

The story ends in the usual way when the Aśvins arrive and agree to heal the sacrifice in exchange for a cup of soma. The head they add to the mutiliated victim is once again the *Pravargya* pot, and any man can similarly replace the head of the sacrifice by performing the *Pravargya* ritual.

(The gods) said to the Aśvins:
'You are doctors; put back the head of the sacrifice.'
The two (Aśvins) said:
'Let us choose a favour. Let a cup be filled here for us also.'
(The gods) filled the Aśvin cup for the two (Aśvins).[62]
The two (Aśvins) put back the head of the sacrifice; (the head) is the *Pravargya*.

When (the gods) sacrificed with that sacrifice, including its head, they received all their wishes, they won the world of heaven.
If someone puts the *Pravargya*-pot on the fire, he puts back the head of the sacrifice. When he sacrifices with that sacrifice, including its head, he receives all his wishes, he wins the world of heaven.
Therefore it seems to provide strength to the Aśvins; it is the *Pravargya*.

(*Taittirīya Āraṇyaka* 5: 1, 6–7)[63]

The story of the *Pravargya* in the *Taittirīya Āraṇyaka* emphasizes the importance of the ritual, but it also explains why the sacrifice was decapitated. In the other accounts, this was taken for granted, but these later Taittirīya scholars felt that it demanded an explanation.

They justify it as a punishment of Makha for violating the principles of the *sattra*. The responsibility for carrying out this violent punishment is transferred onto the ants. In the other texts, the gods thought nothing of beheading a victim or chopping it up, but now it must be made clear both that the violent punishment was justified and that the gods are completely innocent of such violence and bloodshed.

The Beheading of the Sacrifice in the Śatapatha Brāhmaṇa

Yet another explanation of the *Pravargya* was developed by the Vājasaneyin school, and it is found in book 14 of the *Śatapatha Brāhmaṇa*. This book provides us with a long narrative, developing the story of the *Taittirīya Āraṇyaka*, and adding a lot of circumstantial details. It starts off with a roll-call of all the gods who took part in the soma sacrifice (which is once again a *sattra*):

> The gods were sitting down at a *sattra* soma sacrifice – Agni, Indra, Soma, Makha, Viṣṇu,[64] and All the Gods except the two Aśvins. Their divine sacrificial space was Kurukṣetra.
>
> (*ŚB* 14: 1, 1^{1-2})

The gods named here are essential to the story. Soma must be present at his own sacrifice, and Agni, Indra, and All the Gods are the recipients of the three pressings of soma (*ŚB* 14: 1, 1^{16}). Viṣṇu is strangely presented not as the father of Makha, but as Makha himself ('Makha is indeed Viṣṇu,' *ŚB* 14: 1, 1^{13}), so that Viṣṇu is identical with the sacrifice ('Viṣṇu is the sacrifice,' *ŚB* 14: 1, 1^{6}). From this point on, Makha disappears from the story and we will hear only of Viṣṇu. Finally, the absence of the Aśvins is made explicit from the very beginning of the story. Since Soma, Makha, and Viṣṇu will be regarded as identical, the roll-call is reduced to Soma, the gods who drink soma, and the Aśvins who do not.

The story continues as it did in the *Taittirīya Āraṇyaka*, but this time the culpability of Viṣṇu (in other words, Makha the sacrifice) is made explicit. The sacrifice deserves to have its head cut off. The gods make the rules of the *sattra* sacrifice very clear, and Viṣṇu understands that he is violating the rules, but he simply cannot control his desire for glory. The gods also express their resentment immediately. They want to overpower him, they do not wait for the ants to suggest this idea to them (as in the *Taittirīya Āraṇyaka*):

> They said: 'Whichever of us first achieves the goal of the sacrifice by means of his austerity, asceticism, belief, sacrifice, and libations – he will be the best of us; it will be shared by all of us.'
> They said, 'All right.'
> Viṣṇu achieved it first and became the best of the gods. This is why they say that Viṣṇu is the best of the gods.
> ... But Viṣṇu was not able to control his glory. So it seems that even now not everybody is able to control their glory.
> He took up his bow with three arrows and walked away. He stood there, resting his head on the end of the bow. Since they were unable to overpower him, the gods sat around him on all sides.
> (*ŚB* 14: 1, 1^{4-7})

The ants come along and behead Viṣṇu as he stands there in all his glory. When the sacrifice has been beheaded, there is a new development in the story.

> The gods moved towards him like people who want to get treasure. Indra reached him first. He lay beside him, limb by limb, and embraced him. By embracing him, he became his glory, and whoever understands this becomes the glory that Indra became. Viṣṇu is indeed Makha, so Indra became the one who owns Makha (*makhavān*).[65]
> (*ŚB* 14: 1, 1^{12-13})

In the *Ṛgveda*, Indra had beheaded Makha himself,[66] and in the *Śatapatha Brāhmaṇa* he ends up being the winner from the decapitation of Makha–Viṣṇu. In effect, Indra has repeated the actions of Makha–Viṣṇu by taking the glory of the sacrifice, but it is only a partial, headless sacrifice, and he does allow the other gods to participate in this truncated ritual: 'worshipping and working hard, the gods performed this headless sacrifice' (*ŚB* 14: 1, 1[17]). Indra does realize that the sacrifice is incomplete, that the head should be replaced, but he does not want anyone to know this secret (*ŚB* 14: 1, 1[18–19]). So this *Brāhmaṇa* sets up a contrast between Indra and Viṣṇu. Viṣṇu takes into himself all the true glory of the complete sacrifice, and thereby becomes identical with Makha himself. Indra absorbs the incomplete glory of the headless sacrifice into himself and becomes identical with that faded and incomplete glory. Indra is not content, however, to be in second place behind Viṣṇu. He is not happy that Viṣṇu won the entire sacrifice and that he merely possesses its mangled remains. His efforts to hide his failure lead to a very strange development in the story of the Aśvins.

The Head of the Sacrifice and the Head of Dadhyañc in the Śatapatha Brāhmaṇa

The Aśvins had always possessed the secret of the *Gharma* ritual and they gave it to their human protégé, Atri. What they had not possessed was the right to drink soma, and they were given the secret of soma by Dadhyañc. Since the story of Dadhyañc had involved decapitations and head-transplants by the Aśvins, and since the Aśvins had similarly healed the sacrifice by placing a new head (the *Pravargya* pot) on its mutilated body, the authors of the *Śatapatha Brāhmaṇa* boldly conflated these two stories and completely altered the myth of Dadhyañc. In the *Ṛgveda* Indra and Dadhyañc had possessed the secret of soma, and the Aśvins and Atri had possessed the secret of the *Pravargya*. Now we are told that it is Indra and Dadhyañc who possess the secret of the *Pravargya*. This is the only secret worth knowing, this is the 'honey' (*madhu*) that Dadhyañc had revealed to the Aśvins in *RV* 1: 116, 12cd:

> Dadhyañc, the son of Atharvan, proclaimed the honey
> to you, by means of a horse's head.

In *ŚB* 4 these lines were quoted and the honey was correctly identified as soma; the same lines are quoted once again in *ŚB* 14: 1, 1[25] and given a completely new interpretation. Now the honey of Dadhyañc is identified as the hot milk of the *Pravargya*.

This new version of the story of Dadhyañc is cleverly used to explain another feature of the *Pravargya*. In contrast to the original *Gharma* rite of the Atri family, which they later shared with all the priestly families of the Pūru-Bharata tribes,[67] the *Pravargya* of the Kuru-Pañcāla kingdom is a secret ritual, an *āraṇyaka* (forest ritual) that should only be performed in a forest where no villager would intrude. This is why it is discussed in the *Taittirīya Āraṇyaka* and in the *Āraṇyaka* section of the *Śatapatha Brāhmaṇa*. The man who performs it must learn about it in secret, and this education lasts a year, during which the man to be initiated has to obey many tabus (*Baudhāyana Śrauta Sūtra* 9: 19-20; *Āpastamba Śrauta Sūtra* 15: 20, 11–15: 21, 15). At the start of his preparation, the person to be initiated into the mysteries of the *Pravargya* has to move away from his home into the forest.[68]

> He goes out of the village to the east or the north, and he sets up his fire in an empty place from which no roof can be seen.
>
> (*Baudhāyana Śrauta Sūtra* 9: 19)[69]

The new version of the Dadhyañc story explains why the *Pravargya* must be a secret ritual. Indra had imposed this secrecy on Dadhyañc, and this tradition of secrecy has surrounded the *Pravargya* ever since:

> Dadhyañc the son of Atharvan knew about this pure one, this sacrifice, how this head of the sacrifice is put back on, how this sacrifice becomes whole.
> Indra said to him, 'If you tell this to anyone else, I will cut your head off.'
>
> (*Śatapatha Brāhmaṇa* 14: 1, 1^{18-19})

> A man should not tell this to everyone. That is sinful. Otherwise, Indra will cut his head off.
> He could tell it to someone well-known to him, or someone who knows the Vedas well, or someone who is dear to him, but not to everyone.

He should tell it to someone who lives with him for a year.
(*Śatapatha Brāhmaṇa* 14: 1, 1^{26-27})

In spite of these threats, Dadhyañc reveals the secret to the Aśvins, and his story continues in the usual way that we saw in the *Ṛgveda*, with the exchange of human and horse heads, and the restoration of his original human head at the end. There is, of course, the important change that the secret is now the *Pravargya* rather than the soma sacrifice, but in both stories Indra wants to exclude the Aśvins.

So there is a complete changeover from the story in the *Ṛgveda*. As Dadhyañc is no longer the person who tells the Aśvins about the soma sacrifice, somebody else has to teach them instead. This teaching role is taken over by Cyavana. The new version of both stories is finally combined into a complicated and novelistic 'frame story' in the *Jaiminīya Brāhmaṇa*, where the story of Dadhyañc, the *Pravargya* expert, is found inside the story of the Aśvin Cup, which in turn is placed inside the outer story of Cyavana.[70] This arrangement reflects the real world of Vedic ritual, where the *Pravargya*, taught by Dadhyañc, is a part of the outer ritual of the soma sacrifice, with its Aśvin Cup, which is part of a successful life for a morally noble man (*ārya*). Such a man listens to the Vedas, sacrifices to the gods, and has children, like Cyavana. As Witzel points out, Indian priests had plenty of experience in framing rituals inside each other, but the Jaiminīyas use this framing technique as a new literary device. They frame one story inside another, rather than creating hyper-links from one story to the other (as in the *Śatapatha Brāhmaṇa*).[71] The frame-story became a standard device in the classical literature of India.[72]

To sum up the wide range of speculations inspired by the *Pravargya*: it starts off as an offering of hot milk (*Gharma*) by the Atri family, which is later adopted by all the priestly families of the *Ṛgveda*. When it is incorporated into the soma sacrifice as the more elaborate *Pravargya* rite, its presence calls for an explanation. The Aitareya school sees the *Pravargya* as a way of healing the chopped up sacrifice and bringing its fragments together. For the Kauṣītaki school, the sacrifice has been beheaded rather than chopped up, and the *Mahāvīra* pot used in the *Pravargya* is the missing head of the decapitated sacrifice. The Taittirīya school once again identifies the *Pravargya* pot with the head of the sacrifice, but also explains why the sacrifice was beheaded in the first place. Finally, the Vājasaneyin scholars proclaim in the *Śatapatha Brāhamaṇa* that the *Pravargya* is the essential secret ingredient of the soma sacrifice. Without the *Pravargya*, Indra's soma sacrifice is worthless, so this must have been the vitally important secret revealed to the Aśvins by Dadhyañc. Indra remains indifferent when Cyavana tells the Aśvins about the soma sacrifice, but he is ready to behead anyone who reveals the secret *Pravargya*. It is now proclaimed as the central ritual action to which the rest of the soma sacrifice provides a foil and a frame.

The Morning Prayer (*prātaranuvāka*)

The Aśvins are the gods of the *Pravargya*, and they are belatedly offered a cup of soma too, but they are also celebrated in the prayers that mark the beginning and end of the soma sacrifice. Before dawn on the Pressing Day of a soma sacrifice, the Hotar priest recites a very long prayer called the Morning Prayer (*prātaranuvāka*).[73] Ṛgvedic recitation and Samavedic chanting usually take place in the Recitation Hut (*sadas*), but when the Hotar recites this long hymn, he sits between the soma chariots that are parked in the Soma Hut (*havirdhāna*) itself.[74] The prayer is dedicated to the gods of the morning, and consists of selected stanzas from the *Ṛgveda*. It starts off with one stanza (recited three times) to the Water Goddesses (*āpaḥ*). Then come the stanzas celebrating Agni, Uṣas, and the Aśvins. Finally, the very last stanza comes from a hymn to the Aśvins, but it mentions all the morning gods, and like the first stanza it is recited three times:

> Dawn with her brilliant cattle has arisen,
> Agni has been established at the proper time,
> your immortal chariot, o gods of mighty wealth,

has been yoked, o wonder-workers.
O honey-lovers, hear my call.

(*RV* 5: 75, 9)

Vedic ritualists focus on the peculiar features of this Morning Prayer. The ritual texts state that it must be sung before anyone speaks, even before any bird or animal makes a sound,[75] and the *Aitareya Brāhmaṇa* explains that this rule ensures that the first thing heard on that special morning will be this hymn.[76] The prayer to the morning gods strangely begins with the Water Goddesses, and this detail is explained by the Ṛgvedic *Brāhmaṇas*: all of the gods wanted to be mentioned first, so by starting the hymn with a stanza to the Waters, the priest avoids giving offence to any particular god.[77] Finally, the Morning Prayer is unusual because it is recited in the Soma Hut, but the *Kauṣītaki Brāhmaṇa* provides a way of understanding this.

According to this text, the Recitation Hut is the stomach of the sacrifice, and the Soma Hut is its head. All the other hymns are food, so they naturally go to the stomach and are recited in the Recitation Hut. The Morning Prayer, in contrast, is the air that the head needs to breathe, so it has to be recited right beside the head, in the Soma Hut itself.[78] Here we have another allusion to the headless sacrifice, and as usual the texts assert that the ritual under investigation is vitally important because it involves the head of the sacrifice. Usually the head is the *Pravargya*, but in this case it is the Soma Hut, so the Morning Prayer which is recited in the Soma Hut must be greater than all the other hymns.

The Aśvins appear in this hymn as 'gods who come in the morning',[79] along with Uṣas, the goddess of dawn, and with Agni. The fire god is included among the morning gods because the priests energize the sun when they bring the sacred fire back to life at dawn.[80] The *Kauṣītaki Brāhmaṇa* reveals why the hymn is dedicated to these three gods: Agni belongs to this world, Uṣas to the atmosphere in between, and the Aśvins to the heavens.[81] These three gods therefore represent the entire universe,[82] and by combining their power, the Morning Prayer brings about the final victory of the gods over the demons (*asuras*).[83]

The Twilight Chant (*saṃdhistotra*) and the Aśvin Hymn (*āśvinaśastra*)

If a soma sacrifice finishes in one day, it ends with a chant and a hymn honouring Agni after the third and last pressing of soma juice in the evening.[84] Otherwise, it ends at dawn on the following morning with the Twilight Chant and the Aśvin Hymn. Like the Morning Prayer (*Prātaranuvāka*), which started off the soma sacrifice, this chant and this hymn honour the three morning gods, and they initiate the final soma sequence.[85]

While it is still dark, the Udgātar sings the Twilight Chant, which praises Agni, Uṣas, and the Aśvins in that order. According to the *Jaiminīya Brāhmaṇa* of the Sāmavedic priests, the daytime soma sacrifice had defeated the demons by day and forced them to retreat into the night, but they were defeated in this final hide-out by the overnight rites.[86] After defeating the demons by day and by night, the gods joined (*saṃdhā*) the two parts of their victory with the Twilight (*saṃdhi*) Chant.

This chant is followed immediately by the Aśvin Hymn, which must be recited before dawn, because it enables the sun to rise again and start a new day.[87] The Aśvin Hymn is really a special form of the Morning Prayer, which has been expanded to 1,000 verses.[88] As the *Śatapatha Brāhmaṇa* puts it, 'the recital of the Aśvin Hymn has pushed the Morning Prayer from its place'.[89] Vedic thinkers wondered why it bore the name of the Aśvins alone when it was dedicated to all three morning gods. They said that the hymn celebrated the new victory of the gods over the Asuras,[90] or else it was offered as a prize to the guests at a divine wedding.[91] In either case, the gods celebrate this victory or wedding with a chariot race. Agni takes the lead, Uṣas follows, and the Aśvins come last. Their positions at this stage in the race explain the order in which they appear in both the Twilight Chant and the Aśvin Hymn.[92] The Aśvins bribe the other two competitors to let them win by offering one third of the prize to each team, so their name is given to the hymn, but all three morning gods are honoured equally in it.[93] As often happens in explanations of the soma sacrifice, the Aśvins must trick their way into a prominent position.

The *Sautrāmaṇī* (Good Saviour Ritual)

Finally, the Aśvins play a major role in the *Sautrāmaṇī*, a ritual that is dedicated to Indra the Good Saviour (*Indra Sutrāman*), but also to the Aśvins and Sarasvatī. The offering in this ritual is not soma but an alcoholic drink called *surā*, which is made from a mixture of fermented rice and barley.[94] This drink was an antidote to soma, and the *Sautrāmaṇī* ritual cured anyone who had become sick from an overdose of soma. The ritual was also included in the coronation ceremony of a king (*Taittirīya Saṃhitā* 1: 8, 20).[95] The mythical prototype of such patients was Indra himself, who had been cured of his overdose by the Aśvins and Sarasvatī.

The ritual echoes the soma sacrifice: the priests buy the ingredients for *surā*, just as they buy soma, and each of these purchases is included as a part of the ritual; there are three days of preparation, during which *surā* is brewed, just as there are three *Upasad* days in a soma sacrifice; in each case, the important day is the fourth one when the sacred drink (*surā* or soma) is offered to the gods and consumed by the priests. In the mantras for the *Sautrāmaṇī* ritual, *surā* is often called 'soma',[96] which emphasizes the parallel between the two drinks and rituals.

On the first day, a bull is sacrificed to Indra and the *surā* ingredients are mixed together and placed in a pit. The mixture is brewed over the first three days. On the main day of the ritual, a cup of milk and a cup of *surā* is offered to the Aśvins, to Sarasvatī, and to Indra. The same gods also receive animal sacrifices: a goat for the Aśvins, a sheep for Sarasvatī, and a second bull for Indra. After these sacrifices, a throne is set up for the sacrificer, and a broth cooked from the sacrificed animals is poured over him.[97] Finally, there is a ritual bath (*avabhṛta*), as at the end of a soma sacrifice, and the sacrificer makes offerings to his ancestors and sacrifices a third bull to Indra the Strengthener (*Indra Vayodhas*).[98]

Surā is denounced in the Vedas, because it was a popular drink that did not really belong in proper Vedic ritual.[99] So the Aśvins are once again involved in an incongruous ritual, one that is based on a popular drink (milk or *surā*) rather than on the rare and wonderful soma. Both the *Pravargya* and the *Sautrāmaṇī* are parallel to the soma sacrifice and yet form a contrast to it. The story behind the *Sautrāmaṇī* is found in a Ṛgvedic hymn where Indra the Good Saviour (*Sutrāman*) is himself saved by the Aśvins and Sarasvatī.

> O Aśvins, you (took) *surāma*
> together with Namuci, the Asura,
> syphoning it off (*vi-pā*), o lords of splendour,
> you helped Indra in his deeds.
>
> As parents help their son, the two Aśvins
> helped you with their wonderful powers, o Indra;
> when with your might you syphoned off (*vi-pā*) the *surāma*,
> Sarasvatī healed you, o generous god.
>
> Indra is the Good Saviour (*sutrāman*), a good helper. . .
> (*RV* 10: 131, 4–6)

The precise meaning of *surāma* is unclear. Böhtlingk and its Monier-Williams translation take it to mean alcoholic poisoning, and their view is accepted by Bloomfield.[100] This interpretation ignores the verb *vi-pā*, which means 'to syphon off one liquid alone from a mixture of liquids'.[101] *Surāma* must, therefore, be a mixture of drinks containing *surā*.[102] The Aśvins isolate its parts and extract the *surā* from the mixture (*vipipānā*, 4c), as does Indra (*vi apabaḥ*, 5c).

Geldner suggests that Indra was made sick by a mixture of soma and *surā*, and that the Aśvins and Sarasvatī isolated the soma and gave it to Indra.[103] The '*surā* mixture' (*surāma*, 4a and 5c) would therefore mean 'soma mixed with *surā*'. Fowler agrees, and even claims that *surā* was offered with soma rather than with milk at the *Sautrāmaṇī*.[104] This strange statement raises doubts about the original premise. There is, however, another possibility. *Surā* is brewed by pouring milk on a mixture of grains for three days in a row,[105] and the *Sautrāmaṇī* ritual involves offerings of *surā* and of milk. The mixture in *RV* 10: 131, 4a may therefore consist of *surā* and milk, rather than *surā* and soma. As we shall see, later texts always speak of soma as being a dangerous drink (when taken in excess) and *surā* as its cure. It would be strange to mix the poison and its cure in the same cup, whereas to combine the two cures (milk and *surā*) together would make sense. The cautious Aśvin doctors and the weakened Indra decide it would be better to syphon off the *surā* from the milk and take these medicines separately, rather than combine them in a drug cocktail.

Soma Overdose, Surā Treatment

In the *Śatapatha Brāhmaṇa* it is bad soma (not a mixture of soma and *surā*) that makes Indra violently ill and debilitates him completely. His father Tvaṣṭar casts a magic spell on the soma and hides it away from Indra, but Indra steals it and drinks it down, with dire consequences.

> Tvaṣṭar kept the soma with the magic spell on it away from Indra. Indra violated the sacrifice, and violently drank the soma. He fell to pieces, and his strength and courage flowed away from every limb.
>
> (*Śatapatha Brāhmaṇa* 12: 7, 1^{1})

It is only *after* he has been rendered helpless by the magic soma that we hear anything about *surā*.

> Indra used to associate with Namuci, the Asura. Namuci realized, 'This fellow will not make a recovery. Come on, let's steal his strength, his courage, the soma he drinks, the food he eats.' With this *surā*, Namuci stole Indra's strength, his courage, the soma he drank, the food he ate. And Indra lay there in pieces.
>
> (*Śatapatha Brāhmaṇa* 12: 7, 1^{10})

Bloomfield says that Namuci made Indra helplessly drunk by giving him *surā*,[106] but the story makes it quite clear that Namuci does not need to use *surā* or indeed anything else to overpower Indra. Tvaṣṭar has already done this work for Namuci. A passage cited by

Bloomfield from Mahidhara's commentary on the *Vājasaneyi Saṃhitā* explains what is really going on:

> An Asura called Namuci was a friend of Indra's. By means of *surā* together with soma, he always drank Indra's strength. So Indra spoke to the Aśvins and Sarasvatī: 'My strength has been drunk by Namuci.'[107]

The phrase 'with this *surā*, Namuci stole Indra's strength' (*ŚBr* 12: 7, 1[10]) means that Namuci took *surā* to make himself strong, and when he was fortified 'with this *surā*', he stole Indra's soma and strength. *Surā* is not a poison used to weaken Indra; on the contrary, it is a magic potion that strengthens Namuci. Indra could only be cured 'with this *surā*', but Namuci keeps it to himself.

The ritual hand-books and the *Śatapatha Brāhmaṇa* make it clear that medical problems arise from soma, not from *surā*. The *Āpastamba Śrautasūtra* quotes the mantras used in the *Sautrāmaṇī*, graphically explaining their significance.[108]

> 'The soma has rushed through in front.' For someone who has vomited soma (*somavāminaḥ*).
> 'The soma has rushed through behind.' For someone who has been cleaned out by soma (*somātipavitrasya*).
> (*Āpastamba Śrautasūtra* 19: 6, 12)

The *Śatapatha Brāhmaṇa* describes the general condition of the man who has had too much soma.

> His splendour, strength and courage go away from a man when soma cleans him out above or below.
> (*Śatapatha Brāhmaṇa* 12: 7, 2[1])

The *Śatapatha Brāhmaṇa* uses the same words to describe the condition of the weakened Indra and of his human counterpart who needs to be healed by the *Sautrāmaṇī* ritual: '(Indra's) strength and courage flowed away,' '(the man's) splendour, strength and courage go away.'[109] They both have the same medical symptoms, and the very fact that the story of Indra is being used to explain the *Sautrāmaṇī* shows that both Indra and the human patient are suffering from the very physical results of drinking soma improperly. Soma is the problem, *surā* is the cure.

An ordinary man suffering from an overdose of soma can be cured by the priests through the *Sautrāmaṇī*, but in Indra's case a divine medical team, consisting of Sarasvatī and the Aśvins, has to come to the rescue. The scene in which the gods summon the Aśvins and Sarasvatī to heal Indra is very similar to the one in which they had to ask the Aśvins to heal the sacrifice by replacing its head. Once again, the Aśvins drive a hard bargain.

> And Indra lay there in pieces. The gods gathered around him:
> 'He was the best of us, but evil found him out. Come on, let's heal him.'
> They said to the Aśvins, 'You are Brahmin doctors. Heal this god.'
> 'All right,' the two replied, 'but let us have a share.'
> They said, 'This goat is your share.'
> 'All right.'
> This is why the grey goat belongs to the Aśvins.
> (*Śatapatha Brāhmaṇa* 12: 7, 1^{10-11})

The gods go through the same bargaining procedure with Sarasvatī:

> They said to Sarasvatī, 'You are medicine. Heal this god.'
> 'Let me have a share,' she replied.
> They said, 'This sheep is your share.'
> 'All right.'
> This is why the sheep belongs to the Sarasvatī.
> (*Śatapatha Brāhmaṇa* 12: 7, 1^{12})

The story ends happily when the Aśvins and Sarasvatī take everything that Namuci had stolen from Indra and give it back to him.

> The Aśvins and Sarasvatī took away the strength and courage from Namuci, and they put it back in Indra. They saved him from evil. 'We saved (*trā*) him from evil, so he is well-saved (*sutrāta*).'
>
> (*Śatapatha Brāhmaṇa* 12: 7, 1[14])

Namuci's source of strength and courage is his *surā*; Sarasvatī and the Aśvins take it from him, and cure Indra from the bad soma he had taken. In order to do this, they must first extract the *surā* from the mixture (*surāma*) of milk and *surā*. This is what happens during the *Sautrāmaṇī*, where the milk and *surā* are offered in separate bowls,[110] and it is also what is described in *RV* 10: 131, 4–6. The Aśvins join Namuci as he drinks the mixture, but they extract *surā* from it, and use it to help Indra: 'syphoning it off [...] you helped Indra in his deeds.' When he is strong enough ('with his might', *śacībhiḥ*), Indra is able to extract the *surā* from the mixture by himself, and Sarasvatī completes his healing process: 'when with your might you syphoned off the *surāma*, Sarasvatī healed you.' In this hymn, and throughout the *Sautrāmaṇī*, the Aśvins appear in their traditional role of doctors and saviours, assisted by the goddess Sarasvatī, while Indra the Good Saviour (*Indra Sutrāman*) is the one who has to be saved (*sutrāta*). The *Sautrāmaṇī* and the Ṛgvedic hymn celebrate the return of Indra to his proper role as Good Saviour.

Blood and Soma

There was, however, an alternative explanatory myth for the *Sautrāmaṇī* that made Indra responsible for his own recovery. Indra is debilitated, not because he has taken too much soma and made himself sick, but on the contrary because there is not enough soma left for Indra, since Namuci has drunk his entire supply. Indra goes to the Aśvins and Sarasvatī not because he wants medical assistance, but because he needs legal advice on killing Namuci, without violating the promises he had made to him. The Aśvins and Sarasvatī are rewarded with a share in the *Sautrāmaṇī* when they provide Indra with a legal trick that enables him to kill Namuci with impunity (*ŚB* 12: 7, 3[1–3]). Indra beheads Namuci, and retrieves the soma himself, by extracting it from the head of Namuci. In order to do this, he has to 'syphon it off' (*vi-pā*) from the mixture of blood and soma in Namuci's head.

> ... In the head that was cut off, there was soma mixed with blood.
> They (the Aśvins and Sarasvatī) were horrified.
> They saw how to syphon off (*vipānam*) the two liquids.
> 'King Soma, the immortal drink, has been pressed.'
> With that (mantra), they sweetened the soma and put it inside their bodies.
>
> (*Śatapatha Brāhmaṇa* 12: 7, 3^{4})

Once again, Indra needs the Aśvins and Sarasvatī to teach him how to syphon off the correct drink (soma or surā) without taking in any of the other liquids with which it is mixed, in this case Namuci's blood (*ŚB* 12: 7, 3^{4}). Nevertheless, Indra retrieves his strength and courage by his own efforts, and he recovers his health completely by drinking soma from his enemy's head.

This story makes Indra look good, since he recovers not by receiving *surā* from the Aśvins, but by taking his own favourite drink, soma. The story does not work very well, however, as an explanation of the *Sautrāmaṇī*, where Indra should be drinking *surā* and milk instead. The *Śatapatha Brāhmaṇa* tries to get around this difficulty by arguing that the soma he drinks is really *surā* or milk which has been transformed into soma. The priest turns *surā* into 'a form of soma',[111] and even into soma itself.[112] Since it would be inauspicious for a Brahmin to drink *surā*, he has to convince himself that he is really drinking soma.[113] Likewise, the milk offered is really soma.[114] By artificially declaring that soma can appear as *surā* or milk, a story about Indra sucking soma out of his enemy's head can be reinterpreted to explain a ritual in which a man extracts *surā* from a mixture of milk and *surā*.

The same equation of milk or *surā* with soma occurs even in the mantras that are used in the ritual itself, but here the motivation is different. Since there are no mantras referring to *surā* in the *Ṛgveda*, the priests have to take mantras composed for soma and recycle them as mantras about milk and *surā*, so that they can use them in the *Sautrāmaṇī* ritual.[115] The goal of the priests is not really to equate soma with *surā* or milk; they are simply obliged to transform soma mantras into *surā* mantras.[116] This ploy made it easier for the scholars who composed the *Śatapatha Brāhmaṇa* to reinterpret the origins of the *Sautrāmaṇī*. Indra was not 'properly saved' (*sutrāta*) by the Aśvins; being the Good Saviour, *Sautrāman*, he saved himself. He did so by drinking soma from the bloody head of his enemy, but since soma can be considered a form of *surā* or milk, Indra's recovery may be commemorated by drinking *surā* and milk at the *Sautrāmaṇī*. The helpless Indra who was dependent on the Aśvins and Sarasvatī is ignored, and we return to the more familiar image of the god who defeats all his enemies and strengthens himself with soma.

The Aśvin Rituals

The Aśvins are popular gods and they are especially associated with humble offerings of milk and *surā* rather than the great sacrifice of soma. Milk is a very simple gift, offered into the fire at home every morning and evening, in the *Agnihotra* ritual. *Surā* is a strong and not quite respectable drink, the sort of offering that would not be appropriate for a great god like Indra, unless he were ill. These offerings have to be incorporated into the system of solemn *śrauta* rituals, and the stories of the *Ṛgveda* have to be altered or reinterpreted to allow for these radical changes. In the stories behind the *Pravargya* and the *Sautrāmaṇī*, the god Indra must lower himself somewhat, and the other gods are forced into the strange position of asking the Aśvins for help. They have to welcome the Aśvins and their peculiar rituals, they have to accept the *Pravargya* and the *Sautrāmaṇī* as a part of their world. The Aśvins and their rituals do not just arrive as a new element discreetly added to a Vedic sacrifice; they have to be welcomed into the very heart of the soma sacrifice. As a reward for their services, the Aśvins demand their cup at the soma sacrifice, like all the other gods, and they demand an animal victim at the *Sautrāmaṇī*. As a final triumph, their hymn starts off the main day of the soma sacrifice, and if the sacrifice lasts more than one day their hymn marks its end as well.

It is no wonder, therefore, that the stories told to explain the Aśvin rituals are so contradictory and convoluted. An old Vedic story about Dadhyañc and soma is transformed into a late Vedic story about the *Pravargya*, so that the Aśvins and the Adhvaryus may be glorified. Conversely, a story about a helpless Indra being given a dose of *surā* by the Aśvins becomes a story about Indra drinking soma from a skull, so that the glory of Indra the Good Saviour will not be diminished. As the Adhvaryus assume a dominant role in Vedic ritual, the stories told about their divine role-models, the Aśvins, must undergo parallel changes. When the simple milk offering of cowboys is incorporated into the soma sacrifice as the *Pravargya* ritual, it is used as a vantage point from which the Adhvaryus can criticize the rest of the sacrifice and analyse its workings.

The Aśvins are not simple rustics who are only too grateful to be invited to such a splendid event; they act as spokesmen for the Adhvaryus among the gods. The Aśvins are, therefore, ritual experts who readily spot what is wrong with the ritual, and they alone have the power to mend it. The reluctance of the other gods to accept them as equals is only a further demonstration of their ritual incompetence, which the Aśvins have to correct. Their Morning Prayer is the air the sacrifice needs to breathe; the overnight sacrifice ends with their hymn. They heal the soma sacrifice itself; they heal anyone who is overpowered by soma. They have developed into scholars who can provide *brāhmaṇa* explanations, they have become the masters of ritual.

Vedic ritual was purified and regulated by the Aśvins in myth and the Adhvaryus in reality, until it developed into the elaborate *śrauta* system. This innovative 'traditional' system triumphed for the best part of 1,000 years, and it still survives in the southern half of India, but it led to a reaction. There was a complete rejection of the Vedas by the Jains and the Buddhists, but the Hindus themselves also began to move in new directions. The ritual of the mind and the pleasure of pure knowledge came to be far more important than the elaborate world created by the Adhvaryus in the kingdom of the Kuru-Pañcālas. In the new classical age that followed, the Aśvins would be remembered mainly as the fathers of the youngest Pāṇḍavas in the *Mahābhārata.* Personal devotion to the three great gods was already overriding the more evenly divided attentions of the Vedic world, and the Aśvins were once again on the margins of the religious world.

The story of the Aśvins begins among the nomadic horsemen of Central Asia; their adventures were told by the tribesmen of northern India; experts in Vedic ritual honoured the Aśvins and made up myths about them that reflected their own cultural wars for control of the sacrificial arena. In spite of these developments, the Aśvins always retained an independent and youthful manner that reflected an earlier and less complex society. As the tribesmen settled down under the imperial rule of the Mauryas, and as Vedic sacrifice gave way to devotional worship, the world of the Aśvins faded away. Soon they were all but forgotten.

CHAPTER 5

THE CULT OF THE DIOSKOUROI

In Ancient Greece, the twin horse gods are called the Dioskouroi ('the young men of Zeus'). As the name implies, they are young gods (*kouroi*), like the Indian Aśvins (*yuvānā*), but they are highly unusual among the gods of Greece in that they once led a human life on earth. If the Aśvins are gods who associate too freely with human beings, and are therefore looked upon as impure by the other gods, as unworthy of receiving soma sacrifices, the status of the Dioskouroi is even lower than this. These young gods not only associate with humans, they are human themselves, and like all human beings they experience death.

As young men and human gods, they naturally devote themselves to helping adolescents and rescuing people in trouble. They have the special task of looking after two very important Greek institutions: the training of the young men who will form the Spartan army, and the safety of the sailors who man the merchant navies of Ancient Greece. Sparta is their home, and it has the most powerful army in archaic Greece; the Athenians and Ionians are great sailors, and among them the Dioskouroi are famous for rescuing ships in distress. The Dioskouroi are twins, but unlike their Indian counterparts, each of them has his own individual name: Kastōr and Poludeukēs. Along with their sister Helenē, they are usually regarded as the children of Zeus and a human mother, Lēdē.[1] The Dioskouroi and Helenē once lived as humans, and the myths told about them refer to this former human existence. All three of them are worshipped as gods, and this chapter will discuss their cult in Greece. Since Sparta was once the earthly home of the three gods, it is also the centre of their cult, and that is where we shall begin.

The Cult of the Young Men at Sparta

Sparta was renowned throughout the Greek world for its system of military indoctrination, which trained every male Spartan to be a professional warrior from his earliest boyhood.[2] The Spartan citizen is never allowed to grow up; he spends his entire life in the atmosphere of a military school. Brutalized by young men when he is an adolescent, he will bully his juniors when he reaches manhood himself. Even after he has reached maturity at the age of 30, he dines every day with his fellow-warriors for the rest of his life. This austere militarism is directed mainly against 'the enemy within', against their own people, though the Spartans do not regard anyone else in their country as their own people. The state is based on a hierarchy of social groups, with the Spartan citizens at the top, the 'people who live around them' (the *perioikoi*) enjoying limited autonomy, and finally the hated Helots, who are slaves with no rights whatsoever.[3] Fear of the Helots is the main reason for the peculiar nature of the Spartan state, and young Spartans are encouraged to kill any Helots who seem dangerously strong or independent.[4] The religion of the state naturally reinforces the militaristic upbringing of the Spartans and includes a strong focus on youth-festivals.[5] Though Sparta is under the protection of Athēna of the Bronze House, who has her temple on its acropolis,[6] the most important gods for the Spartans are Apollōn and Artemis. They are the gods in charge of young people in Sparta and other Dorian states.[7] The two most sacred shrines in the state are the Throne of Apollōn at Amuklai, with its 14-metre high statue of Apollōn standing on the Throne,[8] and the temple of Artemis Orthia in Sparta itself.[9]

At each of these famous sanctuaries, the connection between the gods and Spartan youth is made clear. There is an altar built into the Throne of Amuklai, which is supposedly the tomb of the hero-god

Huakinthos.[10] He himself is a young god whose youth-festival, the Huakinthia, had been taken over by Apollōn,[11] and later stories made him the boy-friend of Apollōn. His youth-festival begins every year with offerings to Huakinthos and Apollōn at Amuklai.[12] At the other great Spartan shrine, the temple of Artemis Orthia, boys are flogged in an endurance test that initiates them into Spartan manhood.[13] Less brutally, they perform dances with masks, which represent either ideal characters they should imitate (warrior-masks), or caricatures they should avoid (masks depicting old women, gorgons, and satyrs).[14]

The three greatest annual festivals at Sparta are the Karneia, the Huakinthia, and the Gumnopaidiai (the Festival of Naked Boys),[15] and all three festivals honour Apollōn as the god of youth. The major events at each of these festivals are choral songs and dances by Spartan boys and girls. The Karneia honour Apollōn Karneios, and are celebrated in tents outside the city; during the festival, boys and girls dance together and compete in choirs.[16] The Huakinthia, as we have seen, honour Apollōn and Huakinthos, and the highlight of the festival is a competition for boys and girls in choral singing and dancing at the theatre.[17] The third great festival is the Gumnopaidia, with its competitive dancing choirs of boys and adult men in the theatre.[18] The close connection between the religious festivals of Sparta and its military training was recognized in ancient times, and the Hellenistic scholar Demetrius of Scepsis describes the Karneia festival as 'an imitation of the military training system (*agōgē*)'.[19]

Into this world of prolonged adolescence the tradition of the Indo-European horse gods could easily be adopted and treated as genuinely Spartan. The Dioskouroi are 'young men' (*kouroi*) who are content with their subordinate status and quite happy to perform errands for their betters. At Sparta, they are identified with two local figures called the Tundaridai.[20] This mysterious name, which is probably pre-Greek,[21] was interpreted to mean the 'sons of Tundareos,'[22] and Tundareos was a mythical king of Sparta. Whether they are regarded as the sons of the Olympian king Zeus, who reigns over the gods, or the sons of the Spartan king Tundareos, whose tomb was on the acropolis of the city,[23] the Tundaridai play an important role in

Sparta. They are the patrons and role-models for young Spartan men as they go through the various stages of their indoctrination.[24] Their sister Helenā and their wives, the Leukippides, play a similar role as patron goddesses for young Spartan women.[25] The importance and popularity of the Tundaridai is brought out by two details from the everyday habits of the Spartans and from monuments erected in the city. The Tundaridai are so well-known at Sparta that people refer to them simply as 'the two gods' (*tō siō*),[26] and the most important sets of sculptural reliefs from Sparta are Hero Reliefs and Dioskouroi Reliefs.[27] These details from Spartan life reinforce two essential features of the Tundaridai: the Spartans take it for granted that the Tundaridai are gods, and they regard them as role-models for young men and warriors.

The Spartans worship a wide range of heroes. They take over traditional Panhellenic heroes and transform them into Spartan patriots;[28] they also worship historically famous Spartans as heroes, and hold them up as examples for the nation to follow.[29] In the case of the greatest Spartan of all, Lukourgos, the man who set up their military government, they even worship him as a god.[30] All of these Spartan heroes are honoured because of their educational value, and the Dioskouroi fit in well with the others, but being gods they are even better role models.

The main temple of the Dioskouroi is a few miles south of Sparta, in a place called Therapnē, and this village is always considered their home in Greece.[31] Their temple in the village is located in a sanctuary called the Phoibaion.[32] Beside the Phoibaion is another temple, which is dedicated to their sister Helenā and her husband Menelaos.[33] This married couple and the twin horse gods are closely related not just in myth (because of their family connections), but also in the cults of Sparta. In one of his hymns composed for Spartan choirs, Alkman tells how Menelaos 'is honoured in Therapnē with the Dioskouroi'.[34] The Phoibaion sanctuary is named either after Phoibos,[35] another name for Apollōn, or after Phoibē,[36] a goddess who is identified with Artemis and with the undeveloped wetlands that lie beyond the reach of city life.[37] Apollōn is the great god of youth-festivals at Sparta, but Artemis also plays a major role in the initiation of young men and women,[38] and one of her titles throughout the Greek world is 'Nurturer of Adolescents' (*Kourotrophos*).[39] So whichever of the two gods of adolescence owns the Phoibaion, it is perfectly natural that the 'young men of Zeus' would live there.

When the young men of Sparta are ready to become adult citizens, they come out to the Phoibaion and sacrifice a puppy at night to Enualios (another name for the war-god Arēs).[40] A local myth told that the Dioskouroi had brought the first image of Arēs to Therapnē from the exotic land of Kolkhis by the Black Sea.[41] As in all Greek states, but more explicitly so in Sparta, growing up means that a boy must enter the world of the war-god. After performing the sacrifice in the Phoibaion, the boys go back to Sparta and fight a ritual battle in the Plane Grove. The rules even allow them to gouge each other's eyes out.[42] This battle is yet another of the violent tests endured by every young male Spartan. The Phoibaion sanctuary marks a turning-point in his life from the gods of youth, Apollōn, Artemis, and the Dioskouroi, to the god of war and manliness, Enualios.

In addition to the temple they share in the Phoibaion, each of the Dioskouroi also has his own separate sanctuary – Poludeukēs has one outside Therapnē,[43] and Kastōr has a sanctuary with a tomb in Sparta,[44] near the place where Spartan citizens gather for political meetings.[45] They have, however, another shared sanctuary in Sparta. It is located near the Race Course (*Dromos*) where young men practise running. The gods who share this sanctuary with the Dioskouroi are very significant: they are Eileithuia, the Kharites, Apollōn Karneios and Artemis Hēgomenē.[46] Eileithuia is the goddess of childbirth, the Kharites or Graces are the goddesses of growth and fertility, and, as we have seen, Apollōn and Artemis are the patrons of adolescent men and women. Apollōn Karneios is honoured at his festival by a special event (probably at this very Race Course) in which a group of naked young men run after a young man draped in wool. As part of the Karneia, boys and girls also dance and sing in choirs,[47] and Artemis Hēgomenē ('Artemis the Leader') is the goddess who leads girls in dance.[48] At the Race Course, the Dioskouroi are the gods responsible for starting foot-races and are given the special title of

Dioskouroi Starters (*Aphetērioi Dioskouroi*).[49] All of these events, group singing, dancing, and racing, are typical activities of young people going through adolescence. In Sparta itself, as in Therapnē, we find once again that the Dioskouroi are the gods of adolescence, and are naturally associated with gods and goddesses who lead young people across the various thresholds of birth, growth and adolescence until they finally reach adulthood.

The Spartans also honour the Dioskouroi with a special festival of their own, the Dioskoureia. This festival includes dancing by young men, but these dances most probably are war-dances. Plato compares the dances honouring the Dioskouroi at Sparta with the war-dances of the Kourētes on Crete, and this word *kourētes*, like *kouroi*, means 'male adolescents'.[50] In fact, the Dioskouroi are regarded as the inventors of the war-dance, which they perform for the first time when Athēna plays the flute for them.[51] These war-dances are yet another element in the training of young men as warriors.

An inscription from the Roman period reminds us that there are also athletic competitions at the Dioskoureia. It commemorates a man called Sextus Eudamos, who is 'the life-long and hereditary priest of the Dioskouroi and organizer of the athletic competitions of the Great Dioskoureia'.[52] Pausanias also tells us that the Spartans celebrate the Dioskoureia with drinking and games.[53] Pindar goes even further, honouring the Dioskouroi as the patrons of all athletic events in Sparta,[54] and even claiming that Hēraklēs delegated the organization of the first Olympic Games to them.[55] The Spartan cult of the Dioskouroi marks them out as the patrons of athletic events, the guardians of male adolescents, and the gods who lead them into the world of the adult warrior.

The wives of the Dioskouroi, the Leukippides (White Horse Goddesses), were also worshipped in Sparta. This cult of the Leukippides was unique to Sparta,[56] and their temple was near the childhood home of the Dioskouroi.[57] The priestesses in charge of the cult are young unmarried girls, and they too are called Leukippides (White Horse Girls).[58] Along with the Girls of Dionusos (*Dionusiades*), the White Horse Girls worship Dionusos, who is a god of women, not of wine, in Sparta.[59] These girls are under the jurisdiction of a religious official called the Priest of the Leukippides and the Tundaridai.[60] We also hear of a Spartan priestess called 'the Foal of the Two Most Holy Gods,' so she must have some connection with the White Horse Girls and the Dioskouroi.[61] Since young girls going through adolescence are often equated with wild animals and spend a period serving a goddess in a temple,[62] it is clear that the White Horse Goddesses are playing a very similar role to the Dioskouroi. They are helping the White Horse Girls make their way to adulthood.

Sparta was unique in the Greek world not only because of its brutal system of initiation, but also because it was the last surviving monarchy in Greece. Even more perversely, Sparta had two kings from two separate royal families. Given the popularity of the Dioskouroi in Sparta, and the fact that the two royal families of Sparta claimed descent from a set of twin brothers, who were its first Dorian kings,[63] it is not surprising that the two kings identified themselves with the Dioskouroi.[64] The kings of Sparta always went into battle with images of the Dioskouroi: 'Both of these (the Tundaridai) used to accompany them (the kings) as their allies.'[65] When the Spartans changed their laws so that only one king went to battle while the other stayed at home, the same rule applied to the Dioskouroi: 'one of the Tundaridai was left at home.'[66] The idea of a special god who looks after the king and his palace is a very ancient one that goes back to pre-Greek times, and the Spartans give this time-honoured function to the Dioskouroi.[67]

Near the old market-place for selling goods at Sparta there were altars to Zeus Amboulios, Athēna Amboulia, and the Dioskouroi Amboulioi.[68] These titles are remarkably similar to the ones held at Athens by the three gods who looked after the Athenian Council (*Boulē*) – Zeus Counsellor (*Zeus Boulaios*), Athēna Counsellor (*Athēna Boulaia*), and Hestia Counsellor (*Hestia Boulaia*). These Athenian titles, held by the same gods (with Hestia replaced by the Dioskouroi at Sparta), suggest that the title *Amboulios* at Sparta has the same meaning as *Boulaios* in Athens, and that the Dioskouroi watch over the Spartan Council.[69] There is no doubt, however, about their protection of the Spartan kings. The Spartans have adapted the cult of the Dioskouroi to suit the peculiar needs and institutions of their strange kingdom.

Between Gods and Men

As young men of Zeus who are not fully gods, as marginal adolescents, the Dioskouroi are ambiguously positioned between gods and men. In the Greek world, young men or women are so doubtfully human that they are regarded as savage, as belonging to the world of animals.[70] Spartan boys belong to groups called 'herds' (*agelai*) and are commanded by a 'herd-leader' (*bouagos*);[71] they spend a period in the countryside called the 'fox time' (*phouaxir*), and this 'fox time' is a preliminary to the whipping-ordeal that initiates them into manhood.[72] In Attica, young girls are called 'bears' (*arktoi*) and spend a period called the 'bear time' (*arkteia*), during which they go off to serve Artemis at her remote temple in Brauron. This period that they spend as Bear Girls is a preliminary to the marriage that initiates them into womanhood.[73] Violence turns fox-boys into men, marriage turns bear-girls into women. Human adolescents belong to a savage world, a world of wild animals that lies outside the world of adult citizens, but nonetheless leads into that world of adult maturity.

Our low-class young gods are in a similar situation. The fact that they perform lowly services for others and the fact that they are young men are merely two different ways of visualizing the same low status. The word 'boy' can refer (in Greek as in English) both to a servant and to a young male, and this double meaning in and of itself reveals the identification of physical immaturity with social inferiority. Youth and service are two different categories that help to define people who are not full members of the group, and yet cannot be complete outsiders because they are necessary to the very existence of the group. In the case of Greek women, both categories are used with impartiality. Women are childlike,[74] women serve,[75] but in their case this inferior position is permanent. When they try to define the horse gods, the Greeks focus on their youth – this is the factor that explains their low, ambiguous status. These two young gods straddle the line between gods and men, just as young men, women of any age, and slaves of any age or gender are regarded as less than human, as straddling the line between humans and animals.[76] This dual status is an essential characteristic of the Dioskouroi. Their very name combines the most powerful of all gods (*Zeus*) and the most dubious of all humans (*kouroi*). It expresses a theological ambiguity rather than a full possession of divinity.

When modern scholars try to define one of the two poles as the real and original nature of the Dioskouroi, they are merely echoing an ancient discomfort with this strange pair of beings who hover between divinity and mortality. The Greeks themselves use every refinement of mythology in trying to define the status of the Dioskouroi, dividing up their divinity and humanity in a variety of ingenious ways. It would be very convenient if we could state that the Tundaridai were human heroes in Sparta, that their cult spread throughout Greece, and that they were then given the title Dioskouroi and promoted to the rank of gods. Farnell tries to prove that this was indeed the way things happened. He contrasts their 'human-heroic name' Tundaridai with their 'divine name' Dioskouroi, and concludes that they must originally have been human heroes because the name Tundaridai is found earlier than the name Dioskouroi at Sparta.[77] In doing so, Farnell is following the euhemerism of Harris, who cannot believe that people might start off with a conception of the divine as multiple, and therefore concludes that all the extra, superfluous gods (beyond his own one true God) must have arisen because 'primitive' peoples started worshipping human beings, or animals, or natural phenomena.[78] This is too high a price to pay for the dubious privilege of evading ambiguity.

We shall have to accept and respect the contradictory belief of the Greeks that the Tundaridai are the same as the Dioskouroi, and that these strange gods are both divine and human. In Chapter 1, we saw how Harris and his followers tried to explain this ambiguity through their theory of Dioscurism;[79] later we shall see how the Greeks explored this ambiguity in their myths.[80] Here, we are concerned with its significance for their cult and worship. In the *Iliad*, the Tundaridai are normal human heroes who have died and are now buried in their homeland;[81] in Sparta, the local myth tells that the Tundaridai were first worshipped as gods forty years after their death.[82] We must bear in mind, however, that both these witnesses may have special reasons for declaring that the Tundaridai are purely human. In the *Iliad*, Homer likes to keep the worlds of gods and men quite separate, and he is uncomfortable with beings who blur this distinction. So the Tundaridai are completely human, Hēraklēs is completely human, and Homer only once blurts out the word 'semi-divine' (*hēmitheos*), when he looks back at the lost world of the heroes and accidentally reveals the belief of his audience that the heroes are half-gods.[83] The Spartans are also uncomfortable with the ancient gods of the land they conquered. They demote the pre-Greek god Huakinthos to a mortal hero, and hand over his cult to their own god Apollōn, but claim that Huakinthos joined the gods after his death.[84] The way in which they deal with Huakinthos is not so very different from the story they tell about the Tundaridai. It is far from certain that the Tundaridai were originally human heroes.

Any attempt to discover the original prehistoric status of the Tundaridai is futile. The Spartans tell us that the Tundaridai are most definitely gods, but that these gods once led a human life on this earth. When, however, we first hear the Tundaridai being identified as the Dioskouroi, in the *Homeric Hymn to the Dioskouroi*, they are worshipped with *white* lambs,[85] which makes it clear not only that they are gods, but that they are heavenly, Olympian gods rather than chthonic gods of the underworld. If they were really heroes, or were in any way connected with the world of the dead, they would be worshipped with black victims;[86] their sanctuary could not be called a temple (*naos*);[87] and they could not be invited to a banquet at the house of living human beings.[88] The Greeks identify the Dioskouroi with the Tundaridai, but the divinity of the Dioskouroi would be incompatible with a cult of mortal Tundaridai. For this equation to work, there must be something about the Dioskouroi that makes them less than gods,[89] and something about the Tundaridai that makes them more than heroes.[90] The prehistoric status of the Dioskouroi and the Tundaridai is unknowable, but we do know the bewildering belief of the Greeks: the Tundaridai are the Young Men of Zeus, they once led mortal lives, but they are worshipped as Olympian gods, not as heroes.

Even though they could point out the tombs of Kastōr and Poludeukēs to any tourist, the Spartans have no doubt that they were gods and deserve to be worshipped in temples. The Spartan poet Alkman refers to Therapnē as the dwelling-place of the Dioskouroi, the place where they are buried just like human heroes, though they are asleep under the ground, not dead.[91] At the same time, Alkman tells us that they sleep 'the sleep of the gods' and receive 'a divine cult'.[92] Pausanias tells us that their sanctuary at Therapnē is a 'temple' (*naos*),[93] a term that is used only of the dwelling-place of gods. A fifth-century relief of the twin gods makes it clear that in Sparta there is no difference between the Dioskouroi and the Tundaridai (it spells these names in the local Spartan way):

> Pleistiadas erected me, this sculpture, to the Dioskoroi,
> fearing the fury of the twin Tindaridai.[94]

In the rest of Greece, people had no doubt that the divine Dioskouroi were identical to the Tundaridai, so the sixth-century *Homeric Hymn to the Dioskouroi* begins in the following manner that seems disturbing only to us:

> Tell me, glancing-eyed Muses, about the Dioskouroi,
> the Tundaridai, the shining children of Lēdē,
> horse-taming Kastōr and irreproachable Poludeukēs.[95]

The Greeks who worship these gods, and raise statues to them, and sing hymns to them are perfectly happy with this contradiction. Sometimes they feel that the Tundaridai are under the ground in a tomb; sometimes they feel that the Dioskouroi come from the stars; but mostly they feel that the divine twins are beside them, and they trust in their assistance whenever they are in trouble. More sophisticated thinkers wonder whether the Dioskouroi are really gods or humans, which leads to great confusion, as we shall see shortly when we come to discuss their myths. This ambiguous status, this contradictory nature is, however, an essential feature of the two gods, and it accounts both for their immense popularity and for their helpful interventions in human affairs.

Spartan Images

The Tundaridai appear at two of the most sacred spaces of the Spartans, the Throne of Apollōn at Amuklai, which was sculpted by Bathuklēs around 550 BC, and the Bronze House of Athēna on the Acropolis of Sparta, which was built and decorated by Gitiadas sometime before 500 BC. The Tundaridai were depicted on horseback at the top of the Throne, one on either side.[96] Elsewhere on the Throne, which was decorated with lots of scenes from Greek myth, they were shown abducting the Leukippides.[97] The Temple of Athēna also had a representation of this abduction, and once again this was just one of many mythical scenes.[98] The Spartans in the sixth century think of the Dioskouroi in conjunction with the abduction of the two Leukippides, and they consider both the twin gods and their twin victims to be horse gods. These conceptions are related, because as White Horse Goddesses, the Leukippides are 'the feminine counterpart' of the Twin Horse Gods,[99] and it is therefore as horse riders and horse gods that the Dioskouroi abduct them.

The famous Dioskouroi reliefs, in contrast, do not show any mythical events. The oldest one dates from 575–550 BC and is fairly typical.[100] It shows them as two young naked men, facing each other. Three other reliefs from the sixth century show them in the same way, standing naked and facing each other,[101] while a fourth one has them naked and facing each other but standing beside their horses.[102] In all of these archaic reliefs we see the Dioskouroi as typical young men, and if it were not for other clues, we could never guess that they were gods.

Some reliefs indicate that the Dioskouroi could be symbolized by snakes or amphoras. Two of the sixth-century reliefs have snakes (framing the relief on the top or sides, not in the actual relief itself), and this is a common motif on later Dioskouroi reliefs, but the significance of these snakes is unclear. Some modern scholars think they represent the underworld of the dead and show that the Dioskouroi are regarded as dead heroes.[103] Others think that the snakes represent gods of the upper world, and show that the Dioskouroi are being thought of as living protectors of the home,[104] or that the snakes are participating in a festive banquet for the Dioskouroi and attending the event as their representatives.[105] The snakes do not allow us to decide whether they are gods or men. The other common symbol for the Dioskouroi is a pair of amphoras. One of the sixth-century reliefs has two amphoras standing between the Dioskouroi, and a fifth-century Dioskouroi relief simply has two amphoras by themselves.[106] Once again the significance of this symbol is unclear. Are the amphoras being used for libations to dead heroes,[107] or for *Theoxenia* honouring them as living gods?[108] These two symbols were combined on some Spartan coins which show two amphoras, each of them encircled by a snake.[109] Such snakes and amphoras are ambiguous, because they can be associated with the dead, with heroes, or with gods. These symbols share the ambiguity of the Dioskouroi themselves.

The Dioskouroi are also represented by a unique symbol of their own. It is called the *dokana* ('beams'), and it consists of two vertical beams joined together at the top and middle by two horizontal ones. It looks like the letter H with an extra horizontal line on top. This symbol appears for the first time on a fifth-century relief from Sparta.[110] The relief shows the *dokana*, with a snake creeping up each of the upright beams. Once again, the meaning of this wooden structure has always been disputed. Plutarch seems to be alone in his belief that the *dokana* symbolize the brotherly love of the Dioskouroi.[111] A Byzantine dictionary (based on ancient scholarship) interprets the *dokana* as tombs,[112] and some modern scholars accept this explanation.[113] This would suggest that the twins are mortal heroes. Other scholars believe that the *dokana* represent a royal palace and symbolize the function of the Dioskouroi as the protectors of the king's home;[114] or they could be an arch used for initiation rituals, which would symbolize the role of the Dioskouroi as models for the young warriors of Sparta;[115] or a throne, pointing to the divine status of the Dioskouroi.[116] All this scholarly controversy surrounding the symbols that represent the Dioskouroi once again reveals the ambiguous status of the two hero-gods. Their symbols are no less ambiguous, and how we interpret them depends on how we perceive the Dioskouroi themselves. The significant point is that the Greeks have a place in their imaginary world for these beings with dual citizenship, these hero-gods who are equally comfortable among gods and men.

Gods among Men

Military Interventions

Like other Greeks, the Spartans feel that the Dioskouroi are always nearby, and they expect these gods to come to their assistance, but the Spartans, not surprisingly, look for their help in battle. Pausanias tells us how two young men from Messenia, the traditional enemy of the Spartans, took advantage of this expectation. While the Spartans were campaigning against the Messenians, the day of the festival honouring the Dioskouroi came by, and the Spartan soldiers celebrated the event in their camp. The two Messenian tricksters dressed themselves up as the Dioskouroi, wearing white tunics with red cloaks, and rode up to the camp on beautiful horses. 'The Spartans bowed down and prayed to them, thinking that the Dioskouroi themselves had arrived for their sacrifice.' While the happy Spartans were busy praying, the Messenians killed a large number of them and rode away quickly.[117] The real Dioskouroi were, of course, furious at this act of sacrilege and punished the entire Messenian nation for many years to come, but the important point of the story is that the Spartans are fooled so easily: they take it for granted that the Dioskouroi would join their celebration.

Their belief is not unfounded, because the Dioskouroi do not neglect their Spartan homeland. When Aristomenēs led the Messenians in their great seventh-century rebellion against the Spartans, he almost surprised the city of Sparta in an attack by night, but was stopped by the sudden appearance of Helenā and the Dioskouroi.[118] The Dioskouroi also came to the rescue at another great crisis in Spartan history. In 405 BC the Spartans fought the Athenians at Aigospotamoi in a naval battle that decided which of them would win the Peloponnesian War and dominate Greece. As the Spartan commander, Lusandros, was sailing out of the harbour to attack the Athenian fleet, some eye-witnesses saw the Dioskouroi appearing in the form of stars over each of the steering-oars at the back of his ship.[119] After his naval victory, Lusandros commemorated the battle with a set of statues at Delphi. The Dioskouroi must have had a central position in the victory monument because Pausanias mentions them first, both when he is talking about the monument as a whole, and when he describes the individual statues that made it up. The monument showed Zeus and the most important gods of Sparta: the Dioskouroi, Apollōn and Artemis. Beside them were Poseidōn crowning Lusandros, and finally the Spartan general's prophet and his helmsman.[120] Lusandros also dedicated two golden stars to the Dioskouroi at Delphi, but just before Sparta was defeated at Leuctra the stars disappeared.[121] The explanation for this miracle is found in Pausanias. A mysterious messenger told the successful enemy commander, Epaminondas of Thebes, that the ancient anger of the Dioskouroi against the Messenian imposters had finally come to an end.[122]

Human Hospitality

These appearances of the Dioskouroi in the middle of a battle-scene are, of course, extraordinary events, but the Dioskouroi also join in with their human worshippers on more everyday occasions. The Greeks invite them to a banquet called *Theoxenia*, 'entertaining the gods'. This lovely expression literally means that the gods (*theoi*) are being welcomed and entertained as 'friends from abroad' (*xenoi*).[123] These banquets where the gods are invited as real guests are quite different from the normal way of treating the gods in Ancient Greece.[124]

When Greeks want to honour the gods, they usually offer a domestic animal as a victim to the gods who remain distant, rather than asking the gods to come close and join them. At such an animal sacrifice, the ritual emphasizes the gap that separates gods from men, the gods are not physically present;[125] at the *Theoxenia*, the gods are invited as guests, just like all the other human participants who have been invited, and during the party the gods recline on a couch and join in with all the other guests.[126] At a sacrifice, the fat and bones of the victim are burned and sent up to heaven as an offering to the gods, and then the human participants have a separate meal here on earth; at the *Theoxenia* they eat together, the gods participate as ordinary friends.[127] A sacrifice always takes place outside; the *Theoxenia* are usually celebrated inside a house or temple.[128] The *Theoxenia* are, therefore, much closer in spirit to the rituals of Vedic India, where the gods sit down on a carpet of sacred grass among the worshippers,[129] than they are to normal Greek religious celebrations.[130] *Theoxenia* are celebrated for Apollōn at Delphi,[131] which is his summer home, and a couch is set up for *Zeus Philios* (Zeus of Friendship) at parties in Athens,[132] but the favourite guests at *Theoxenia* are the Dioskouroi.[133]

Terracottas from the Spartan colony of Taras (modern Taranto) in southern Italy show the Dioskouroi riding through the sky on horseback, naked except for the cloaks billowing behind them, and coming toward a table laden with food.[134] Their sister Helenā is often invited too, as we see from a poem by Pindar that celebrates the *Theoxenia* offered by Thērōn of Akragas (modern Agrigento), a Dorian city in Sicily. Pindar's ode begins as follows:

> I pray that I may please the Tundaridai with their love of
>   hospitality
> and Helenā with her beautiful hair,
> as I praise famous Akragas.[135]

In Sparta itself, Helenā is often invited along with her brothers. There are a number of Dioskouroi reliefs from Sparta that commemorate *Theoxenia*. They were raised by Spartans who celebrated these banquets and wanted to have their *Theoxenia* remembered. The ones that survive date from the second or first century BC, and show the Dioskouroi as naked young men standing on either side of an archaic-looking statue of the goddess Helenā.[136] These monuments provide us with information about the people who organize the event.[137] They are called the Diners (*Sītēthentes*),[138] and they are headed by the Priest of the Dioskouroi and the Priestess of Helenā, each of whom is given the title 'Welcomer of the Gods' (*Sidektas*).[139] This association of Diners includes musicians, a dance-teacher, tailors who make the ceremonial costumes, and finally a cook and a baker.[140] Some of its members are freedmen, some are even slaves.[141] The *Theoxenia* banquet is therefore an event that breaks down the boundary between the human and divine worlds, and even some social boundaries inside the human world. It is not so much an offering to the Dioskouroi as a celebration in which they participate along with their worshippers.

The Dioskouroi come to attend the *Theoxenia*, but they also make unexpected visits. In Sparta, they behaved rather badly to one of their hosts, a man called Phormiōn. He happened to be living in the house that had originally belonged to their father, and they wanted to spend the night in their old bedroom. They arrived there from Cyrene, and Phormiōn welcomed the two young strangers, but told them they could not have that bedroom because his daughter was sleeping there. On the following morning, the two young men had disappeared with his daughter, leaving behind in her bedroom statues of themselves and some silphium (a sacred plant from Cyrene).[142]

In neighboring Arcadia, the Dioskouroi visited Euphoriōn, a member of the Greek elite who lived sometime around 600 BC,[143] and they changed his life in a more positive way. He welcomed the Dioskouroi in his own home, and from then on he entertained any strangers who came along.[144] A final story from nearby Argos probably refers to a mythical ancestor, rather than a historical miracle. It tells how Pamphaēs welcomed the Dioskouroi, and he and all his descendants were rewarded as a result with athletic excellence.[145] Whether these stories were told about real people, or made up about mythical characters, the attitude of the Greeks to the Dioskouroi is consistent. They expect these gods to be near them. This unusual closeness of the twin horse gods to the human world is a feature we have also noted in India; of all the gods in Greece and in India, they are literally the most down-to-earth.

The Cult of the Dioskouroi throughout Greece

Invitations to Dinner

The Dioskouroi are invited to *Theoxenia* not just in Sparta but all over the Greek world. Powerful rulers like Thērōn of Akragas invite them to feasts in their palaces, and such hospitality to the gods is celebrated by Pindar:

> My heart encourages me to say that glory has come
> to the Emmenidai family and to Thērōn, as a gift from the Dioskouroi
> with their fine horses, because that family welcomes them
> with more hospitable dining-tables than any other mortals do.[146]

The poet Bacchylides of Ceos wrote similar poems praising Thērōn and other members of the Panhellenic elite, but he could not afford such luxury himself. Nevertheless, he feels it would be all right for him to invite the Dioskouroi to a humble party in his own house:

> I have no whole oxen here, and no gold,
> and no purple carpets,
> but I do have a kind heart,
> and a pleasing Muse, and sweet wine
> in Boeotian cups.[147]

In democratic Athens they are invited every day for breakfast at the city hall (the *Prutaneion*), where they are served a simple meal of 'cheese, pastry, ripe olives, and leeks'.[148] *Theoxenia* are depicted on Attic vases from around 500 BC, so the custom of entertaining the Dioskouroi at the city hall must date from the sixth century BC at the latest.[149] The earliest such Athenian vase-painting (before 500 BC) shows them wearing clothes and sitting down at an outdoor table laden with food, while a worshipper serves them; a pillar beside the table has a picture of them on horseback.[150] Another vase-painting shows them running naked through the sky, while a worshipper sets the table.[151] The most common type, however, shows them arriving for their meal on horseback, wearing nothing but the cloaks flying behind them.[152]

The Dioskouroi were called the *Anakes* (kings, or lords) in Athens, and they had a sanctuary called the *Anakeion*, which was probably located to the north-east of the Acropolis.[153] The Athenians told a story that Peisistratos had assembled the citizens either in the Anakeion or the Thēseion,[154] sent in his agents to disarm them, and made himself dictator. Even if this story is not true, it does at least imply that the Anakeion had already been built by the sixth century BC. Pausanias calls it 'the ancient temple of the Dioskouroi', and it had statues of the Dioskouroi standing and of their sons on horseback. It was decorated around 475 to 450 BC with paintings by Polugnōtos and Mikōn, two famous artists.[155] Polugnōtos did a painting of the Dioskouroi marrying the Leukippides, and Mikōn's painting showed the Argonauts. The Dioskouroi must have been entertained with *Theoxenia* at this temple too, because there is a group called the *Parasitoi* (Fellow-Banqueters) at the temple.[156] The Anakeion is the oldest temple of the Dioskouroi in Athens, but there was another shrine of the Dioskouroi near the Agora, at the headquarters of the Athenian cavalry. This must date to the 450s BC, when Athens set up its new cavalry,[157] which replaced its small mounted border patrol.[158] The Athenians also celebrate a festival called the Anakeia, which honours the Dioskouroi with horse-races.[159]

Athens does not have the harsh initiation system for young men that we found in Sparta, and on Attic vase-paintings the Dioskouroi are visualized as young adult warriors in a domestic setting. Several paintings, dating from about 550 to 510 BC, show them getting their horses ready and saying goodbye to their family before they head off to war, and, as in Spartan reliefs, they are usually naked except for their cloaks.[160] The people saying goodbye to them are their father Tundareos[161] and their sister Helenē,[162] but on some paintings we see the Dioskouroi without their family, and accompanied instead by several of the gods.[163] These paintings, again like the Spartan reliefs, do not show mythical scenes; the Dioskouroi are represented in everyday situations. They appear as prosperous Athenians, because horse riding is now a rather fashionable and high-class activity. They are cavalry soldiers in most of these paintings, but two vases depict them as 'mounted hoplites' who are using their horses just as a means of getting to the battlefield.[164] The old-fashioned aristocratic chariot appears on one vase alone,[165] so the Dioskouroi represent the prosperous horsemen of Athens rather than its noblemen.[166]

There are curious similarities between the cult of the Dioskouroi in Athens and in Argos. In Argos too they are worshipped as the *Anaktes* (the older and more corect form of the word *Anakes*).[167] Their temple in Argos has likewise a family group of statues with the Dioskouroi, their wives Hilaeira and Phoibē, and their sons Anaxis and Mnasinous.[168] When we come to the myth of Helenē's abduction, we shall see that there are further connections between Athens and Argos at this sacred site.[169]

Rescues at Sea

The Dioskouroi are, of course, worshipped by all Greeks and they are especially revered as Saviours (*Sōtēres*). Their father too is often called Zeus the Saviour (*Zeus Sōtēr*), both because he saves cities in wartime, and also because he saves individuals who are in trouble, and especially people who are travelling by sea.[170] On reaching dry land safely, the voyagers gratefully make an offering to Zeus the Saviour, and for this purpose a temple of his is conveniently located at the harbour of Athens, the Peiraieus. The title of Saviour has the same implications for the Dioskouroi. As we have seen already, they intervene to save their friends on the battlefield,[171] but they are also famous for rescuing ships that are caught in a storm at sea. The first time they are called Saviours is in the sixth-century *Homeric Hymn to the Dioskouroi*, which celebrates the birth of the Dioskouroi and their rescue of a ship lost at sea:

> She (Lēdē) gave birth to boys who are Saviours of earth-dwelling
> men
> and of fast-sailing ships, when the winter storms rage
> on the implacable sea.[172]

The hymn goes on to describe a typical storm, and when the decks are being flooded, the crew-members rush to the stern to pray and offer sacrifice to the Dioskouroi. The response is immediate.

> Suddenly they appear
> rushing through the air with dark wings,
> and at once they stop the blasts of the dreadful storm-winds,
> and calm the waves on the surface of the whitened sea,
> beautiful signs to the sailors from their trouble.[173]

The last lines address the Dioskouroi as 'Tundaridai, riders of swift horses', so the poet probably visualizes them as riding through the air. During a storm at sea, static electricity creates a flashing light around the masts of a ship, and this phenomenon is known as St Elmo's fire. The 'beautiful signs' of line 16 must refer to these flashing lights.

Alcaeus, from the island of Lesbos, explicitly visualizes the Dioskouroi as horsemen and as flashing lights in his poem to the two gods:[174]

> Come here to me, leaving the island of Pelops,
> strong children of Zeus and of Lēdē,
> appear with caring hearts, Kastōr
> and Poludeukēs.
>
> Across the wide earth and the entire sea
> you go on your swift-footed horses,
> and you easily free men from
> sorrowful death,
>
> jumping onto the top of their well-decked ships,
> shining from far away, running along the ropes,
> bringing light in the dreadful night
> to the black ship.

In this short poem, Alcaeus presents a different vision of the Dioskouroi in each of the stanzas: first, we see young Spartans, at home in a specific geographical location, the Peloponnese, the 'island of Pelops'; next, we find the horse gods, who are equally at home everywhere, riding across land and sea; finally, we have the flashing lights that suddenly appear in the night, and play about the mast and rigging of a ship in distress. Although it is a popular theme in Greek literature, their apparition at sea is shown on only one vase from the classical era. This rare painting shows the Dioskouri galloping through the air, and it could easily be mistaken for a depiction of normal riders were it not for the waves and the dolphin beneath them.[175]

It is only natural that a sea-faring people like the Greeks would place a very high value on gods who could save men at sea, and that the supreme example of salvation is rescuing a ship at sea. This function of rescuing ships at sea is completely absent from the Indian picture of the horse gods. The only thing that is remotely comparable is the case of Bhujyu, but his situation is quite different. He has been abandoned and is alone in the sea; we are not dealing with a ship and its crew. In Greece, by contrast, the rescue of a ship at sea is the typical way in which the Dioskouroi help humanity. The two poems we have just seen date from the sixth century, but the belief that the Dioskouroi appear as St Elmo's fire must have been very old and well established by this time, because the contemporary philosopher Xenophanes goes out of his way to condemn it:

> Xenophanes says that the sort of fires that appear on ships – which some also call the Dioskouroi – are tiny clouds glowing because of the sort of motion they have.[176]

The Dioskouroi have travelled a long distance from their world of dead heroes and their earthy graves in Sparta to these flashing lights of salvation that suddenly appear from heaven. It is this ability of theirs to transcend mortality and yet reach back down from their divinity and touch humans once again that makes them so popular throughout the Greek world. If the Dioskouroi can feel comfortable in such a wide variety of situations, if they can traverse with ease the worlds of gods, heroes, and mortals, it is little wonder that the Greeks were happy to worship them, to ask them for help, to invite them into their homes.

CHAPTER 6

THE MYTHS OF THE DIOSKOUROI

The Status and Parentage of the Dioskouroi

The Dioskouroi Tundaridai are both gods and men. The Greeks ponder this contradiction in their myths, and use the story of their birth to pin down their status. In the *Iliad*, Homer regards them as ordinary human beings, who died and were buried in their homeland; we are told that they have the same mother as Helenē,[1] but nothing about their father. Even if Zeus had fathered them, they would still be mortal, like all the other heroic sons of Zeus. Their sister Helenē looks out from the walls of Troy and wonders why she cannot see them:

> So she spoke, but the life-giving earth had already possessed them,
> Back in Lakedaimōn (Sparta), in their own dear country.[2]

Helenē's ignorance of their death makes it all the more poignant; there is no doubt about their mortality. The *Iliad* is, however, a tragic poem, and part of what makes it so tragic is that Homer emphasizes the humanity of his characters. He is not at all happy with people who cross the line that separates gods from men, and he deliberately makes them stay on the human side of the line.[3] Homer studiously avoids mentioning hero-cult or semi-gods;[4] Helenē is a very beautiful woman, but by no means a goddess; her brothers are fine young men, but definitely mortal; Hēraklēs too is a human being, whose fate is no different from that of Akhilleus.[5]

Things are a little different in the *Odyssey*. Homer does not quite say that Helenē is a goddess, but he does tell us that she is the daughter of Zeus, and that her husband Menelaos, simply because he is married to her, will not die like other men but will go straight to Ēlusion instead.[6] Hēraklēs had once been a human, and his 'image' (*eidōlon*) is left behind in the Underworld with the other human ghosts,[7] but he is now recognized as a god and lives with the goddess Hēbē on Olumpos.[8] A similar, but very peculiar, compromise is reached with the Tundaridai. This time, we are told the names of both their parents – they are the children of Lēdē and Tundareos.

> And I saw Lēdē, the wife of Tundareos,
> who gave birth to two strong-minded sons under Tundareos,
> horse-taming Kastōr and the great boxer Poludeukēs.[9]

When Homer tells us about their status, however, he starts off with the same expression that the *Iliad* had used about the life-giving earth possessing their bodies,[10] but then he continues very mysteriously:

> The life-giving earth possesses them, but they are both alive:
> Even under the earth, having this honour from Zeus,
> Every second day they are alive at one time, but at another time
> again
> They are dead: they have gained an honour equal to that of the
> gods.[11]

As sons of the mortal Tundareos, it makes sense that they are buried, but they experience mortality and immortality every second day. Zeus bestows this favour upon them, but merely because he respects them; not because he is in any way related to them. It seems that the power he grants them is confined to the grave, and that they stay inside it even on the days they are alive, which would make them local and chthonic powers. Homer does not tell us, unfortunately, whether their power is heroic or divine. He finishes off his evasive account of the Tundaridai with a wonderfully ambiguous formula that catches their essence perfectly, 'they are honoured just like the gods'. Does he mean that they are identical to gods, that they are gods (at least every second day)? Or does he mean that they are merely honoured as if they were gods, that they are not really gods themselves?[12] In dealing with the Tundaridai, there is no way of evading this ambiguity; the question will always be open.

The first place we see them called Dioskouroi is a text from the beginning of the sixth century. The *Homeric Hymn to the Dioskouroi* recognizes them as proper Olympian gods,[13] and describes their birth as follows:

> Tell me, glancing-eyed Muses, about the Young Men of Zeus (*Dioskouroi*),
> the Tundaridai, the brilliant children of Lēdē with her beautiful ankles,
> horse-taming Kastōr and irreproachable Poludeukēs,
> whom she bore under the top of the great mountain, Taügetos,
> after mingling in love with the dark-clouded son of Kronos.[14]

Both of the Tundaridai are the sons of Zeus and of Lēdē, and they were born in Lakōnia, the Spartan homeland of Tundareos and Helenē.[15] The Dioskouroi are now regular Olympian gods, so they are not confined to their grave in the earth. They can freely travel through the air on their horses, and they appear to sailors in the form of flashing lights. They come to the rescue whenever a ship is in trouble, not just every second day. This new conviction that the Dioskouroi are gods is not just a poetic fancy; a contemporary athlete, who won a discus-throwing competition, dedicated his prize-winning bronze discus to them:

> *Ekhsoida(s) m' anetheke Diwos qoroin megaloio*
> *khalkeon, hoi nikase Kephalanas megathumos.*

> Exoidas dedicated me to the two Young Men of Great Zeus,
> a bronze (discus), with which he defeated the great-hearted Kephallenians.[16]

The sixth-century *Catalogue of Women* brings the neglected Tundareos back into the picture by stating that Lēdē had three daughters with him,[17] but Kastōr and Poludeukēs are her sons by Zeus.[18]

These myths solve the problem of the Tundaridai–Dioskouroi by explaining that they are mortal (in the *Iliad*), divine (in the Homeric hymn), or something in between (in the *Odyssey*).[19] The real problem, however, is that the Tundaridai–Dioskouroi are both human and divine, and the Greek poets have to resort to considerable creativity in order to sort this out.

The sixth-century Greek poet from Italy, Ibycus of Rhegium, told the same story that the locals did in Sparta,[20] and said that the Dioskouroi had originally been human, but were then promoted to the status of gods.[21] Ibycus has separated their mortality and divinity into two consecutive phases of a single career, so that they can have a normal human life and still be worshipped as gods without any misgivings. This is an elegant solution to the problem, which preserves the Homeric tradition that the twins are of equal status. It is not, however, the answer that wins the approval of the Greek world.

The approach that eventually wins general acceptance was first taken by the seventh-century poet, Stasinus of Cyprus. He is the first to separate the two brothers, and instead of dividing their mortality and immortality across time, he divides it between the two brothers. His solution to the problem of their status will become the standard version:

> Kastōr is mortal, and he is destined for death,
> but Poludeukēs, that branch of Arēs, is immortal.[22]

Greek artists sometimes present one of the brothers with a beard and the other brother as beardless; perhaps they too are indicating that the one with the beard is aging, whereas the other is ever young and immortal.[23]

It is possible that Stasinus, in order to justify this distinction, made Kastōr the son of Tundareos and Poludeukēs the son of Zeus, but Pindar is the first author we know who explicitly makes this connection. In one of his odes, Pindar tells us that Kastōr has just died and the immortal Poludeukēs is understably upset; Zeus comes along and explains how each of them was born.

> So he (Poludeukēs) spoke. Zeus came up to him
> and said these words: 'You are my son;
> later, her heroic husband
> came to your mother and begat this man as mortal seed.'[24]

As a special favour to Poludeukēs, Zeus agrees that he may share his immortality with his brother:

> 'If you intend to share everything with him equally,
> then you could stay breathing under the earth half the time,
> and the other half you could be in the golden homes of heaven.'[25]

Pindar specifies elsewhere that their time under the earth will be spent in Therapnē, and that they will spend every second day in each place.[26] This recalls the arrangement in the *Odyssey*, and Pindar is the first thinker since Homer to face up to the fact that the Dioskouroi are chthonic heroes living under the ground. The *Odyssey*, however, stated that they were always chthonic beings in Therapnē, dead in their graves one day, alive in their graves the next day. Pindar, in contrast, boldly asserts that they are both chthonic heroes and Olympian gods, dead in their graves at Therapnē one day, alive in heaven the next. Pindar's elaborate compromise became the standard version of the story, but after going to all the trouble of working out this theory, he still calls *both* Kastōr and Poludeukēs 'sons of gods' (*huioi theōn*)![27]

The significant thing about all these solutions to the mystery of the Dioskouroi is their variety itself, and their agreement on one point – the obvious ambiguity in the status of the Dioskouroi. In Burkert's words, the Dioskouroi 'reach with equal ease in to the heroic-chthonic domain and the domain of the gods, and it is this which gives them their special power.'[28]

The Birth of Helenē

The Egg of Nemesis

All this speculation ultimately gave rise to the well-known Hellenistic version of the birth of the Dioskouroi. Lēdē sleeps with her husband Tundareos and with the great god Zeus, who appears to her in the form of a swan. As a result of this exciting night, Lēdē lays two eggs from which two sets of twins emerge. One egg contains Kastōr, the mortal son of Tundareos, and Poludeukēs, the immortal son of Zeus; the other contains the divine Helenē and the human Klutaimnēstra.[29] From the third century BC onward, Kastōr and Poludeukēs were depicted in Greek art wearing a felt-cap called a *pilos*,[30] and the Hellenistic poet Lycophron identifies these felt-caps as the egg-shells from which they had been born:

> The split oval of an egg covers their foreheads,
> as protection against a bloody spear.[31]

Two striking features of this story are the metamorphosis of Zeus and the birth from an egg, but they do not appear in the birth-story of the Dioskouroi until the third century BC.[32] Originally, Helenē alone was born from an egg, but this is a very different myth, and in this version she is not the daughter of Lēdē. The story first appears in the sixth-century *Cypria*, which tells us that both of Helenē's parents are gods; she is the daughter of Zeus and Nemesis. Here is how Stasinus of Cyprus tells it:

> Nemesis with her beautiful hair gave birth to her, after mingling in love
> with Zeus the king of the gods, under brutal force.
> She kept trying to escape, she did not want to mingle in love
> with father Zeus, the son of Kronos; her mind was torn by embarrassment

> and indignation (*nemesis*); across the land and the black barren water,
> she kept running and Zeus kept chasing; in his heart he was longing to take her.
> Sometimes in the waves of the loud-crashing sea
> she would appear as a fish and churn up lots of sea-water,
> sometimes she would go by the river Ocean and the ends of the earth,
> and sometimes she would go on the fertile solid earth; she was constantly changing
> into the various animals that the solid earth nurtures, so that she might evade him.[33]

The rest of the story is recorded by a later Greek author:

> The man who wrote the *Cypria* says that he changed into a gander, chased her, and mingled with her. . . she produced an egg, from which Helenē was born.[34]

Nemesis has presumbly changed into a goose herself, and Zeus foils her attempts to evade him by turning into a gander.[35] Even though Stasinus of Cyprus is our source for this story about Zeus, Nemesis, and Helenē, it is actually an Athenian myth that was told in the temple of Nemesis at Rhamnous.

So far, the story told by Stasinus has nothing to do with Lēdē, but she comes on to the stage now. Sappho knew about this episode:

> They say that Lēdē once discovered
> a hyacinth-coloured egg.[36]

This part of the story was also told by the locals at Rhamnous. It was depicted on the base of the statue of Nemesis, frequently painted on vases, and well known to all Athenians.[37] There are no less than 14 Attic vases from the fifth century depicting the story of Helenē's egg.[38] The abandoned egg is at the centre of the scene, sitting on an altar. Lēdē has just discovered it and raises her hands in surprise;

Tundareos, standing behind her, betrays no emotion; the Dioskouroi are there too, gazing at the egg from the other side of the altar.[39] This is the moment described in Sappho's poem, and the comic poet Cratinus tells us how Lēdē has to sit on the egg and keep it warm.[40] Finally, Helenē hatches out of the egg, a scene that appears on two non-Athenian vases.[41]

Lēdē takes the baby, nurses her, and raises her until she reaches adolescence.[42] The final scene in this story was depicted on the pedestal of the new statue of Nemesis, the one sculpted by Pheidias when the temple was renovated in 430 BC.[43] The pedestal showed Lēdē bringing Helenē back to Nemesis, accompanied by Lēdē's immediate family (Tundareos and the Dioskouroi). They were also joined by Helenē's future male relatives through marriage. These men were her brother-in-law Agamemnōn, her husband Menelaos, and her son-in-law Neoptolemos, who happened to be great warriors on the Greek side during the Trojan War. Pheidias, like Stasinus before him, was obviously thinking about the role of Nemesis in causing the Trojan War by bringing Helenē into the world.

At first sight, this story looks like a clumsy attempt to adapt the Athenian myth of Helenē and Nemesis to the Spartan story about Helenē and Lēdē.[44] The tale of her adoption is remarkably similar, however, to the purely Athenian myth of Erikhthonios and Athēna; it is the feminine counterpart to a very masculine story.

The Athenians told that their ancestor, Erikhthonios, was born when Hēphaistos tried to rape the virgin goddess Athēna. She evades his attentions, and when he ejaculates onto her dress, she rejects his semen and throws it onto the earth. Gaia the earth goddess acts as a surrogate-mother, and when the child, Erikhthonios, is born she hands him over to Athēna.[45] In this story, the boy's social mother, Athēna, withdraws before he is born, leaving the masculine semen behind her; and Erikhthonios, the first Athenian, is produced from the earth in a masculine birth and he emerges from that semen alone. He has no real mother. Helenē's biological mother, Nemesis, likewise withdraws before Helenē is born, leaving the feminine egg behind her; and Helenē, the goddess of young girls and fertility, is the product of a purely feminine birth from this egg.

The Athenians are very happy with their myth of autochthony, of a masculine birth from semen alone, but they would find the idea of a feminine birth from an egg alone quite disturbing. Aristotle evades this possibility by declaring that even eggs are purely masculine, that they are formed from semen alone![46] If we were to follow Aristotle, we would have to conclude that the story of Helenē and the egg of Nemesis is really a story about her birth from the semen of Zeus, so Helenē's birth would therefore be identical with the birth of Erikhthonios from the semen of Hēphaistos. The stories are quite different, however, and the contrasts between them help to define the roles of male and female in Athenian thought. Erikhthonios belongs to his country, he arises from its earth, he is rooted in its land. Paintings of his birth show the upper body of Gaia, only partly rising from the earth, handing him directly to Athēna.[47] Hēphaistos has fertilized the earth with his semen, Erikhthonios is a product of what is literally his native land, and therefore belongs to the social world of Athēna, who is the goddess of that political unit.[48] Helenē, in contrast, never touches the earth; even at the moment of her birth, her egg is perched on an altar, removed from the soil. Unlike Erikhthonios, she is not a product of her native land, and therefore she does not have an Athenian identity, she has no citizenship. She never becomes a child of Athēna; instead, she is picked up casually by a foreign family that wants to adopt a baby girl.

Athenian women are only loosely attached to their family and their country as they will be married off and sent away to a husband elsewhere. Like the egg in Helenē's story, they hover above the land without coming into contact with it. This is in striking contrast to their goddess Athēna, who will remain in Athens with Erikhthonios, both of them rooted in the land of Attica. Athēna remains on the Acropolis only because she is a virgin goddess. She will not be married off, she will never leave home, she will never reproduce. Her virginity means that Athēna is masculine, patriotic, and barren. Helenē, however, is overpoweringly feminine, but in exchange for this gift, her presence will always be unreliable, temporary, seasonal.[49] The autochthonous birth of Erikhthonios guarantees the succession of male Athenian citizens; the strange birth of Helenē symbolizes the disquieting nature of women and of sexual reproduction for the Greeks. Who can predict what might come out of that egg? Who can predict what a woman will give birth to?[50] The myths of the first king and the young goddess form a natural but quarrelsome pair.

Later, the Greeks become uncomfortable with the contradictory stories about Helenē's birth, so they eliminate Nemesis from her story and make Lēdē her biological mother. Zeus, in the form of a swan, mates with Lēdē, and it is she who lays Helenē's egg.[51] Later still, they have Klutaimnēstra hatching from the same egg, and the Dioskouroi emerging from a second egg, both eggs produced by Lēdē. The result is the erotic Hellenistic fantasy of Lēdē and the Swan, with which we began this section.

The Birth of the Horse

Dēmētēr Erinus of Thelpousa (Arcadia)

Due to her feelings of shame and indignation (*nemesis*)[52] at the advances of Zeus, Nemesis, whose very name means 'indignation', had tried to evade him by adopting various animal forms. As Burkert points out, 'here she is very clearly a double of the raging Demeter Erinus'.[53] They are both primeval goddesses with similar functions: Nemesis, Indignation, the daughter of Night, is the goddess of moral outrage; Erinus, the Fury, born from the castrated Sky, is the goddesss of vengeance.

The stories of Dēmētēr the Fury (*Dēmētēr Erinus*) and Nemesis are almost identical too. Nemesis tries to evade Zeus by changing into animal form, and Dēmētēr the Fury tries to escape being raped by Poseidōn the Horse God (*Poseidōn Hippios*) in the same way.[54] Pausanias heard this story from the locals who lived near the temple of Dēmētēr the Fury at Thelpousa in Arcadia.

> They say that Poseidōn followed Dēmētēr, being full of lust to mate with her. So she changed herself into a mare, and grazed along with the other mares belonging to Onkos.[55] But Poseidōn realized that he had been tricked, so he changed himself into a stallion and mated with Dēmētēr.

> ... They say that Dēmētēr bore a daughter to Poseidōn, but they believe it is wrong to reveal her name to the uninitiated, and also a horse, Areiōn. This is why they were the first of the Arcadians to name the god Poseidōn Hippios.[56]

The story lacks the complicated analysis of gender and reproduction that we found in the myths about the births of Helenē and Erikhthonios, but if the experience of *Dēmētēr Erinus* relives the rape of Nemesis, complete with its animal metamorphoses, other details in the story bring it closer to the birth of Erikhthonios, for they reveal that the horse is likewise a chthonic creature, a product of the earth. *Dēmētēr Erinus*, in the Arcadian myth, is not the bright, familiar Olympian goddess of grain production and harvest celebrations. She is a dark underworld goddess, with all the characteristics of an Erinus.

Erinus of Tilphousa (Boeotia)

In the Boeotian version of this story, the goddess who produces the first horse is simply Erinus herself. The sixth-century *Thebais*, the epic of Boeotia, tells us that Erinus is raped by Poseidōn near the spring of Tilphousa in Boeotia, and gives birth to the first horse, Areiōn.[57] Erinus is the darkest and most frightening of all the underworld deities, and her chthonic nature is vividly captured by Homer when he tells the story of Althaia and her son Meleagros. Althaia beats the earth with her hands, and calls upon Hadēs and Persephonē to punish her son, but it is the terrifying Erinus who listens to her cries and emerges from hell to kill Meleagros.[58] The Boeotians are telling us that horses come from hell.

Dēmētēr Melaina of Phigalia (Arcadia)

The very name *Dēmētēr Erinus* sounds like a contradiction; how can the benevolent Olympian goddess be a Fury of the Underworld? In another part of Arcadia, on one of the mountains surrounding the remote town of Phigalia, the local myth expresses this contradiction by calling the raped goddess Black Dēmētēr (*Dēmētēr*

Melaina). In Phigalia, Black Dēmētēr gives birth to a daughter alone, not to a horse, but this myth is important for our understanding of the goddess *Dēmētēr Erinus* who did give birth to the first horse. Even though the people of Phigalia do not call Black Dēmētēr a Fury (*Erinus*), this is what they have in mind, because this goddess shares several features with the Furies. She wears black just like the Furies,[59] and such black garments distinguish the Furies from the 'white-robed' Olympian gods.[60] It is Dēmētēr's fury that makes her black, and such a 'black wave of anger' is an essential aspect of the Furies.[61] Finally, both Black Dēmētēr and the Furies live in caves.[62]

The Arcadians explain the fury of Black Dēmētēr by saying that it must have arisen because of her rape by Poseidōn, or because of the rape of her daughter, Persephonē, by Hadēs.[63] This strangely sensitive analysis explains how a shining Olympian goddess could be so traumatized, and so alienated from her own identity, as to become a black goddess, an underworld demon. The Arcadians are uncomfortable with this Black Dēmētēr, and reassuringly declare that she is not really a Fury, that her alienation is merely temporary. Her story would not, therefore, be so very different from the familiar one of the bright Olympian goddess, Dēmētēr, who temporarily withdraws her gifts from the human race. Black Dēmētēr is a saddened goddess of the upper world rather than a terrifying goddess of the Underworld. This Dēmētēr is soon persuaded by Zeus and the Fates to put aside her wrath, to return to her usual, benevolent self.[64] And the story told by the Arcadians ends happily... almost: Dēmētēr is once again a beautiful Olympian goddess... but she has the head of a horse, with snakes coming out of her hair![65]

The Earth

For the myth of the first horse, however, the important point is that Areiōn is produced by the Underworld, and this chthonic origin is explicit in other versions of the myth. From Thelpousa in Arcadia, there was yet another story about the first horse, which is recorded by the poet Antimachus of Colophon (*c.* 400 BC):

Adrastos, son of Talaos, descendant of Krētheus,
was the first of the Danaoi to drive his two praiseworthy horses,
swift Kairos and Areiōn from Thelpousa;
near the grove of Apollōn Onkaios,
AUTĒ GAIA sent him up, a wonder for mortals to see.[66]

Dēmētēr the Fury is absent from this version. We could interpret the words *AUTĒ GAIA* as 'the Earth Goddess herself (*autē Gaia*)', or 'the earth itself (*autē gaia*)', because *AUTĒ GAIA* could be either. Gaia is the least anthropomorphic of all the gods. She is almost indistinguishable from the earth itself, *gaia*. In the story of Erikhthonios, Hēphaistos does not sleep with her, as gods usually do with goddesses or mortal women. His semen merely falls onto her, or rather onto it, because it is the physical earth that receives his semen, even though both the earth itself and the Goddess Earth send up his offspring to Athēna. As we have already seen, only the upper body of Gaia appears on paintings of this event; her womb is the earth itself. Erikhthonios himself is a child of the physical earth, the soil (*khthōn*) of Attica. He is 'very much a man of the soil' (*Eri-khthon-ios*), he is born 'from the soil itself' (*auto-khthōn*). So the *GAIA* in the lines by Antimachus can be the goddess Gaia as well as the physical soil (*khthōn*) or earth (*gaia*) of Arcadia. It is not clear that there was any father in this version, because the word *autē* could imply that the goddess or soil produced Areiōn all by herself or itself.[67]

In other regions of Greece, the goddess is dispensed with. There is no mother involved, no feminine contribution to the birth of the first horse. It is produced by the god Poseidōn from the physical earth itself. At Horse Hill (*Hippios Kolōnos*) near Athens, Poseidōn the Horse God (*Poseidōn Hippios*) merely ejaculates onto the ground, and this is how he produces the horse Skirōnitēs; in Thessaly, Poseidōn the Rock God (*Poseidōn Petraios*) does the same thing, and from the rock emerges the horse Skuphios.[68] Thessaly is, of course, a land strongly indebted to the power of Poseidōn as the god of earth-quakes. It lay underneath a lake, until Poseidōn shattered the mountains around it and created the new land of Thessaly.[69] He opened up the earth to create Thessaly, and opened up Thessaly to create the first horse, so that it comes from underneath the soil of a country that itself came from below the ground. In Attica, Horse Hill was also a gateway to the Underworld. It had a hero-shrine to Peirithoos and Thēseus, to Oidipous, and to Adrastos,[70] all of whom entered the Underworld while still alive. The horse comes from the very depths of the Underworld.[71]

There may be a Mycenean background to these myths. The horse was, after all, a recent arrival into the human world, and had to be assimilated somehow into their culture and religion. When the Egyptians learned how to use horses from their neighbours to the east, they took the easy way out. Instead of trying to find a place for the horse in the Egyptian pantheon, they simply imported the foreign patron gods of the horse, and expected them to look after these strange animals in their new home. The west Asian gods Reshef, Ishtar and Anat were the gods of the horse in Egypt.[72] In Greece, however, the horse was adopted by local gods, who had to be transformed into horse gods for this purpose. Burkert speculates that Poseidōn may have become a horse god around 1600 BC, when the Mycenean Greeks started using the chariot,[73] but there is no evidence for any masculine Mycenean horse god. The Palace at Pylos does have a tablet with the words *Potiniya Iqeya* (*Potnia Hippeia*), the Mistress of Horses, which makes it clear that there was already a goddess of horses in Mycenean times.[74] Athēna was also worshipped in the Mycenaean period as *Atana Potiniya* (*Atana Potnia*), the Mistress of Atana.[75] At some stage, the Greeks must have equated these two goddesses, so *Athēna Potnia* and *Potnia Hippeia* became *Athēna Hippia*. The Mycenean backgrounds of *Poseidōn Hippios* and *Athēna Hippia* must remain speculative, but we do know what the later Greeks thought about these two gods.

The myths about the birth of the horse bring out one essential point: the horse is a chthonic creature, it is born of the earth; and yet it is also a product of sexuality, begotten by a pair of gods.[76] These dangerous gods, the earth-shaker *Poseidōn Enosikhthōn*, the rock god *Poseidōn Petraios*, and the outraged earth *Dēmētēr Melaina*, *Dēmētēr Erinus*, or simply Erinus, transform themselves into horse gods and then produce the first horse. For humans, autochthony claims that they belong to the land, and conversely asserts their claim to own that land; but for horses it asserts a derivativion from, and an equation with, the violent and destructive forces of the earth. This dangerous aspect of the horse emerges from other Greek myths.[77] Poseidōn becomes the father of the winged horse Pēgasos when he sleeps with another terrifying goddess, Medousa.[78] Pēgasos strikes the earth so violently when he first gallops off that the blow creates the spring Hippokrēnē (Horse Spring),[79] a miracle that is often repeated by the horse's equally violent father, Poseidōn.[80] Pēgasos displays his dangerous character again when he throws his owner, the great horseman Bellerophōn, who is a ruined man ever afterwards.[81] The even more terrifying horses of Diomēdēs tear men to pieces and devour them.[82]

As with the other dangerous forces of the earth, the horse is placed under the control of human technology by the goddess Athēna. Poseidōn may have produced the horse Pēgasos, but Athēna gives Bellerophōn the first bridle, which will allow him to ride Pēgasos.[83] In Bellerophōn's homeland, Corinth, she is worshipped as Athēna the Bridle Goddess (*Athēna Khalinitis*).[84] Poseidōn may have given men the horses to draw their chariots, but Athēna teaches men how to build the first chariot,[85] and how to drive it.[86] She is indeed Athēna the Horse Goddess (*Athēna Hippia*), but she is a very different kind of horse deity from Poseidōn. Athēna the Horse Goddess represents the technical skill that enables humans to master horses, whether riding them or driving them in a chariot; Poseidōn the Horse God represents the wild unpredictability of the horse, and the strength that we still call 'horse power'.[87]

The god Poseidōn violates an outraged goddess or the earth itself and produces the first horse. The god Zeus violates a goddess of outrage and produces Helenē. The Dioskouroi will end up being the gods of the horse and the brothers of Helenē, benevolent saviours strangely connected with deeds of primitive savagery by Olympian gods. This connection has very deep roots.

Goddesses on the Run

The ugly tale about Poseidōn the Horse God and his rape of the earth is not just an old story of the Greeks; it is also an Indo-European myth. The Greek story told us about a masculine birth of the horse, but the Dioskouroi had nothing to do with it; in the feminine story about Nemesis giving birth to Helenē, the Dioskouroi are not directly involved. They arrive later on the scene to witness the adoption of their new sister. When we turn to the Indian version of this story, the bestial rape and the horse gods are brought together, because that is how the Aśvins are born. As we saw in Chapter 2, this story is recorded in the *Great Book of the Gods* (the *Bṛhaddevatā*). The goddess Saraṇyū, daughter of Tvaṣṭar, has married Vivasvant, but after giving birth to the first humans, the twins Yama and Yamī, she gets bored with her mortal husband and decides to leave him:

> Without her husband's knowledge,
> Saraṇyū created a woman of similar appearance (*savarṇā*);
> she entrusted her two children to this substitute,
> became a mare, and departed.
>
> (*Bṛhaddevatā* 7: 1)

The story of Saraṇyū involves two main episodes: the substitute and the metamorphosis. Both of these elements are found in the story of Helenē, and many scholars (myself included) have been so impressed by these similarities, that they have derived the names Saraṇyū and Helenē from Proto-Indo-European, **Selenā*.[88] Unfortunately, the great names in Indo-European linguistics – Pokorny, Mayrhofer, and Watkins – do not accept this etymological connection between the two goddesses.[89] In any case, the thematic connections are still quite striking. If the names are, in fact, unrelated, we are dealing with a changed name rather than a new personality, with what Watkins calls 'lexical substitution' rather than 'semantic change'.[90] Saraṇyū, like Helenē, is married off to a man, produces a family, gets bored with her husband, and disappears. Like Helenē again, she leaves a substitute to cover her absence.[91] Hesiod was the first Greek poet to tell about

Helenē's substitute (*eidōlon*),[92] but the episode became famous because of what happened to Stesichorus of Himaera. He had written a poem called *Helenā* telling how she had run away with Paris.[93] The goddess Helenē had been insulted and had struck him blind. He wisely wrote some new poems called the *Palinodes*, in which he retracted his previous statements and declared that Helenē had never gone anywhere with Paris. The Trojan War had been fought over her *eidōlon*, and Helenē had nothing to do with Paris or Troy.[94] Impressed by the repentance of Stesichorus, Helenē restored his sight.[95]

In both the Greek and the Indian stories, the substitute leads an adventurous life. Saraṇyū's substitute sleeps with Vivasvant and gives birth to Manu, an alternative ancestor of the human race.[96] Helenē's substitute runs off with Paris and starts the Trojan War, saving the world from overpopulation.[97] The episode of the substitute in Saraṇyū's story establishes her identity with Helenē, but the episode of the metamorphosis is more immediately relevant to the birth of Helenē and the birth of the horse in Greece.

In India, a goddess changes into a mare and gives birth to the horse gods. In Greece, one goddess (*Dēmētēr Erinus*) changes into a mare and gives birth to the first horse, Areiōn; another goddess (Nemesis or Lēdē) changes into a bird and gives birth to Helenē; in a later version of the story,[98] she gives birth to the horse gods also, as in India.

If we return to the Greek story of the violated earth, we shall find that it shares some further details with the Indian one. Poseidōn the Horse God turns into a stallion and rapes a goddess, or else he ejaculates his semen onto the ground. Both these details are combined in the *Bṛhaddevatā*. As in Greece, the goddess turns into a mare to escape her male stalker. The stalker sees through the trick, and turns himself into a horse. The Indian and Greek versions run as follows:

> When, however, Vivasvant had become aware
> that Saraṇyū had departed in the shape of a mare,
> he quickly went after the daughter of Tvaṣṭar,
> having become a horse of the same type.
>
> (*Bṛhaddevatā* 7: 3)

> But Poseidōn realized that he had been tricked, so he changed himself into a stallion and mated with Dēmētēr.
>
> (*Pausanias* 8: 25, 5)

The stallion (Vivasvant) ejaculates his semen onto the ground, as Poseidōn does in some Greek versions, but Saraṇyū artificially inseminates herself with it.

> When Saraṇyū recognized Vivasvant
> in the form of a stallion,
> she approached him for sexual intercourse,
> and he mated with her there.
>
> Then in their excitement,
> the semen fell on the ground,
> and the mared sniffed up that semen,
> in her desire to become pregnant.
>
> (*Bṛhaddevatā* 7: 4–5)

Such artifical insemination is a common narrative device in Indian stories, but in Greek myth it is not necessary.[99] If semen falls onto the ground in Greece, there is no need for a woman to act as a surrogate mother; the earth itself is fertilized by the semen and produces a horse like Areiōn, a man like Erikhthonios.[100] The only case of anything resembling artificial insemination or surrogate motherhood in the myths of Ancient Greece involves a male god, Zeus himself. He gives birth to Athēna from his head, to Dionusos from his thigh. In Greek myth, the male reproduction dreamt of by Hippolutos is a real possibility, and women can be eliminated from the reproductive process.[101] In Indian stories, however, reproduction is nearly always sexual, so a surrogate mother has to come to the rescue and inseminate herself (Saraṇyū, Adrikā).[102] These are, however, unusual procedures, only to be used in an emergency. Usually, there is no need to resort to the pregnant earth of Greece or the rented wombs of India.[103]

In the case of Saraṇyū, we seem to have a conflation of two stories: her escape from Vivasvant is overdetermined. The metamorphosis is quite unnecessary, because she has already managed to get rid of Vivasvant through the more convenient device of a surrogate (same type, *savarṇā*, and same appearance, *sadṛśī*). Helenē had left a similar surrogate at Troy for Paris to play with, and back in Sparta 'her ghost ruled the home', and Menelaos was left with 'beautiful statues'.[104] These goddesses can easily slip out of a man's arms, leaving him with nothing but his fantasies. The *Ṛgveda* describes Saraṇyū's disappearance as follows:

The mother of Yama, being married,
the wife of great Vivasvant, disappeared.

They (the gods) hid the immortal woman from the mortals,
and creating a similar (*savarṇā*) woman, they gave her to Vivasvant.
She gave birth to the Aśvins when this happened.
Saraṇyū abandoned her two twin children.

(*RV* 10: 17, 1–2)

Saraṇyū is married, she is the mother of Yama and Yamī, but she abandons her twin children and disappears. She is remarkably similar to Helenē, not just in the clever trick of the surrogate, but also in her behaviour and character. The Helenē described by Aeschylus and Sappho is a Greek version of Saraṇyū:

She walked lightly through the gates,
daring an undareable deed.

(Aeschylus, *Agamemnon* 407–408)

Leaving behind the best of men,
she went and sailed off to Troy,
she did not think at all
about her child or dear parents.

(Sappho, fr. 16 Campbell, 8–11)

Helenē is married, she is the mother of Hermionē, but she abandons her child and disappears without a care in the world. These light-hearted, free-spirited goddesses never settle down.

Saraṇyū's sexuality and fertility were temporarily placed at the disposal of Vivasvant, and she becomes the ancestor of the human race through her twin children, Yama and Yamī. This is the sole purpose of her marriage, and once it has been accomplished she feels free to leave. Her own daughter, Yamī, calls Saraṇyū 'the young girl (*yoṣā*) of the waters',[105] implicitly comparing her with one of the Apsarasas, the water nymphs who spend all their time playing music, dancing, and sleeping around. Helenē's beauty was sold twice over: she was set up as a prize for the most prestigious suitor in Greece, she was awarded to Paris as a fee for his judgement, and so she became, through no fault of her own, 'a woman of many men'.[106] Her main function in life is to cause a war and relieve the earth of its excess population.[107] Once the war has started, she is irrelevant to the gods, so she reverts to her carefree manner.[108] The nonchalance that is an essential aspect of her characterization is best seen when Homer shows her casually making a tapestry of the war, fought, as he remarks, 'on account of her'.[109] Saraṇyū's beauty and fecundity are utilized to create the human race; Helenē's saves the human race from its own excessive fertility. Even though these goddesses are perpetually young and immature, they are forced to play a vital role in the future of the human race, a role that is imposed on them by their overpowering fathers: by the laws (*vratāni*) of Saraṇyū's father Tvaṣṭar; by the plan (*boulē*) of Helenē's father Zeus.[110]

The Abduction of Helenē

When Saraṇyū had done her duty by producing the first human couple, Yama and Yamī, 'the gods hid this immortal woman from mortals', as the *Ṛgveda* tells us. The gods did a fairly good job of it, because apart from the episode in which she mates with Vivasvant and gives birth to the Aśvins, nothing more is known about her. There is more to Helenē, however, than 'Helen of Troy', the woman who carried out the plan of Zeus by starting the Trojan war. She is also a goddess who is honoured in Athens and Sparta, and she forms a trinity with the Dioskouroi, just as Sūryā does with the Aśvins in Indian myth. Her abduction to Troy was probably modelled on the local stories of her disappearance from Attica and Laconia. I would like to start with the abduction that is not so well known, the Athenian story.[111]

Helenē of Attica

Helenē was regarded by the Athenians as one of their own goddesses, born from the egg of Nemesis at Rhamnous on the north coast of Attica, and worshipped at the ancient Mycenaean site of Thorikos, on the southern tip of the state.[112] According to the Athenian myth, Thēseus the king of the land marries Helenē, the beautiful young goddess. They have a daughter together, and her name is Iphigeneia.

The story is first mentioned by Stesichorus (632–566 BC), who tells us that Iphigeneia was the daughter of Thēseus.[113] At Troizen in the Argolid, the mythical birthplace of Thēseus, there was a sanctuary of Aphroditē the Bride (*Aphroditē Numphia*), and according to Pausanias, 'Thēseus built it when he made Helenē his wife'.[114] There is only one vase-painting that presents the Athenian version of Helenē's marriage to Thēseus. It shows Thēseus and Peirithoos standing at an altar, while Helenē stands beside them with her mother, Lēdē, who presumably approves of this marriage with Thēseus. There are two young men present as well, who might be the Dioskouroi; if so, they are also giving their blessing to the marriage of Thēseus and Helenē.[115]

As a king, Thēseus is responsible for the fertility of his land, and he should guarantee this by his own correct behaviour, which in Homer and Hesiod means honouring the gods and upholding justice.[116] By marrying Helenē, a young goddess of earthly and human fertility, Thēseus is taking a short cut to produce the desired result. Their marriage is, of course, fruitful and their daughter is the 'mighty birth' Iphigeneia.[117] Her name resembles that of Kalligeneia, 'beautiful birth', the new-born goddess worshipped at the Athenian fertility festival of the Thesmophoria.[118] For Thēseus and Helenē and Athens, Iphigeneia represents the new, life-giving fertility of the land.

Iphigeneia was worshipped under several names throughout the Greek world: as Artemis Iphigeneia in Hermione near Troizen;[119] as Artemis or as Iphigeneia in the Temple of Artemis at Aigeira, in Achaea;[120] and according to the *Catalogue of Women*, she was honoured as Artemis of the Cross Roads (*Artemis Enodiē*),[121] and also as Hekatē.[122] Iphigeneia, Artemis Iphigeneia, Artemis of the Cross-Roads, and Hekatē are all forms of Artemis in her chthonic aspect. Her titles once again show that Iphigeneia, like Kalligeneia, is a young goddess of the earth who guarantees its fertility.

Iphigeneia is also visualized as a young girl on the verge of becoming a woman. The Temple of Artemis at Brauron was the place where little girls served the goddess as 'Bears' before returning home to face puberty and marriage; it was Iphigeneia who had brought the cult-statue of Artemis to Brauron.[123] The Temple of Artemis Orthia at Sparta played the same role for young Spartan girls, and once again it was Iphigeneia who had brought the cult-statue of Artemis Orthia to the temple.[124] According to the Spartan myth, Helenē had danced at the Temple of Artemis Orthia when she was a girl, and it was from this temple that Thēseus had abducted her, brutally forcing her into the world of women.[125] Iphigeneia, in contrast, has nothing to do with human fecundity or reproduction. She always remains a young girl; she never becomes an adult woman.[126]

Helenē of Argos

The Athenians rarely depicted their side of the story, because it was the Spartan version that prevailed. According to the Spartans, Helenē was a Spartan goddess, so she belongs to their king and country. An interesting compromise between the two stories appears in Argos, half-way between the two states. At Argos, there was a sanctuary of the birth-goddess Eileithuia, founded by Helenē: 'they say that she was pregnant and gave birth in Argos; she then built the sanctuary of Eileithuia, and gave her new-born girl to Klutaimnēstra.'[127] Helenē has borne Thēseus a daughter, as if they were in a serious relationship (as in the Athenian story), but she leaves him and her daughter behind, and comes back home to Sparta, as if it had only been a temporary affair (as in the Spartan version). She gives birth to Iphigeneia neither in Attica nor in Sparta, but in Argos, so even if her reproductive powers are derived from Sparta and are activated by an abduction to Athens, her fertility benefits the land of Argos because she gives birth there, and her child will be raised in Argos by the queen of the land, Klutaimnēstra.

Helenā of Sparta

In Sparta, it is naturally their own king, Menelaos, who marries the adolescent fertility goddess of his land, Helenā. This Spartan story became part of the Panhellenic tradition, and their wedding is celebrated in the Hesiodic *Catalogue of Women*. This marriage was also accepted by Athenian artists. An archaic wedding vase from Attica shows Helenē standing on a chariot with an unidentified husband, and removing her veil. The Dioskouroi are there too, standing on a second chariot.[128] It was they, after all, and not her parents, who had arranged the marriage of Helenē, inviting suitors from all over Greece, and finally choosing Menelaos.[129]

The wedding-night of Helenā and Menelaos is celebrated in the eighteenth *Idyll* of Theocritus, where a group of adolescent girls sing outside Helenā's bridal-chamber, and wish that she could remain a girl and play with them.[130] The marriage takes place in the spring,[131] the trees in the meadows have put out their leaves,[132] and the young girls feel like new-born lambs.[133] They commemorate Helenā's marriage by putting a garland on a plane-tree, pouring oil on its base, and writing on it, 'Worship me: I am Helenā's tree'.[134] They are the first girls to do this,[135] and Spartan girls will maintain the custom every year.[136] Clearly, this is not just an ordinary wedding, but the marriage of a king with his fertile land. Their marriage is, of course, fertile, but their daughter Hermionē is just a normal human being, who dutifully produces a male heir to the throne of Sparta a generation later.[137]

As we saw on the Attic wedding vase, the Dioskouroi take care to attend the ceremony. And with good reason. For the Spartan goddess

Helenā has a tendency to disappear. Her youthful fertility is a transient thing, and she is a local Spartan version of the vanishing fertility goddess, Persephonē. Just as Persephonē disappears to the Underworld with Hadēs every winter and the earth refuses to produce food in her absence, so Helenā disappears and abandons the land of Sparta. Helenā follows the sun to the east, abducted by Thēseus to Attica[138] and by Paris to Troy;[139] or else she follows the sun to the south and ends up in Egypt, brought there by Paris or Menelaos,[140] or simply removed there by order of the gods.[141] If her marriage to the king of the land represents its continuing productivity, her disappearance represents the loss of its life-giving force. This explains why her relationship with Thēseus is viewed from completely opposite perspectives in Athens and Sparta. For the Athenians, it is a marriage and a blessing to their land. For the Spartans it is an abduction, a loss that must be recuperated. So the Dioskouroi go off to rescue their sister, to bring Helenā back from the east. The Dioskouroi invade Attica, and find their sister in Aphidna, in the north-east of the country. They punish Thēseus for his crime by attacking Athens itself, enslaving his mother, Aithra, and replacing him as king of Athens with Menestheus.

This story of Thēseus and Helenē, viewed from a Spartan perspective, is a very old and famous one, and it became part of the Panhellenic epic tradition. Homer knew it, because Aithra is still Helenē's slave in the *Iliad*;[142] it also appears in the *Cypria* of Stasinus, who tells us that Helenē was carried off to Aphidna and that the Dioskouroi plundered Athens.[143] Arctinus must have known the story too, because he tells us in the *Sack of Ilion* that the sons of Thēseus joined the war against Troy with the specific purpose of securing their grandmother's release.[144] At the Panhellenic sanctuary of Olympia, the Kupselos Chest depicted the Dioskouroi bringing Helenē back home to Sparta. They have enslaved Aithra, who is 'thrown to the ground under Helenē's feet'. An inscription written in Doric Greek explained what was going on:

> The Tundaridai are bringing Helenā away and they are dragging Aithra from Athens.[145]

Alcman, being a Spartan poet, knew the whole story and recorded it in his poetry.[146] The Athenians naturally were not too fond of it, because it presented their king and hero, Thēseus, in such a bad light.[147] Only one vase survives that possibly depicts the Dioskouroi rescuing Helenē, and it is in fragments (its date is around 520 BC). One piece shows a chariot driven by Phorbas (the charioteer of Thēseus); another fragment has an unidentified young man in armour; a third one has the Dioskouroi. The only story that unites Thēseus and the Dioskouroi is the abduction of Helenē, so Köhne feels confident in identifying this as the theme of the vase.[148]

Even the Athenians were eventually forced to accept the common opinion of the Greeks, and the abduction of Helenē appears in the first history of Athens, the *Atthis* of Hellanicus, written around 400 BC. Historians at this time were rigidly applying the new science of chronology to Greek myths, and since Thēseus belonged to the ancient generation of the Lapiths and Centaurs whereas Helenē was still a young woman during the Trojan War, Hellanicus concluded with cold mathematical logic that Thēseus must have been 50 and Helenē only seven at the time of her abduction.[149] This is, of course, a particularly absurd age for a Spartan girl, since they married 'not when they were small and unready for marriage, but when they were in their prime and ripe for it',[150] which was around 18 to 20 years old.[151] The goals of Hellanicus were purely antiquarian, but through this difference in their ages, Thēseus becomes merely a force of old age and decay that is snatching youth and brightness away from the world. His role is identical to that of Hadēs in abducting the young Persephonē to the realm of the dead,[152] and there was, in fact, another myth where Thēseus tried to replace Hadēs. He went down to the Underworld with his friend Peirithoos and they attempted to abduct Persephonē herself.[153]

The significance of Helenē's abduction by Thēseus is clear, and in rescuing her the Dioskouroi are not only bringing their sister back home; they are also bringing back life and growth to the land. Helenē's story is Indo-European, because it is also found in the Baltic lands and in India.[154] In Latvia, the *Dieva dēlī*, the two Sons of the sky god Dievs, elope with a goddess called the Maiden of the Sun (*Saules*

Meita), who is the daughter of the sun goddess, Saule.[155] In Indian myth, we again find a sun-goddess who is called simply Sūryā (Sun Goddess) or the Daughter of the Sun (*Sūryasya Duhitā*), and the Aśvins elope with her during the middle of her wedding to another god. Finally, we have Helenē herself, who once again runs away with the horse gods, but this time they are her brothers and they are rescuing her, not eloping with her. Their role as husbands is taken over by the brothers Agamemnōn and Menelaos,[156] who rescue her for the last time after the death of her brothers.

These thematic parallels are supported by an alternative etymology of Helenē's name, which derives it from the root **swel*, 'to burn, smoulder'. Helenē could, therefore, be a conflation of Helenē and Whelenē,[157] of 'swift' *Selenā and 'sunny' *Swelenā, of Saraṇyū and Sūryā. Helenē's sunny name identifies her with the Sun Goddess Sūryā-Saule, who is found in the company of the same twin horse gods, the Young Men of Zeus (*Dios kouroi*), the Grandsons of Dyaus (*Divo napātā*), the Sons of Dievs (*Dieva dēlī*). Their relationship may be explained in different ways – they can appear as siblings, friends, or spouses – but the trinity formed by the Twin Horse Gods and the Sun Goddess is an Indo-European theme that has survived in Greece, India, and the Baltics.

The Adventures of the Dioskouroi

The White Horse Girls

The stories told in Greece and India about the birth of the horse gods or their adventures with a goddess may preserve Indo-European elements, but the later career of the Dioskouroi is purely Greek. When Hesiod describes the age of heroes, he says that they died 'for the sheep of Oidipous',[158] and 'for Helenē with her beautiful hair'.[159] Raiding livestock and abducting women are the main achievements of a Greek hero, so it is not surprising that the heroic Tundaridai abduct their future wives, the Leukippides. Twins can be viewed either as one person appearing twice, or as two different individuals. The first is clearly the case in the myths of the Indians, where the horse gods do not have separate names or identities. They are simply called the Aśvins or the Nāsatyas. It is only natural, therefore, that they would share one wife between them, the Sun Maiden, Sūryā. The Greek twin gods, however, are regarded as separate people. Even in Homer, the Dioskouroi already have their own individual personalities and names: Kastōr is an expert in horses, and Poludeukēs is an athlete,[160] or more specifically a boxer:

> Kastōr the tamer of horses and Poludeukēs the great boxer.[161]

Each of the Dioskouroi will inevitably have his own individual wife with her own particular name. Their wives are called the Leukippides, which means 'daughters of Leukippos' (White Horse),[162] though the *Cypria* makes them daughters of Apollōn instead.[163] The Spartan poet Alcman mentions their abduction in one of his poems.[164] He gives their names as Phoibē and Hilaeira, and he probably thought of Apollōn as their father.[165]

The story of their abduction was well known in Sparta by the sixth century, since it is depicted on two of the most important sacred monuments in the land, the Temple of Athēna of the Bronze House, on the acropolis of Sparta, and the Throne of Apollōn at Amuklai.[166] As we saw in the previous chapter, however, these two White Horse Goddesses (Leukippides) are worshipped by the White Horse Girls (Leukippides), and these girls are under the authority of the Priest of the Tundaridai and the Leukippides. This priest is therefore responsible for the devotion of unmarried girls to the Girls of Leukippos, and of unmarried boys to the Boys of Tundareos.

This connection between the Leukippides and girlhood can be seen in a poem called 'The Leukippides'. It was written by the fifth-century poet, Bacchylides of Ceos, and it starts off as follows:

> We are performing a beautiful dance
> and a new song
> for violet-eyed Kupris.[167]

These lines describe the moment when adolescent girls have taken their leave of Artemis, the goddess of the wildnerness, and have entered the new world of Kupris (Aphroditē).[168] While they are still in the realm of Artemis, they are viewed as wild and untamed. In Attica, they are the Bear Girls (*Arktoi*); in Sparta, they are the White Horse Girls (Leukippides). We find the same image of horse girls in a poem by Anacreon, where a girl is visualized as an untamed foal (*pōlos*) who must be subjected to bridle and reins.[169] This use of the metaphors 'tame' and 'yoke' for marriage is commonplace in Greek. Spartan girls are wild horses who must be tamed to bear the yoke of marriage, just as Spartan boys are wild foxes who must be tamed by the yoke of war.[170]

The abduction of the Leukippides by the Dioskouroi is a popular theme in vase paintings.[171] In Greek myth, girls are usually abducted from the dancing chorus of the virgin goddess Artemis, but two of the vase paintings that depict the abduction of the Leukippides show the girls being taken away from a temple of Aphroditē.[172] As in the poem of Bacchylides, the Leukippides have already left Artemis behind; they are dancing and singing for Aphroditē. Many of these paintings show the two goddesses being carried off on chariots by the Dioskouroi in elaborate scenes crowded with figures. Some include gods, who look on with approval at this forced marriage.

The use of the chariot in these paintings implies that the abductors intend to marry their victims; when men run after women on foot, they want to rape them.[173] On one mixing-bowl, the abduction of the Leukippides in chariots on the upper panel of a vase is explicitly contrasted with a scene of Satyrs running after Maenads on the lower panel, where the goal is immediate sex rather than any long-term relationship.[174] On other vases, however, the violent and sexual nature of the abduction is brought to the fore, and the Dioskouroi, armed with spears, pursue the Leukippides on foot, as in a rape scene. In one particularly violent example, a Son of Zeus drags one of the Leukippides by the hair,[175] a form of violence against women that is otherwise only depicted on battle-scenes where Greeks are killing Amazons.[176]

This violent 'initiation' into marriage is typical of heroic society. Helenē is abducted from the temple of Artemis, the Leukippides are abducted from the temple of Aphroditē. At Sparta, however, it had a special significance, because even in historical times it was normal for a Spartan man to abduct his bride.[177] It was yet another of the archaic institutions that Sparta alone had preserved. Spartan boys and Spartan girls receive a brutal and violent initiation into the adult world. Whether they are human or divine, the young women are always abducted, the White Horse Girls by Spartan men, the White Horse Goddesses by the Dioskouroi. Their story is equally at home in heroic myth and in Spartan reality.

The Battle with Idas and Lunkeus

The second great activity of the heroic world, according to Hesiod, is cattle-raiding. Such a cattle-raid forms the last episode in the mythical biography of the Dioskouroi. Idas and Lunkeus were the Apharētidai, the sons of Aphareus, and they lived in Messenia, the neighbouring state and traditional enemy of Sparta. The sons of Aphareus and the sons of Tundareos join forces for a cattle-raid. This story was known throughout the Greek world, and the Sicyonian Treasury at Delphi (570–550 BC) shows the four of them using their spears to drive the cattle home.[178]

After this victory, the two sets of twins start to fight over the cattle they have won. The Dioskouroi hide in a hollow oak tree, hoping to ambush Idas and Lunkeus and kill them when they pass by. Unfortunately for them, Lunkeus happens to possess the magic gift of being able to see everything, no matter how distant it may be. He and his brother go up to the oak tree and attack the Dioskouroi. Poludeukēs kills Lunkeus, Idas kills Kastōr, and Zeus blasts Idas with a thunderbolt, leaving Poludeukēs as the sole survivor. In later times, visitors to Sparta could see the tombs of the Apharētidai[179] and the trophy erected by Poludeukēs to celebrate his victory.[180] The story of their combat was obviously well-known in Sparta,[181] and it became a part of the Panhellenic tradition, since it appears in the sixth-century *Cypria*.

And Lunkeus quickly
went up to Taügetos, relying on his swift feet.
Going up to the very top, he looked throughout the entire Island

> of Pelops son of Tantalos, and the glorious hero soon saw
> with his amazing eyes the two of them inside the hollow oak tree,
> horse-taming Kastōr and the champion athlete Poludeukēs.
> Going right up to the huge oak tree, he stuck his spear through
> it. . .[182]

That is as far as our quotation from the *Cypria* goes, but the ending of the story is recorded by a later author:

> The poet who composed the *Cypria* wrote that Kastōr was speared to death by Idas, son of Aphareus.[183]

The full story is given by Pindar, who tells us that Poludeukēs agreed to share his immortality with Kastōr, who was then raised from the dead by Zeus. They spend one day alive under the earth, and the next day 'in the golden homes of heaven'.[184] And that marks the end of their earthly biography. The Sons of Tundareos die as local heroes after a very ordinary cattle-raid.

Other Adventures

Even though they were the brothers of Helenē, the Dioskouroi were regarded as belonging to the generation before the Trojan War, and they participated in two of its great Panhellenic adventures, the voyage of the Argō and the boar-hunt of Calydon.

The Sicyonian Treasury at Delphi (570–550 BC) gives us an idea of how the Dioskouroi were viewed by Greeks in general. It shows the Dioskouroi on horseback in front of the Argō;[185] even on a sea voyage they remain horse gods. From Greek vase paintings, we see that the Dioskouroi only play a minor, supporting role in the story of the Argō. One of the Dioskouroi holds the hand of King Phineus, while Iasōn cures him of blindness.[186] The Dioskouroi pinion the giant Talōs, so that Mēdeia can kill him without interference.[187] At the funeral games for King Pelias, Kastōr comes second in the chariot-race on a Corinthian vase,[188] but on the Kupselos Chest at Olympia, it is Poludeukēs who competes in this chariot-race.[189] The Homeric formula that makes Kastōr the horse-tamer must not have been universally accepted, but the tradition of the Argō story does know that Poludeukēs is a great boxer. The only significant achievement by either of the Dioskouroi is when he defeats the barbarian king Amukos of the Bebrukes in a boxing-match.[190] So the Dioskouroi are relatively minor figures in the story of the Argō saga. Their participation was, however, well-established, because the Spartans believed that their statue of Arēs Thēritas had been brought back from Kolkhis by the Dioskouroi.[191]

The other Panhellenic adventure they took part in was the boar-hunt of Calydon, where they simply go along with all the other hunters.[192] Since the Greek elites enjoyed boar-hunting, the Calydonian hunt was a popular theme on Greek vases.[193] In both of these Panhellenic expeditions, there is little to distinguish the Dioskouroi from the general mass of heroes, or to suggest that they are gods.

As sons of king Tundareos, the Dioskouroi also play a small, secondary role in the mythical history of Sparta itself. When their wicked uncle Hippokoōn drove Tundareos from the throne, Hēraklēs helped them to restore their father.[194] Other versions of the story attributed the restoration of Tundareos to Hēraklēs alone.[195] In Athens, the Dioskouroi deposed Thēseus to punish him for his abduction of Helenē, and made Menestheus king instead. It seems fitting that their role was to help others reach the throne rather than become kings themselves: they remain adolescents.

The Young Horse Gods in Greece

The most striking feature about the young horse gods in Greece is their ambiguity: they have two names, Tundaridai and Dioskouroi; they have two natures, chthonic heroes and Olympian gods. Some of the stories about their earthly existence treat them as generic heroes – the voyage of the Argō, the boar-hunt of Calydon. It does not matter much that they are the sons of Tundareos, it only matters that they are heroes of some kind. Other stories treat them as very specific heroes, the sons of Tundareos, who belong to a particular place, Sparta, and show them deeply immersed in its local mythology – the abduction of the Leukippides, the final battle with the Apharētidai. These deeds could only have been carried out by local Spartan heroes. And some let us glimpse their divinity – the story of their birth, the rescue of Helenē. In these stories, they are neither heroes nor Spartans. They associate with other gods, they are playing a divine role, but one that is unique to them.

The gap between the two sides of their nature comes out most clearly at the points where they must meet, at birth and in death. The Greeks try to eliminate this gap by dividing their double nature between them, assigning all the chthonic heroic mortality to Kastōr, and all the Olympian divine immortality to Poludeukēs; but instead of removing the problem, this solution creates a new one. We may have solved the mystery of the twins, but we now have to face the even greater mystery of Poludeukēs. The Greeks are familiar with the births of gods, but what does it mean for the god Poludeukēs to be born as a human being, and to go through life without ever knowing that he is a god? Zeus only reveals this to him when his brother Kastōr dies. And what happens to Poludeukēs after Kastōr dies? The Greeks are silent on this point, but he must have died in some sense or other, because he ends up being buried with his brother. This is quite different both from the apotheosis of a human being like Hēraklēs, and from the usual temporary human disguises that the gods adopt, a trick of theirs that exasperated Plato.[196] Poludeukēs is more than a human being who becomes a god, and more than a human form that is adopted by a god; he is neither simply a human being nor simply a god.

When it comes to the cult of the Dioskouroi, however, the Greeks definitely err on the side of divinity. The Dioskouroi do indeed possess a tomb, but they are worshipped as Olympian gods. In their story that the Dioskouroi led normal human lives, and were then worshipped as gods 40 years after their deaths, the Spartans are merely expressing a metaphysical gap in terms of a time gap. They are trying to build a bridge between the life of two heroes and the worship of two gods. The essence of the Dioskouroi, however, lies in those 40 years, in that gap between mortality and divinity.

It is easier to talk about their function. They are male adolescents (*Kouroi*), that bridge of ten years or so between boys and men. They are horsemen, that necessary bridge beween warlords in chariots and ordinary soldiers on foot. They are Saviours (*Sōtēres*), that mysterious bridge between gods and men. These functions all mesh together – their rescues, their service, their youth. In Greece, as in India, a god who focuses so much on rescuing mankind is something less than a god. In India, he is a god who does not deserve to drink soma with the other gods; in Greece, he is a part-time god – one day god, one day dead. These young horse gods do not ride out in glory like cavaliers; they are only fit to be sent on errands. They do not carry out their missions in dignified grandeur, like Hermēs or Iris; they obey instantly, rescuing a shipload of sailors, saving an army of soldiers, putting a king on a throne, escorting a goddess back home. And all of this is an aspect of their youth. For in Greece as in India, adolescence is a time of poverty and obedience, a time when a young man is an outlaw and almost a slave.[197] They come from Sparta, a land where this ancient conception of adolescence was maintained for longer and in a more extreme form than in any other Greek state,[198] and it defines the Dioskouroi. They never grow up; they remain Tundaridai, the sons of Tundareos, and Dioskouroi, the young men of Zeus.

It is hard to grasp these gods; they are ambiguous and, as Plato says about all ambiguity, they summon thought and awaken the understanding.[199] It is even hard to think of them as gods, for Plato has told us that the eternal should be absolute,[200] but the very essence of the Dioskouroi is their relativity. They are divine in relationship to men, and earthly in relationship to the Olympians; they are heroic adventurers in comparison to childish boys, and immature tricksters in comparison to heroes; to their human worshippers, they are Dioskouroi; to the gods, they are Tundaridai.

CHAPTER 7

THE GREEK HORSE GODS IN ITALY

In Italy, there was no independent tradition of worshipping twin horse gods. This cult was an import from Greece. It first appeared among the Greek colonies of southern Italy in the sixth century BC, and later spread to their Oscan-speaking neighbours. In northern Italy, the Etruscans and Latins were worshipping the Dioskouroi by the end of the sixth century BC, but it is not clear whether this cult came from southern Italy or from Greece itself. After the Dioskouroi had been naturalized as Latin gods, they were adopted by the Romans at the beginning of the fifth century BC. Although they had been brought in from overseas, the Dioskouroi were quickly assimilated as native gods by the Etruscans and the Latins, and they produced a profound and lasting impression on these peoples.

The Dioskouroi in Southern Italy

The Dioskouroi first came to Italy from Sparta by boat in the middle of the sixth century BC, and not surprisingly their first Italian home was in a city founded by Greeks. This city, the Greek colony of Lokroi Epizephurioi (modern Locri), was involved in a dispute with its powerful neighbour, Krotōn (modern Crotone). The dwellers of Lokroi sent messengers back to the homeland to ask for assistance, but they only received moral and religious support. Their relatives in

Lokris Opountia sent them the help of the Lokrian hero, Aias the son of Oileus; the Spartans, exhausted by their own wars,[1] could only send the Dioskouroi in their direction. These divine helpers were placed on a couch on board a ship and sailed for Italy. When the gods arrived, they enabled the armies of Lokroi Epizephurioi to achieve a stunning victory over Krotōn at the Battle of the River Sagra, which took place sometime in the first half of the sixth century BC.[2]

At this time, both the Spartan colony of Taras (modern Taranto, on the heel of Italy) and the northern Greek colony of Lokroi Epizephurioi (on the toe of Italy) were being threatened by a common enemy: the expansionist league of Achaean colonies (Krotōn, Subaris, and Metapontion) that lay between them along the Gulf of Taranto.[3] The Battle of the River Sagra put an end to the westward expansion of this league, and in gratitude the Locrians set up altars to the Dioskouroi on the banks of the river.[4] Statues of the Dioskouroi have been found in fifth-century temples at Lokroi itself.[5] The Dioskouroi had been invited to Italy as Spartan war-gods to help the Locrians win an important battle. Except in Etruria, the martial aspect of these gods will be their most important characteristic throughout Italy.

The Dioskouroi were equally kind to the vanquished after the Battle of the River Sagra. When Phormiōn, one of the defeated generals, was celebrating the *theoxenia* in honour of the Dioskouroi at Sparta, they appeared to him in person and advised him to migrate to North Africa rather than returning home to Krotōn. Given that he was responsible for the disaster to his country, this was probably good advice, and Phormiōn moved to Libya and settled in the Greek city of Cyrene.[6]

Leōnumos, another defeated general from Krotōn, was recovering from his wounds at the mouth of the Danube,[7] when the goddess Helenē appeared to him to announce her displeasure with the poet Stesichorus.[8] Helenē trusted Leōnumos to pass this message on to Stesichorus, because the poet also came from the Greek community of southern Italy and Sicily.[9] As we saw in the last chapter,[10] the goddess had been insulted by his poem about her role in the Trojan War, so Stesichorus apologized to her by writing two new poems (his *Palinodes*) denying everything he had said. Stesichorus may also have celebrated the role of her brothers at the Battle of Sagra.[11]

These stories make it clear that the Dioskouroi were already well-known and popular throughout southern Italy in the middle of the sixth century BC. Their worship may, however, have been private, except in the case of Lokroi. Taras was a Spartan colony, founded at the end of the eighth century BC, and we would naturally expect the city to have a public cult of the Dioskouroi. There is little evidence for such a cult, however, until the fourth century BC, when the Dioskouroi appear on the gold coins that were used by the city to pay its army.[12] The new importance of the cavalry in the battles between the Greek colonies and the native Italians may have led to a renewed interest in the horse gods among the governments of the Greek states in southern Italy during the fourth century BC.

These battles also spread the cult of the Dioskouroi among the Italians themselves. Around 400 BC, the Greek state of Poseidōnia was conquered by the Lucanians.[13] For most of the fourth century BC, the coins of the city retain its old Greek name, *Poseidan(ia)*, but around 300 BC the Lucanians issue coins with the Oscan version of its name, *Paistano*.[14] These explicitly Lucanian coins depict the Dioskouroi on horseback, and show that the Lucanians of *Paistano* have taken over this cult from their Greek fellow-citizens and made it their own.[15]

The cult of the Dioskouroi spread throughout central Italy during the third century BC, when this region was already under Roman control.[16] In central Italy the Dioskouroi were called 'the Sons of Jupiter' (*Iovios Puclois*, *Ioveis Pucles*), a title they never receive in Latin.[17] So even though the central Italians were under Roman rule, they must have imported the cult of the Dioskouroi from their Greek neighbours rather than from their Roman masters. In spite of the language difference, the central Italians should be included with the Greeks of southern Italy in their worship of the Dioskouroi.

The *Tinas Cliniar* of Etruria

The Etruscans were familiar with the Dioskouroi from the Greek vases that they had been importing since the middle of the sixth century BC. The twin gods appear on the François Vase of 560 BC at Chiusi (Etruscan *Clevsin*) and the Exekias Vase of 540 BC at Vulci

(Etruscan *Velch*), both of which are purely Greek artefacts that were acquired by Etruscans.[18] The Greek artists may have worshipped the Dioskouroi, but such works of art do not prove that there was any cult of these gods in Etruria. It is not until the end of the sixth century BC that we find convincing evidence for Etruscan worship of the Dioskouroi. At this time, they are fully assimilated as Etruscan gods, and are called *Tinas Cliniar*, 'the Sons of Tinia'. Tinia is the chief god of the Etruscans, so this phrase is a direct translation of the Greek name, *Dios kouroi*. The individual names of the Dioskouroi were adopted under the forms *Castur* and *Pultuce*, and their sister Helenē became *Elinai*.[19]

The title *Tinas Cliniar* first appears on an inscription that is our first evidence for their cult and for their assimilation: 'Venel Atelinas gave this to the Sons of Tinia.'[20] These words, in Etruscan, were written on a Greek cup that was presented as an offering to the Dioskouroi, and it was found in an Etruscan grave at Tarquinia (Etruscan *Tarchnal*). The painting on the cup has nothing to do with the Dioskouroi, so the inscription expresses the personal faith of the Etruscan writer, and was not inspired by anything on the vase itself. The *Tinas Cliniar* are already popular in Etruria, they are accepted as Etruscan gods, their cult is not regarded as an exotic Greek import.

The Sons of Tinia appear frequently on bronze mirrors from Etruria, and these date mainly from the fourth and third centuries BC.[21] Usually the two gods appear standing on either side of a beam (a simplified version of the Greek *dokana*), a star, or an amphora.[22] Sometimes they are shown with their shields or horses in the background.[23]

The story of Helenē's birth from the egg appears quite often on Etruscan artefacts.[24] Several images show the egg being presented to Tundareos (Etruscan *Tuntle*) by the twin gods, but sometimes Hermēs (Etruscan *Turms*) gives him the egg,[25] so we are already moving away from the normal Greek story. In one strange example, a female figure identified as Urphea receives Helenē's egg from Hermēs.[26] This Orphic connection may explain why the story of Helenē's egg is so popular in Etruria; it has been adopted as an allegory by the Orphics and Pythagoreans.[27] De Grummond suggests that the egg may have been a symbol of the Afterlife, and this would explain why Hermēs

(*Turms*) is the one who hands the egg to Tundareos (*Tuntle*), since he is the god who escorts people to the Underworld.

Helenē's story was used in a similar way by the Pythagoreans of southern Italy. In a late fifth-century BC tomb at Metapontion, a rich Pythagorean woman was buried with an image of a baby emerging from an egg. This was a representation of the birth of the Orphic deity Phanēs from the original cosmic egg, but since Phanēs was bisexual, he could be represented either as the god Erōs or as the goddess Helenē.[28] Helenē's birth from the egg of Nemesis can represent the birth of Phanēs from the egg of the cosmos.

Both in southern Italy and in Etruria, the simple story of Helenē's egg has acquired this new meaning for the followers of Orpheus and Pythagoras. On Etruscan mirrors, one or both of the *Tinas Cliniar* may be present when Helenē's egg is found or delivered, but this story has been removed from its original mythical context, and it has little to do with the earthly career of the Greek Dioskouroi.

The only adventure of the Dioskouroi that is commonly represented in Etruscan art is the boxing match between Poludeukēs (Etruscan *Pultuce*) and Amukos (Etruscan *Amuce*). This is an episode from the story of Iasōn and the Argonauts. Amukos, King of the Bebrukes, guards a sacred spring, and will not allow anyone to drink from it without a boxing-match. Poludeukēs accepts the challenge, defeats Amukos, and ties him to a tree. The rest of the Argonauts are now free to drink as much as they want from the spring.[29]

This episode is very popular on Etruscan artefacts and appears on the famous Ficorini *cista* from Praeneste (modern Palestrina). The Ficorini *cista* is a beautiful cylindrical box made of bronze, and it dates from the fourth century BC. Although it was made in Rome by a Latin artist, Novios Plautios, for a lady who lived in Praeneste, Dindia Macolnia, the work is very Etruscan in its style. The prophet of the Argonauts, Mopsos, is depicted with wings, so he was regarded as divine by the artist.[30] He is presented as an Etruscan prophet, standing with one leg higher than the other, resting it on a stone.[31] He is looking down at a prophetic head on the ground, which is another Etruscan feature.[32] As with many Etruscan artefacts, this Latin work was found in a tomb. It was dedicated to 'the daughter', but we are not quite sure whose daughter this was. It could have been a gift from Dindia Malconia to her own daughter, or perhaps an offering to Proserpina, the Daughter of the Underworld.[33]

Wiseman believes that the Latins may have associated Amukos with their own city of Amunclae,[34] but this would not explain the popularity of the story among the Etruscans. However we might explain this choice, the important point is that the Etruscans are not merely importing Greek myths about the Dioskouroi; they are deliberately seeking out stories that will fit in with their own religious preoccupations. The very strangeness of their choice makes it clear that the story of Amuce is no longer the Greek episode of Amukos. It is now an Etruscan myth, with Etruscan characters behaving in an Etruscan manner.

The Etruscans did indeed borrow the Dioskouroi and their story from the Greeks, but they focused on two obscure episodes from the myth of the Dioskouroi and interpreted them in their own way. The Egg of Elinai is not quite the same as the egg from which Helenē was born, and the obscure episode of Poludeukēs and Amukos, from an epic tradition to which the Dioskouroi are only very loosely attached, acquires a strange new importance when it becomes the story of Pultuce and Amuce. As Wiseman remarks of Novios Plautios: 'I imagine he didn't think of Amykos and Ajax as particularly Greek, any more than we think of Cinderella as Italian or Snow White as German.'[35] The *Tinas Cliniar* may be of Greek origin, but they have become thoroughly Etruscan in their new homeland, and the man who wrote their name on the Greek cup at the end of the sixth century BC was dedicating a foreign object to the horse gods of his own country.

The *Quroi* in Latium

While the Etruscan was writing his graffito on the Greek vase, another man was writing a similar inscription in a very different language. In the Latin city of Lavinium, this anonymous writer was producing our first evidence for the cult of the Dioskouroi in Latium, by writing the following words (badly spelled) on a bronze plaque:

Castorei Podlouqueique Qurois. It should read *Castorei Poldoukeique Qorois*, 'to the Young Men Castor and Poldoux'. The strange word *Quroi* is his way of spelling *Qoroi* or *Qōroi*, the Western Greek version of *Kouroi*. This makes it clear that the cult of the Dioskouroi came from a Greek source, and not from Etruria. The word *Quroi* is strange not just in its spelling, but also in the way it is used. The Latin writer does not say 'to the Young Men of Jupiter'; he simply writes 'to the Young Men'. Everywhere else in Italy, the horse gods are called the sons of the supreme god: *Dios Kouroi* in southern Italy, *Ioviois Puclois* and *Ioveis Pucles* in central Italy, *Tinas Cliniar* in Etruria. The Latins, in contrast, refrained from calling them the 'Sons of Jupiter', and this title never appears in their language.[36] As Dumézil rather forcefully puts it: 'At Rome, on the other hand, every connection with Jupiter is severed.'[37] This indicates that the Dioskouroi have already been assimilated as Latin gods and have to respect the local rules.

Archaeologists have not found a temple of Castor and Pollux at Lavinium,[38] but Weinstock has shown that they were identified with the *Penates Publici*, the household gods of the state. The small temple of the *Penates* at Lavinium appears centuries later on the *Ara Pacis* of the Emperor Augustus in Rome, and from this depiction we see that the two Penates were visualized as young men with spears, just as the Dioskouroi were in Greece.[39] From ancient writers we know that the *Penates* were also represented by jars,[40] which once again was typical for the Greek cult of the Dioskouroi at Sparta and Taras.[41] This assimilation of the Dioskouroi to the native *Penates* of Latium would be no more surprising than their being called *Tinas Cliniar* on the other side of the Tiber in Etruria.

Castor and Pollux were worshipped as the *Penates*, and they had a temple at Lavinium, which Roman magistrates had to visit for sacrifices every year, but we do not know its date or location. The Latin town of Ardea also had a temple of Castor and Pollux, and archaeologists have uncovered three temples dating from 500–450 BC, one of which must belong to the two gods.[42] From first-century BC sources, we know that they had another temple at Tusculum, where they were worshipped in the Greek fashion with *Lectisternia* – the statues of the twin gods were placed on couches and a banquet was held in their honour.[43] These *Lectisternia* are the Latin equivalent of the Greek *Theoxenia*. Finally, at Cori, archaeologists have found a temple of Castor and Pollux which was built around 100–90 BC, though it probably replaced an older one.[44] So the Dioskouroi arrived at Lavinium in the sixth century BC, at Ardea and also at Rome in the fifth century BC, and were worshipped in all the major cities of Latium by the first century BC.

The *Castores* in Rome

The Dioskouroi first came to Italy to help a city in wartime; they come to Rome for the same reason. In the early days of the Republic, the Romans fought against the other states of the Latin League at Lake Regillus. The Romans commemorated this battle every year on 15 July, but they were not sure of the year in which it took place; it was either 499 or 496 BC. The other Latins were more than a match for the Romans, so the dictator Aulus Postumius Albus had promised that he would build a temple to the Latin gods, Castor and Pollux, if they granted him victory in this battle. His request was granted, and the Romans won. This is Livy's sober version of what happened (Livy 2:21), but popular accounts claimed that Castor and Pollux had suddenly appeared on horseback at the critical moment of the battle and had led the Romans to victory.[45] After the battle, the two gods turned up once again in the Roman Forum, watered their horses at the Pool of Juturna, and announced to the curious bystanders that the Romans had won at Lake Regillus.[46] These stories about the miraculous intervention by Castor and Pollux were probably inspired by Greek tales of the Battle on the River Sagra.[47]

In 484 BC, the Romans finally carried out their promise and dedicated the Temple of Castor and Pollux in the Roman Forum itself.[48] The temple was dedicated to both gods, but was always known as 'the Temple of Castor' in Rome.[49] This may simply have arisen from laziness, but the twin gods were associated with the cavalry at Rome, and Castor was the horse-tamer of the two, so they may have deliberately emphasized the importance of Castor. When they were referring to both gods, they called them the *Castores*. The Romans did not build temples to foreign gods inside the sacred boundary of their city (the *pomerium*), and the cult of the twin gods was not supervised by the officials in charge of foreign rituals (the *Decemviri Sacris Faciundis*, the Committee of Ten for Performing Sacrifices), so Castor and Pollux came to Rome as *Latin* gods, not as foreign Greek gods.[50] This makes it clear that their cult must have been well-established throughout Latium by 484 BC.

In Rome, they were worshipped as gods of the cavalry, and this connection was formalized in 304 BC by the censor Quintus Fabius Rullianus. He established a new public ceremony in Rome, to be celebrated on 15 July, the anniversary of the Battle of Lake Regillus. On this day, the entire Roman cavalry rode into the city and stopped before the two censors, who were seated on a podium in front of the Temple of Castor. Each horseman was inspected by the censors and then he was invited to pass on, or else he was dismissed from the cavalry. The ceremony was recorded by Dionysius of Halicarnassus, who was very impressed by the sight.[51]

The Temple of Castor was also an important place for ordinary Roman citizens. The people voted in front of it, and leaders addressed public meetings from its high podium.[52] The two gods themselves were a part of everyday life. From 211 to 120 BC they appeared on Roman coins,[53] and Romans commonly exclaimed '*edepol*' (by Pollux) or '*ecastor*' (by Castor) when they wanted to add emphasis to their statements.[54]

The popular character of the gods is brought out in the story of another apparition, which we noted in Chapter 1. In 168 BC, a Plebeian man from Reate called Publius Vatinius was going to Rome when he saw two handsome young men riding toward him.[55] They were, in fact, the horse gods Castor and Pollux, and they announced that the Romans had just defeated King Perseus of Macedonia. Vatinius ran off to the Senate House to tell the senators what had happened, but they did not believe him and he was sent to jail. The horse gods also appeared before other members of the general public at this time. They were seen at the Pool of Juturna in the Forum, and the doors of the Temple of Castor opened miraculously.[56] When the

Senate discovered that Vatinius was telling the truth, it ordered his release and rewarded him.[57] These apparitions reveal the intimacy of Castor and Pollux with the Roman people, and the distance of the Senate from popular religion. The horse gods are quite happy to confide in a humble Plebeian like Vatinius, and to mingle with ordinary Romans in the city centre, at the Pool of Juturna, or at their own temple. The Castores may have been invited to Rome as gods of the cavalry, but they stayed there as gods of the people.

The horse gods were imported into Italy from Greece, and their images, names, and stories were entirely Greek. They were welcomed, quite naturally, as Spartan gods by the Greek colonists of Lokroi Epizephurioi and Taras. Their cult spread to Latium and Etruria in the sixth century BC, and to central Italy in the third century BC. They are worshipped as Greek gods with Greek rituals by the Latins in Tusculum, but elsewhere in Etruria and Latium they are fully assimilated as local gods. In Etruria, they may at first have been admired on Greek works of art, but as soon as the Etruscans take up their cult, they worship the twins as Etruscan gods, as the *Tinas Cliniar.* The Romans likewise worship the Castores as Latin gods alone. They welcome them into the heart of their city, as a manifestation of their own Latin *Penates*, and make them a part of Roman life. The Castores participate in Roman battles, in the public ceremonies of Rome, in the political life of the city, in the everyday life of its people. They are the gods of the Roman cavalry, but they are also the gods of ordinary Romans in the marketplace. They have little to do with Jupiter, they are close to the Latin goddess Juturna, who comes from Lavinium, and they are identical with the *Penates*, who are likewise from Lavinium. The *Penates* are the most intimate gods in the life of a Roman, and if the Castores could be identified with them, they had obviously found a place, not just in the heart of the city, but in the hearts of the Roman people themselves.

Their popularity was destined to last for a very long time. Pope Galasius I (492–496) was shocked to discover that they were still being worshipped at the end of the fifth century,[58] but in the days of Pope Gregory XIII (1572–1585), the Romans had fallen under the spell of the Castores once again. Two statues of the Castores, which had once been in a temple of theirs at the Circus Flaminius, were rediscovered in the middle of the sixteenth century. Inspired by the old story of Lake Regillus, the city government of Rome held a special meeting in 1582, and it decided that these two statues should dominate the entrance to the new Capitol created by Michelangelo.[59] The statues were restored and finally installed in 1601,[60] so that they stood at the top of the *cordonata*, the monumental stairs that lead up to the Campidoglio itself. They still overlook the city of Rome today.

CONCLUSION

Warlords and Priests

In early societies, a few people own almost everything, and the majority get by on their left-overs. The observation that the many are cheated by the few was made with brutal accuracy by Vedic thinkers 3,000 years ago: 'The warlord eats, the people are his food.'[1] A peasant expressed the same idea in Ancient Greece when he described his lords as 'gift-eaters',[2] and in a brief moment of radicalism, the great warlord Akhilleus denounces his overlord Agamemnōn as a 'people-eater'.[3] The early cattle-raising societies of Greece and India were dominated by ranchers who acquired such large herds that they could exercise political and military power, and they used this power to acquire even larger herds of cattle. This is what Vedic priests pray for, this is what Greek warriors fight for. Successful chieftains employed priest-poets to make sense of their new world order. The priest-poets explain the universe, and they reassure everyone that their society is in harmony with that ultimate reality.

There will inevitably be some tension between the warlords and the men who create stories to justify their power and perform rituals to sanctify it. The priest-poets may decide that they are the ones who legitimize the chieftains, and that they should take precedence over them. They may even be so bold as to claim that they owe allegiance to no earthly king, that they serve God alone. This is what the Vedic

Brahmins do when they say, during the coronation ceremony, 'Soma is the king of us Brahmins'.[4]

In reality, however, they are completely dependent on the chieftains for their livelihood. A lofty Vedic hymn, in which the poet communicates directly with the gods, will ultimately come back to earth and end with some humble verses 'praising the gift' (*dānastuti*), thanking the warlord for whatever wages he sees fit to grant his loyal priest and poet. In Vedic India, the brahmins may have performed the elaborate coronation ritual (*rājasūya*), but of course they did not decide which man they should crown; they merely attended as his employees. Even in modern England, the Archbishop of Canterbury may crown the monarch, but he must walk behind all the members of the royal family in the Order of Precedence.[5] The relationship between warlord and priest is equally clear in East Africa. The Nuer ranchers felt they could safely dispense with the priestly elite altogether, so they seceded from the Dinkas to form their own nation of cattle-owning warlords.[6] This was, indeed, an extreme measure, but one that reveals who holds the real power in such societies. When Viśvāmitra expressed misgivings about the Bharatas overthrowing the Pūrus, his warlord Sudās lost no time in replacing him with the more malleable Vasiṣṭha.[7] Priest-poets work with the kings and for the kings. The real division in society is not between the leaders and their apologists, but rather between this elite and those whose lives are ruled by what they do and say.

The Third Estate

Ordinary people are those whose cattle may be raided with impunity, or those who never had any in the first place. They are not a separate race with a different language and culture, as nineteenth-century scholars used to think. They are simply people who are locked into a different social category – *dasyus* and *vaiśyas* in India, peasants and Helots in Greece, clients and provincials in Rome, Dinkas in east Africa. It is the arbitrary categories of their superiors that determine whether they are alien or fully human, not their language, culture, or 'race'.

Cowboys and farmhands belong to this great underclass. The stories told by priest-poets in such a society will explain why the sun rises in the east and sets in the west, how the gods give us cattle and milk, why chieftains are powerful and priest-poets can see the gods, and why cowboys must work hard and accept their lot. When the cowboys learn to ride in the fourth millennium BC, this new technique is associated with a pair of horse gods, but since horse-riding is a low-class activity, these gods are of low status, like the cowboys themselves. In India, the lowly horse gods receive a simple offering of hot milk, boiled on a cowboy campfire; they were not originally honoured at the great sacrifices of soma to the gods of the kings and Brahmins. In Greece, the horse gods are worshipped at a picnic shared with their humble devotees; the gods that rule Olumpos are honoured at great animal-sacrifices.

When chariots are invented at the start of the second millennium BC, the speed of wheeled transport increases tenfold, and the chieftains who alone can afford these new racing-cars become even more powerful and dangerous than they had been before. The priest-poets tactfully alter their stories, and proclaim that every god drives a chariot. This new age of racing gods and kings is the one in which we first hear of the horse gods in India. The Aśvins follow the new trend and drive a chariot themselves, a special three-wheeler, and they also participate in the soma-sacrifices. Their old cowboy drink of hot milk is now incorporated into the soma-sacrifice, as an optional and secret element, and they themselves are finally deemed worthy of a cup of soma. The stories told about them make it clear that they are new-comers, and that they are only accepted into the world of soma-drinking gods with considerable reservations.

Finally, in the first millennium BC, riding becomes the sport of kings. In India, the ideal of the chariot-driving god or goddess is now a fixed element of their mythical heritage, and there is no change in the divine image of the Aśvins. In Greece, most of the gods and goddesses retain their chariots, but the Dioskouroi were always horse-riders. They had been ignored by the epic tradition and had never been provided with chariots; in the sixth century BC, their horse riding is suddenly declared to be elegant and fashionable. The

Dioskouroi continue to ride horses, and they still prefer picnics over sacrifices, but throughout Greece and Italy, prosperous horsemen now worship them, as well as the ordinary people who always, quite literally, swore by them.

The Horse Gods

The image of the horse gods and their favourite goddess changes considerably over time, and it also differs dramatically according to its location, just as the Indo-European languages differ greatly from each other. Even though the creativity of the various linguistic traditions is remarkable, even though the horse gods may travel across the land of India and the seas of Greece,[8] the survival of some common themes can still be discerned behind all this variety.

In both India and Greece, the horse gods are young. They are always sons and boys, because they never achieve the completely independent and mature status of a priest like Agni or a king like Indra;[9] they are always restricted to the marginal status of men who are necessary to society, but never quite join it as full and equal participants. They devote themselves to serving others, because they are the divine representatives of a group of people whose sole purpose is to serve. They are accepted with great reluctance by the other gods, and they are especially close to the human race. In fact, they are half-way between divine and human, just as their mortal counterparts, the young and the poor, straddle the world of men and beasts. They live with the sun goddess, as her lovers or as her step-brothers, but they have to fight for this privilege. In India, the Aśvins steal her from Soma; in Greece, they take her from Nemesis, and adopt her as their sister. She belongs to a higher world.

The traditional themes of this story are rather simple ones. The horse gods are born, they get married, they help out. They are not involved in any great events of cosmic significance. Nor are they involved in any act of rebellion against the other gods, for their main goal is to try to fit in. They intervene only to soften the rigour of the powerful gods. So their story does not offer the majority who live at the bottom of society any hope of escaping from their lot. It was, after all, a story told by priests and poets who enjoyed a leisure that was denied to most people. And yet it may, perhaps, have given ordinary people some sort of consolation to know that the story of their lives would not be completely unparalleled in the world of the gods, that the Aśvins and the Dioskouroi were their gods too.

NOTES

Chapter 1 Horses, Twins, and Gods

1. Piggott, Stuart, *Wagon, Chariot and Carriage. Symbol and Status in the History of Transport* (London: Thames and Hudson, 1992), pp. 79–80.
2. The cavalrymen played a major role in overthrowing Athenian democracy and supporting the oligarchy of 404–403 BC. See Bugh, Glenn Richard, *The Horsemen of Athens* (Princeton, NJ: Princeton University Press, 1988), pp. 122–9; Spence, I.G. *The Cavalry of Classical Greece* (Oxford: Clarendon Press, 1993), pp. 216–24.
3. Alföldy describes the Equestrians as 'the *nouveaux riches*, who began to form themselves into a separate social group, the equestrian order': Alföldy, Géza, *The Social History of Rome*, translated by David Braund and Frank Pollock (Baltimore, MD: The Johns Hopkins University Press, 1988), p. 45.
4. 'The horse [. . .] became a part of the mystique of kingship', Piggott: *Wagon, Chariot and Carriage*, p. 74. In Classical Athens, Xenophon notes the psychological impact of a horseman on the general public (*De Re Equestri* 11: 8–9), and that horsemen are well-off and govern most states (Xenophon, *De Re Equestri* 2, 1).
5. The 'stables of Augeias' were cow-sheds, which makes this Labour even more difficult and revolting.
6. Valerius Maximus 1: 8, 1. See Chapter 7 for this and other stories about the horse gods in Rome.
7. See below, 'Horses'.
8. To this very day, if anyone is born between 22 May and 21 June, the horse gods help them decide what to do with their lives, because they are the twins of the zodiac sign Gemini.

9. Farnell, Lewis Richard, *Greek Hero Cults and the Ideas of Immortality* (Oxford: Clarendon Press, 1921), pp. 179–80; Gonda, Jaan, *The Dual Deities in the Religion of the Veda* (Amsterdam: North-Holland Publishing Company, 1974), pp. 49–50; Zeller, Gabriele, *Die Vedischen Zwillingsgötter. Untersuchungen zur Genese ihres Kultes* (Wiesbaden: Otto Harrassowitz, 1990), pp. 15–22, 47, 151, 154, 158.
10. Harris, James Rendel, *The Cult of the Heavenly Twins* (Cambridge: Cambridge University Press, 1906), p. 152.
11. Sternberg, Leo, 'Der antike Zwillingskult im Lichte der Ethnologie', *Zeitschrift für Ethnologie* 61 (1929), pp. 152–200 (this is a German translation of his Russian article, which appeared in 1916); Sidney Hartland, Edwin, 'Twins', in the *Encyclopaedia of Religion and Ethics* (New York, NY: Charles Scribner's Sons, 1955), pp. 491–500.
12. Farnell calls Harris's work 'among modern treatises by far the most hopeful and helpful', Farnell: *Greek Hero Cults*, p. 179. Ward accepts his notion of 'Universal Dioscurism'. See Ward, Donald, *The Divine Twins* (Berkeley, CA: University of California Press, 1968), pp. 3–8. Gonda cites him frequently. See Gonda: *Dual Deities*, pp. 34–7. Zeller regrets that 'the significance of Harris' rich material and conclusions are still unrecognized in Indology', Zeller: *Die Vedischen Zwillingsgötter*, p. 17. Wiseman alone is sceptical, though he is concerned only with Harris's theory about the Roman twins, Romulus and Remus. He declares, somewhat prematurely, that 'Rendel Harris is a forgotten man': Wiseman, T.P., *Remus: A Roman Myth* (New York, NY: Cambridge University Press, 1995), p. 30.
13. Harris: *Heavenly Twins* appears in the bibliography to Bianchi's article on twins. See Bianchi, Ugo, 'Twins', in Jones, Lindsay (editor), *Encyclopedia of Religion* (Detroit, MI: Macmillan, 2005), vol. 14, p. 9418. In Chemery's article on meteorological beings, the *Cult of the Heavenly Twins* and *Boanerges* of Harris are praised as 'two old but still fascinating studies': Chemery, Peter C. 'Meteorological Beings', in Jones, Lindsay (editor), *Encyclopedia of Religion* (Detroit, OH: Macmillan, 2005), vol. 9, p. 5996. *The Cult of the Heavenly Twins* has been cited above (note 6), *Boanerges* is Harris, James Rendel, *Boanerges* (Cambridge: University Press, 1913).
14. Harris, James Rendel, *The Dioscuri in the Christian legends* (London: C.J. Clay, 1903), pp. 20–2.
15. Harris: *Dioscuri in Christian legends*, pp. 38–9.
16. Harris: *Heavenly Twins* and *Boanerges*.
17. In *Boanerges*, he argues for a primitive trinity of the thunder-god and his twin assistants. He believes that polytheistic belief is ultimately based on the fear of thunder and the fear of twins. 'We might almost say that on these two dreads hang nine-tenths of subsequent religion,' Harris: *Boanerges*, p. 30. Harris himself believes in a future Reformation that will free Christianity from its Dioscuric 'veil of error', Harris: *Heavenly Twins*, p. 154.
18. Krappe, Alexandre Haggerty, *Mythologie Universelle* (Paris: Payot, 1930).

19. Harris: *Boanerges*, pp. 198 and 208. He uses the term 'Assessor' in its literal meaning of 'one who sits beside' (God).
20. Harris: *Boanerges*, pp. 20–48. Krappe believes that the worldwide twin gods were originally worshipped indifferently as horses, woodpeckers, or oaks. See Krappe: *Mythologie Universelle*, pp. 67–80. Krappe also emphasizes that the Indo-Europeans must have worshipped them in all three forms before they dispersed to their later habitations. See Krappe: *Mythologie Universelle*, pp. 71, 76–7 and 79–80.
21. Harris: *Heavenly Twins*, p. 152.
22. Leis, Philip E., 'The Nonfunctional Attributes of Twin Infanticide in the Niger Delta', *Anthropological Quarterly* 38 (1965), p. 98. On the one hand, Peek encourages us to look at positive attitudes to twins in Africa, and Lawal points out that the Oyo Yoruba had originally killed twins, but started to honour them by the nineteenth century. On the other hand, Renne notes that twin infanticide was still occurring among other Yoruba peoples in the twentieth century, and that conversion to Christianity played a major role in its abolition. See Peek, Philip, 'Introduction: Beginning to Rethink Twins', in Peek, Philip M. *Twins in African and Diaspora Culture. Double Trouble, Twice Blessed* (Bloomington: Indiana University Press, 2011), pp. 6 and 19–20; Lawal, Babatunde, 'Sustaining the Oneness in Their Twoness: Poetics of Twin Figures (Ère Ìbeji) among the Yoruba', in Peek, *Twins in African and Diaspora Culture*: pp. 87–90; Renne, Elisha R. 'The Ambiguous Ordinariness of Yoruba Twins', in Peek, *Twins in African and Diaspora Culture*: pp. 307–9. Harris had noticed the great diversity in attitudes to twins, but he had attributed it to 'the perplexing and contradictory mind of primitive man' (Harris: *Heavenly Twins*, p. 22). He was perplexed that their behaviour was contradicting his grand theory.
23. Ball, Helen L., and Hill, Catherine M. 'Reevaluating "Twin Infanticide"', *Current Anthropology* 37 (1996), p. 857.
24. For evidence of contemporary twin infanticide, visit the website omochild.org, and see Alessandra Piontelli, *Twins in the World. The Legends They Inspire, the Lives They Lead* (New York: Palgrave Macmillan, 2008), pp. 65–6 (nineteenth-century Japan), p. 80 (*Indios* of Venezuela), pp. 101–6 (Ethiopia), p. 110 (Philippines), pp. 120 and 127 (Madagascar), pp. 131–3 (Laos), pp. 141–2 and 147–8 (Gran Chaco), pp. 153–6 (Guinea Bissau). Piontelli, a medical doctor with vast experience in this field, gives a very humane account of the inhuman conditions endured by people at the bottom of the global economy. Her work is a breath of fresh air (and a dash of cold water) to people like myself who tend to romanticize or intellectualize the world views of people located at a safe distance. I am grateful to Kimberley Patton for introducing me to this moving book.
25. Sternberg: 'Der antike Zwillingskult', pp. 166–9; Krappe: *Mythologie Universelle*, pp. 53–99 ('le Dioscurisme'); Ward: *Divine Twins*, pp. 3–8 ('Universal Dioscurism').

26. Pots often act as surrogate wombs in Vedic thought. See Jamison, Stephanie, *The Ravenous Hyenas and the Wounded Sun. Myth and Ritual in Ancient India* (Ithaca, NY: Cornell University Press, 1991), pp. 231 and 236–9.
27. Vasiṣṭha is called *Maitrāvaruṇa* at *RV* 7: 33, 11a, and both Agastya and Vasiṣṭha are *Maitrāvaruṇi* in later texts (commentaries and epic).
28. Agastya finds a family for Vasiṣṭha, by having him adopted by the Tṛtsus, the family of the Bharata kings whom the upstart Vasiṣṭhas will serve as royal priests (*purohitas*): 'Agastya brings you to the people (*viś*),' *RV* 7: 33, 10d; 'respect him benevolently, Vasiṣṭha is coming to you, Pratṛds', *RV* 7: 33, 14cd. The Pratṛds are the Tṛtsus (the Vasiṣṭhas are called Tṛtsus at *RV* 7: 83, 8). The Vasiṣṭhas needed to be introduced to this family because they were recent immigrants from Eastern Iran. See Witzel, Michael, 'Rgvedic History: Poets, Chieftains and Polities', in Erdosy, George, *The Indo-Aryans of Ancient South Asia. Language, Material Culture and Ethnicity* (Berlin: Walter de Gruyter, 1995), pp. 334 and 335, and note 80 on p. 335. In a later work, Witzel suggests that the Vasiṣṭhas may have belonged to or been adopted into the Agastya family, which once again indicates a subordinate position to Agastya and his family. See Witzel, Michael, 'The Development of the Vedic Canon and its Schools: The Social and Political Milieus', in Witzel, Michael (editor), *Inside the Texts, Beyond the Texts* (Cambridge, MA: Harvard University Press, 1997), p. 289 note 145.
29. *Taittirīya Saṃhitā* 5: 1, 5^5; *Taittirīya Saṃhitā* 7: 1, 1^2; *Aitareya Brāhmaṇa* 4: 9, 3; *Śatapatha Brāhmaṇa* 6: 3, 1^{23}.
30. It is not immediately clear from the *Taittirīya Saṃhitā* itself whether humans are like male asses or mares, whether the ability to produce twins lies in the man who has his 'double semen', or the woman who is 'doubly reproductive'. In either case, only one father would, of course, be required to produce twins. Other texts make it clear that the power to produce twins does, in fact, belong to the mother.
31. For relevant texts and discussions see Tewari, Premvati, *Āyurvedīya Prasūti-Tantra Evaṃ Strī-Roga. Part I. Prasūti-Tantra (Obstetrics)* (Delhi: Chaukhambha Orientalia, 1986), pp. 173–7. I would like to thank Martha Selby at the University of Texas at Austin for this reference.
32. Homer tells us that they are brother and sister (*Iliad* 20: 71) and that Lētō is their mother (*Iliad* 24: 605–609). The first explicit description of them as twins (*didumoi*, a relatively rare word in early and Classical Greek and nowhere used of the Dioskouroi!) appears in Pindar, *Olympian Odes* 3: 35, which dates from 476 BC.
33. Krēthōn and Orsilokhos (*Iliad* 5: 548–549) are the twin sons of Dioklēs; Aisēpos and Pēdasos are the twin sons of Boukoliōn (*Iliad* 6: 21–26).
34. They are called twins (*didumoi*) at *Iliad* 23: 641; sons of Aktoriōn and Molionē (*Aktoriōne Molīone paide*) at *Iliad* 11: 750. They are the sons of Poseidōn implicitly at *Iliad* 11: 751, and explicitly in the Hesiodic *Catalogue of Women*, fr. 17b MW = fr. 14 Most. The Moliones are depicted as conjoined twins in Greek art and in later Greek literature (*Catalogue of Women*, fr. 18 MW = fr. 15 Most).

35. Krēthōn and Orsilokhos are killed by Aineias (*Iliad* 5: 541–542); Aisēpos and Pēdasos are killed by Eurualos (*Iliad* 6: 21–28); the Moliones are killed by Hēraklēs (Ibycus fr. 285 Campbell; Pindar, *Olympian Odes* 10: 26–34).
36. Herodotus 6: 52.
37. The only comparable case is that of Zeus and Semelē, the mother of Dionusos. In this case too 'a mortal woman gave birth to an immortal', as Hesiod says at *Theogony*, 942.
38. Pindar, *Nemean Odes* 3: 22.
39. Homer is already aware of this paradox, and he tells us that the ghost of Hēraklēs is down in the Underworld with all the other dead mortals, but Hēraklēs *himself*, the god Hēraklēs, is among the other gods with his wife Hēbē (*Odyssey* 11: 601–604).
40. In the *Iliad* (18: 117), he is human, but he is a god in the *Odyssey*, so his divine cult has already been established by the eighth century BC, though the more conservative *Iliad* chooses to ignore it.
41. Homer, *Iliad* 14: 323–324 and *Iliad* 19: 97–105; Hesiod, *Theogony* 943–944. Hesiod does, however, mention Iolaos (the son of Iphiklēs) as the companion of Hēraklēs at *Theogony* 317.
42. Hesiodic *Shield of Hēraklēs* 53–56. It is Iolaos, the son of Iphiklēs, who acts as the charioteer and constant companion of Hēraklēs.
43. Homer, *Iliad* 3: 236–244. According to the rules of Ancient Greek myth, if a mother is mortal, it does not matter whether the father is human or divine. In either case, the offspring would be human. According to the rules of Dioscurism, this could only happen if the fathers of both twins were human. Greek myth violates both the Dioscuric principle that all twins must have a human father and a divine one, and the Dioscuric principle that the divinity of a father must lead to the birth of a divine son.
44. Homer, *Odyssey* 11: 298–304.
45. It does refer to them as *Tundaridai* in line 2, but the narrative makes it clear that Zeus is their father.
46. Hesiodic *Catalogue of Women* fr. 24 MW = fr. 21 Most.
47. Homeric Hymn 33 (to the Dioskouroi): 10.
48. Burkert, Walter, *Greek Religion*, translated by John Raffan (Cambridge, MA: Harvard University Press, 1985), p. 200
49. Stasinus, *Cypria* fr. 9 West.
50. In their great work on Asklēpios, the Edelsteins contrast real kings and heroes with a physician like Asklēpios. See Edelstein, Emma J., and Edelstein, Ludwig, *Asclepius* (Baltimore, MD: The Johns Hopkins University Press, 1998), vol. 2, pp. 2–5 and 9–10. The same objection applies to the sons of Asklēpios. 'Machaon and Podalirius are physicians rather than warriors, craftsmen rather than kings,' Edelstein and Edelstein: *Asclepius*, vol. 2, p. 9.
51. *Taittirīya Saṃhitā* 6: 4, 9^{1-2}.
52. 'The glorious hero is also a slave, a woman, and a madman. The son of Zeus is no Zeus-honoured king, but is from the very outset subject to Eurystheus, the

king of Mycenae, who is in turn subject to Hera, the goddess of the Argolid.' Burkert: *Greek Religion*, p. 210.

53. As we shall see later, it is not really certain that the sons of Zeus are divine or that the sons of Tundareos are mortal. See below, Chapter 5, 'Between Gods and Men'.
54. *Atharva-Veda* 3: 28, 1–2.
55. *Atharva-Veda* 3: 28, 2–4. Harris discusses this passage, but spends most of his time denouncing the Brahmins for their greed in confiscating the cow, which he assumes to be the main purpose of this practice. See Harris: *Boanerges*, pp. 183–4.
56. *Aitareya Brāhmaṇa* 7: 9.
57. Yamī not unreasonably points out to her brother that he is the only male human in the world, and that she has no option but to sleep with him (*RV* 10: 10, 3). Yama rejects her proposal, but the hymn does not explain where humans came from in that case. There is a similar problem with the children of Adam and Eve, but the composers of Genesis seem to have accepted the inevitability of primitive incest with quiet Stoicism.
58. Zeller: *Die Vedischen Zwillingsgötter*, pp. 47–8.
59. The circuit (*vartis*) of the Aśvins is 'man-saving' (*nṛpāyiyam*), *RV* 8: 9, 18d and 8: 26, 14b.
60. Homer describes their team-work in a chariot-race – one works the reins while the other uses the whip (Homer, *Iliad* 23: 641–642). A contemporary vase-painting (735–720 BC) shows the conjoined twins climbing onto a chariot in a battle-scene (*LIMC* (*Lexicon Iconographicum Mythologiae Classicae*), vol. 1, part 1: 473; *LIMC*, vol. 1, part 2: 364, image 3).
61. When they beat Nestōr in a chariot-race, he complains, 'they got ahead of me by force of numbers' (Homer, *Iliad* 23: 638–639), but they fill him with envy rather than horror.
62. Herodotus 6: 52. The more prestigious Agiad family was descended from Eurusthenēs, the twin who was born first; the other royal family, the Eurupontidai, derived from the second twin, Proklēs.
63. The saying is attributed to 'inspired poets born long ago' (*viprāso* [. . .] *purājāḥ*, *RV* 1: 118, 3d).
64. They save several heroes from a trap (Antaka, Atri, Saptavadhri and Vandana), and two from the sea (Bhujyu, and Rebha).
65. They supply dehydrated devotees with water (Gotama and Śara) and with milk (Atri, and Śayu).
66. They rejuvenate Cyavana and Kakṣīvant.
67. They arrange happy marriages for Ghoṣā, Puraṃdhi, and Vadhrimatī.
68. They replace one devotee's leg (Viśpalā) and restore eye-sight to others (Kaṇva, Ṛjāśva).
69. They bring to life Dadhyañc (who had been beheaded) and Śyāva (who had been cut to pieces).
70. *Taittirīya Saṃhitā* 6: 4, 9^{1-2}. See *Śatapatha Brāhmaṇa* 4: 1, 5^{14}.

71. 'Therefore a Brahmin should not practise medicine, for the physician is impure, unfit for a sacrifice.' *Taittirīya Saṃhitā* 6: 4, 9^2.
72. It was based on a lost Greek original, and we know that several Greek playwrights produced comedies called *Twins* (*Didumoi*).
73. Plautus, *Menaechmi* 18–21.
74. Some Indian thinkers felt that the Aśvins as a pair represented the twilight, so they could be analysed separately as gods of night and day. The nighttime twin was the son of Vivasvant (later worshipped as a sun-god) and Vasāti (Night), and the daytime twin was the son of Dyaus (Sky) and Uṣas (Dawn). See Yaska, *Nirukta* 12, 2 and Geldner, Karl Friedrich. *Der Rig-Veda, aus dem Sanskrit ins Deutsche übers. und mit einem laufenden Kommentar versehen von Karl Friedrich Geldner* (Cambridge, MA: Harvard University Press, 1951), vol. 1, p. 261.
75. Keith, Arthur Berriedale, *The Religion and Philosophy of the Veda and Upanishads* (Cambridge, MA: Harvard University Press, 1925), p. 329.
76. Turner, Victor W., 'Paradoxes of Twinship in Ndembu Ritual', in *The Ritual Process*, pp. 44–93 (Chicago, IL: Aldine Publishing Company, 1969), p. 45.
77. This discrepancy disappears when Poludeukēs voluntarily surrenders his immortality so that he may die with his brother (Pindar, *Nemean Ode* 10, 57–59), and both of them become part-time gods, spending every second day on Olumpos (Pindar, *Nemean Ode* 10, 55–57).
78. Piggott: *Wagon, Chariot and Carriage*, p. 43. The Greeks knew that horses were happier on open plains. See Griffith, Mark, 'Horsepower and Donkeywork: Equids and the Ancient Greek Imagination', *Classical Philology* 101 (2006), p. 197 note 49.
79. Anthony, David W., *The Horse, the Wheel, and Language* (Princeton, NJ: Princeton University Press, 2007), p. 136.
80. Levine, Marsha, 'The Origins of Horse Husbandry on the Eurasian Steppe', in Levine, Marsha et al., *Late Prehistoric Exploitation of the Eurasian Steppe*, (Cambridge: McDonald Institute for Archaeological Research, 1999), p. 24.
81. Anthony, David, and Brown, Dorcas R., 'The Origins of Horseback Riding', *Antiquity* 65 (1991), p. 32; Levine: 'Origins of Horse Husbandry', p. 5; Anthony: *Horse, Wheel, and Language*, p. 247.
82. Anthony and Brown: 'Origins of Horseback Riding', p. 32; Anthony: *Horse, Wheel, and Language*, pp. 247–8. Originally, Anthony and Brown had also believed that the inhabitants of Dereivka invented horseback riding but this turned out to be incorrect. See Anthony: *Horse, Wheel, and Language*, pp. 213–16.
83. Levine points out that if horses are being raised for their meat (as still happens in Kazakhstan and Mongolia), they will not be killed off during their prime reproductive years from four to fifteen. See Levine: 'Origins of Horse Husbandry', pp. 24, 27, and 31. At Dereivka, in contrast, most of the horses were killed and eaten between the ages of five and eight, which suggests that

they were not domesticated. See Levine: 'Origins of Horse Husbandry', p. 36; Hyland, Ann, *The Horse in the Ancient World* (Westport, CT: Praeger, 2003), pp. 3–5.

84. Using the same methodology, Levine had concluded that the horses at Botai in Kazakhstan (3700–3000 BC) were hunted. See Levine: 'Origins of Horse Husbandry', pp. 43–4. Recent archaeological discoveries show, however, that they were domesticated. See Outram, Alan K. et al., 'The Earliest Horse Harnessing and Milking', *Science* 323 (2009), pp. 1332–5.
85. Anthony: *Horse, Wheel, and Language*, pp. 216–20; Outram: 'Earliest Horse Harnessing and Milking'.
86. Anthony: *Horse, Wheel, and Language*, p. 200.
87. Khazanov (an expert on pastoral nomads) is quoted at Levine: 'Origins of Horse Husbandry', p. 14. See Anthony: *Horse, Wheel, and Language*, p. 221.
88. Levine: 'Origins of Horse Husbandry', p. 10.
89. The size of the horses shows that they were domesticated. See Outram: 'Earliest Horse Harnessing and Milking', p. 1333. Dental damage reveals that they had been ridden with bits. See Outram: 'Earliest Horse Harnessing and Milking', pp. 1333–4. Since the bit would have been made of organic materials such as rope or leather, some scholars do not believe that it could have caused this dental damage. See Hyland: *Horse in Ancient World*, p. 55; Drews, Robert, *The Coming of the Greeks* (Princeton, NJ: Princeton University Press, 1988), pp. 19–20 and 83–5.
90. Traces of fat from mare's milk were found on the pottery. See Outram: 'Earliest Horse Harnessing and Milking', p. 1334–5.
91. Hyland: *Horse in Ancient World*, p. 5.
92. Ludwig, Arne et al., 'Coat Color Variation at the Beginning of Horse Domestication', *Science* 324 (2009), p. 485.
93. The first rigid saddles were developed in Siberia between the fifth and third centuries BC. See Levine: 'Origins of Horse Husbandry', p. 52; Piggott: *Wagon, Chariot and Carriage*, p. 75. They reached China by the fourth century AD and Western Europe by the ninth century AD. See Piggott: *Wagon, Chariot and Carriage*, p. 75.
94. The stirrup was invented in India in second century BC. It was widely used in China by the fifth century AD, and came to Western Europe in the eighth century AD. See Hobson, John, *The Eastern Origins of Western Civilization* (Cambridge: Cambridge University Press, 2004), p. 103; Piggott: *Wagon, Chariot and Carriage*, p. 89.
95. Piggott: *Wagon, Chariot and Carriage*, p. 16; Anthony: *Horse, Wheel, and Language*, pp. 69–72.
96. Piggott points out that the heavy solid-wheeled ox-cart cannot have developed on the steppes or in a semi-desert region. See Piggott: *Wagon, Chariot and Carriage*, p. 17.
97. Piggott: *Wagon, Chariot and Carriage*, p. 18.
98. Piggott: *Wagon, Chariot and Carriage*, p. 18.

99. Hodges, Henry, *Technology in the Ancient World* (New York, NY: Barnes and Noble, 1970), p. 86; Piggott: *Wagon, Chariot and Carriage*, pp. 39–40; Anthony, David, and Vinogradov, Nikolai B., 'Birth of the Chariot', *Archaeology* 48 (1995), p. 40; Hyland: *Horse in Ancient World*, p. 9.
100. Hyland: *Horse in Ancient World*, p. 9.
101. The stiff horse collar was invented by the Chinese in the third century AD, and it reached Europe by the tenth century AD. See Piggott: *Wagon, Chariot and Carriage*, pp. 67 and 137; Hobson: *Eastern Origins*, p. 102.
102. As with oxen, the main function of the horse was to provide milk and meat. See Drews, Robert, *Early Riders: the Beginnings of Mounted Warfare in Asia and Europe* (New York, NY: Routledge, 2004), pp. 12–14 and 24–5.
103. Anthony and Vinogradov: 'Birth of Chariot', pp. 36–41.
104. Anthony: *Horse, Wheel, and Language*, pp. 222–3; 460.
105. Drews: *Early Riders*, p. 51.
106. Falk, Harry. *Bruderschaft und Würfelspiel. Untersuchungen zur Entwicklungsgeschichte des vedischen Opfers* (Freiburg: Hedwig Falk, 1986), p. 54.
107. Falk: *Bruderschaft und Würfelspiel*, pp. 64–5.
108. Boyce, Mary, 'Priests, Cattle and Men', *Bulletin of the School of Oriental and African Studies* 50 (1987), p. 513.
109. Falk, Harry, 'Das Reitpferd im vedischen Indien', in Hänsel, Bernhard, and Zimmer, Stefan (editors), *Die Indogermanen und das Pferd. Festschrift fur Bernfried Schlerath* (Budapest: Archaeolingua Alapítvány, 1994), p. 95.
110. Falk: 'Das Reitpferd im vedischen Indien', p. 101.
111. Piggott: *Wagon, Chariot and Carriage*, pp. 18 and 48; Drews, Robert, *The End of the Bronze Age* (Princeton, NJ: Princeton University Press. 1993) p. 104.
112. Anthony and Vinogradov: 'Birth of Chariot', pp. 36–8.
113. Anthony and Vinogradov: 'Birth of Chariot', p. 38; Anthony: *Horse, Wheel, and Language*, pp. 376 and 402.
114. Anthony and Vinogradov: 'Birth of Chariot', p. 38.
115. Marsha Levine makes an important distinction between the invention of the chariot, and our first discovery of chariots as socially (and archaeologically) visible articles that are preserved in graves. The chariot must have been invented long before the chariot-burials. See Levine: 'Origins of Horse Husbandry', pp. 9–10.
116. Their trotting speed would have been 10–14 km/h. See Piggott: *Wagon, Chariot and Carriage*, p. 18s.
117. From the root *ar*, 'construct'. In Mycenaean, *harma* means 'wheel'. See Plath, Robert, 'Pferd und Wagen im Mykenischen und bei Homer', in Hänsel, Bernhard, and Zimmer, Stefan (editors), *Die Indogermanen und das Pferd. Festschrift fur Bernfried Schlerath* (Budapest: Archaeolingua Alapítvány, 1994), pp. 110–11. See also *DELG* (*Dictionnaire étymologique de la langue grecque*), p. 106.
118. Oldenberg, Hermann, *Die Religion des Veda* (Berlin: Hertz, 1894), p. 2 note 1.
119. Speaking of northern India, Staal points out that 'chariots were imported there by a small number of people *through their minds*': Staal, Frits, *Discovering*

the Vedas. Origins, Mantras, Rituals, Insights (New Delhi: Penguin Books India, 2008), p. 17. Drews also notes that the *formulas* for horse-training must have been brought to the Hurrians of Mitanni. 'Being illiterate, Aryan speakers must in person have brought such terms as *aika vartanna* to the attention of the Hurrians': Drews, Robert, *The Coming of the Greeks* (Princeton, NJ: Princeton University Press, 1988), p. 145. The horse-trainers actually spoke Indic, not Indo-Iranian (which Drews calls 'Aryan'). See Parpola, Asko, 'The Problem of the Aryans and the Soma: Textual-linguistic and Archaeological Evidence', in Erdosy, George, *The Indo-Aryans of Ancient South Asia. Language, Material Culture and Ethnicity* (Berlin: Walter de Gruyter, 1995), p. 358; Staal: *Discovering the Vedas*, pp. 11–13; Watkins, Calvert, *How to Kill a Dragon: Aspects of Indo-European Poetics* (New York, NY: Oxford University Press, 1995), p. 159; Witzel, Michael, 'Early Indian History: Linguistic and Textual Parameters', in Erdosy, George, *The Indo-Aryans of Ancient South Asia. Language, Material Culture and Ethnicity* (Berlin: Walter de Gruyter, 1995), pp. 109–10.

120. Drews: *Coming of the Greeks*, pp. 90 and 145. The Hittite translation is the only version of Kikkuli's work that survives.
121. Piggott: *Wagon, Chariot and Carriage*, p. 48; Kuhrt, Amélie, *The Ancient Near East* (London: Routledge, 1995), p. 104.
122. Kuhrt: *Ancient Near East*, p. 298.
123. Drews: *Coming of the Greeks*, pp. 44–5.
124. Anthony and Vinogradov: 'Birth of Chariot', p. 40.
125. Piggott: *Wagon, Chariot and Carriage*, p. 69; Hyland: *Horse in Ancient World*, p. 15.
126. Hyland: *Horse in Ancient World*, p. xv.
127. The Kassites used them to defeat the Babylonians around 1600 BC. See Hyland: *Horse in Ancient World*, p. 21.
128. Piggott: *Wagon, Chariot and Carriage*, p. 57; Hyland: *Horse in Ancient World*, pp. 14–15.
129. Hyland: *Horse in Ancient World*, p. 13.
130. Piggott: *Wagon, Chariot and Carriage*, p. 60; Dickinson, Oliver, *The Aegean Bronze Age* (Cambridge, England: Cambridge University Press, 1994), p. 203.
131. The Hittites had 3,500 chariots at the Battle of Kadesh in 1285 BC. See Drews: *End of Bronze Age*, pp. 132–3; Hyland: *Horse in Ancient World*, pp. 86–7. Knōssos on the island of Crete had 1,000 chariots, and even the little Greek state of Pulos had several hundred. See Drews: *End of Bronze Age*, pp. 107–10.
132. Drews believes that it is the Sanskrit word *marya* with a Hurrian suffix, but Boyce and Kuhrt believe that it is a Hurrian word. See Drews: *Coming of the Greeks*, p. 155; Boyce: 'Priests, Cattle and Men', p. 509; Kuhrt: *Ancient Near East*, p. 298.
133. Piggott: *Wagon, Chariot and Carriage*, pp. 45–8; Drews: *End of Bronze Age*, pp. 110–13.

134. Piggott: *Wagon, Chariot and Carriage*, p. 57; Decker, Wolfgang, 'Pferd und Wagen im Alten Aegypten', in Hänsel, Bernhard, and Zimmer, Stefan (editors), *Die Indogermanen und das Pferd. Festschrift fur Bernfried Schlerath* (Budapest: Archaeolingua Alapítvány, 1994), p. 263; Hyland: *Horse in Ancient World*, pp. 75–6.
135. For the Mycenean world, see Chadwick, John, *The Mycenean World* (Cambridge: Cambridge University Press, 1976), p. 164 (Mycenean Greece); Plath: 'Pferd und Wagen im Mykenischen', p. 113 (Homeric description, but Plath believes it is based on Mycenean tradition); Dickinson: *Aegean Bronze Age*, p. 203 (Mycenean Greece and West Asia). For West Asia, see Piggott: *Wagon, Chariot and Carriage*, p. 57; Falk: 'Das Reitpferd im vedischen Indien', p. 101.
136. Drews: *End of Bronze Age*, pp. 119–29. Anthony shows that chariots were already used by archers in the Sintashta culture. See Anthony: *Horse, Wheel, and Language*, pp. 397–405. Drews points out that northern Greece was 'a society of infantrymen', so it would have been impossible for the epic tradition to have preserved any accurate knowledge of chariot warfare. See Drews: *End of Bronze Age*, pp. 117–18.
137. Drews: *End of Bronze Age*, p. 117.
138. Piggott: *Wagon, Chariot and Carriage*, p. 48.
139. Piggott: *Wagon, Chariot and Carriage*, pp. 45–8 and 56–7; Decker: 'Pferd und Wagen im Alten Aegypten', p. 265.
140. Falk: 'Das Reitpferd im vedischen Indien', p. 95–6.
141. Piggott: *Wagon, Chariot and Carriage*, p. 47.
142. Piggott: *Wagon, Chariot and Carriage*, p. 57–8.
143. 1 Kings 1: 5.
144. 'In general, the chariot pulled by two horses is above all a status symbol, that cannot be dispensed with if someone wants to display his social rank.' Decker: 'Pferd und Wagen im Alten Aegypten', p. 264.
145. Decker: 'Pferd und Wagen im Alten Aegypten', pp. 264–5.
146. Decker: 'Pferd und Wagen im Alten Aegypten', pp. 263–5.
147. Dickinson: *Aegean Bronze Age*, p. 49.
148. Falk: 'Das Reitpferd im vedischen Indien', pp. 95 and 98.
149. Köhne, Eckart, *Die Dioskuren in der Griechischen Kunst von der Archaik bis zum Ende des 5. Jahrhunderts v. Chr* (Hamburg: Verlag Dr. Kovač, 1998), p. 173.
150. Falk: 'Das Reitpferd im vedischen Indien', p. 98.
151. As Falk points out, the reference to heels make it clear that someone rode the horse rather than drove it in a chariot. See Falk: 'Das Reitpferd im vedischen Indien', p. 93.
152. Riding into a place to steal a few cows is disreputable; invading a territory in chariots and stealing all its cows is a glorious achievement. Vedic wars are cattle raids. See Rau, Wilhelm, *Staat und Gesellschaft im alten Indien. Nach den Brāhmaṇa-texten dargestellt* (Wiesbaden: Otto Harrassowitz, 1957), p. 102.

Similarly, the Greek heroes at Thebes die 'fighting for the sheep of Oidipous' (Hesiod: *Works and Days*, p. 163).

153. Falk: 'Das Reitpferd im vedischen Indien', p. 98.
154. Falk: 'Das Reitpferd im vedischen Indien', pp. 95 and 99.
155. This use of the word *marya* to mean 'servant' brings out the difference between the low status of a young man (*marya*) and the social success of the mature chariot-owner.
156. When a Vedic student becomes a graduate (*snātaka*), he drives a chariot. A Vedic sacrificer should ideally travel by chariot. See Heesterman, J.C., *The Broken World of Sacrifice: An Essay in Indian Ritual* (Chicago, IL: University of Chicago Press, 1993), p. 170. His chariot ride 'is the impoverished remnant of the royal chariot-borne raid', Heesterman: *Broken World*, p. 163. The admirable cattle raid of a king driving a chariot can be imitated by the impoverished chariot-ride of a sacrificer; both are quite different from the disgraceful cattle raid of a young man riding a horse.
157. Falk: 'Das Reitpferd im vedischen Indien', p. 98.
158. Hopkins, Edward W., 'The Social and Military Position of the Ruling Caste in Ancient India, as Represented by the Sanskrit Epic', *Journal of the American Oriental Society* 13 (1889), p. 263.
159. Hyland: *Horse in Ancient World*, p. 79.
160. Hyland: *Horse in Ancient World*, p. 73.
161. Schulman, Alan Richard, 'Egyptian Representations of Horsemen and Riding in the New Kingdom', *Journal of Near Eastern Studies* 16 (1957), pp. 264 and 271; Hyland: *Horse in Ancient World*, p. 79.
162. Schulman: 'Egyptian Representations of Horsemen', p. 267.
163. Decker: 'Pferd und Wagen im Alten Aegypten', p. 264 footnote 53.
164. There were some experiments with mounted warriors in Mycenaean Greece. See Worley, Leslie J., *Hippeis. The Cavalry of Ancient Greece* (Boulder, CO: Westview Press, 1994), pp. 7–11. There is, however, no real cavalry until the eighth century BC. See Worley: *Hippeis*, pp. 19–20.
165. 'The art of riding [...] was deliberately excluded by the author from his depiction of the heroic age,' Plath: 'Pferd und Wagen im Mykenischen', p. 110. Delebecque specifies that Homer was excluding *military* riding from his epics, rather than riding in general. Homer would therefore be correct in believing that the *military* use of horses was a recent innovation. See Delebecque: *Cheval dans l'Iliade*, p. 236.
166. Homer's account of Bronze Age behaviour is supported by Ancient Egyptian sources. A chariot could easily crash, so the horses were trained to accept riders too. Even if the chariot was lost, the warrior and charioteer could escape on horseback. See Decker: 'Pferd und Wagen im Alten Aegypten', p. 264; Drews: *Early Riders*, pp. 52–3.
167. Pausanias tells us that cavalry was used in the First Messenian War (Pausanias 4: 7, 4–5) and Aristotle that it was used in the Lelantine War (Aristotle fr. 98 Rose = Plutarch, *Erotikos* 17). Both of these wars occurred in Homer's

lifetime. The Assyrians had abandoned the military use of chariots by 700 BC. See Drews: *Early Riders*, p. 66.

168. Sappho, fr. 16 Campbell.
169. Köhne: *Dioskuren in der Griechischen Kunst*, p. 173 and footnote 649.
170. Homer feels obliged to account for their absence – they died before the Trojan War (*Iliad* 3: 243–244).
171. Our first evidence for the Dioskouroi comes from Sparta (which was always regarded as the homeland of the Dioskouroi) and Ionia (where they were viewed as sea-faring gods).
172. Parpola, Asko, 'The Nāsatyas, the Chariot and Proto-Aryan Religion', *Journal of Indological Studies* 16–17 (2004–2005), pp. 10–12.
173. Burkert: *Greek Religion*, p. 107.
174. Watkins, Calvert, 'New Parameters in Historical Linguistics, Philology, and Culture History', *Language* 65 (1989), pp. 784–785.
175. Indo-European **wiro peku* → *pecudesque virosque* (Latin), *pasu-vīra* (Avestan), *vīra-pśa* (Sanskrit). See Benveniste, Émile, *Indo-European Language and Society*, translated by Elizabeth Palmer (Coral Gables, FL: University of Miami Press, 1973), pp. 40–2; Watkins, Calvert, *The American Heritage Dictionary of Indo-European Roots* (Boston, MA: Houghton Mifflin, 2000), p. 63. The same idea lies behind the contrast between Greek *tetrapodon* (four-footer) and *andropodon* (man-footer = slave), and between Sanskrit *catuspad* (four-footer) and *dvipad* (two-footer = slave).
176. For the general theme, see Watkins, Calvert, *How to Kill a Dragon: Aspects of Indo-European Poetics* (New York, NY: Oxford University Press, 1995), pp. 297–303. Stories based on this theme will usually include formulaic words that derive from **oghi* (snake) and **g^{w}hen* (kill).
177. Erdosy, George, 'Ethnicity in the Rigveda and its Bearing on the Question of Indo-European Origins', *South Asian Studies* 5 (1989), pp. 35 and 37–8. Erdosy and Arvidsson cite Müller's famous attack on the conflation of race with language, in which he asserted that linguistic racism and racist linguistics are equally absurd: 'it would be as wrong to speak of Aryan blood as of dolichocephalic grammar.' See Erdosy: 'Ethnicity in the Rigveda', p. 35; Arvidsson, Stefan, *Aryan Idols* (Chicago, IL: University of Chicago Press, 2006), p. 61.
178. Poliakov, Léon, *The Aryan Myth. A History of Racist and Nationalist Ideas in Europe*, translated by Edmund Howard (New York, NY: Basic Books, 1974), pp. 191–202.
179. Poliakov: *Aryan Myth*, p. 193.
180. Poliakov: *Aryan Myth*, p. 191; Arvidsson: *Aryan Idols*, p. 108 note 122.
181. Schlegel himself incorrectly believed that it was related to the rather more aristocratic German notion of *Ehre* (honour). See Poliakov: *Aryan Myth*, p. 193; Arvidsson: *Aryan Idols*, pp. 20–1.
182. Witzel points out that India itself, the homeland of the *aryas*, has always been relatively free from 'race-madness' (*Rassenwahn*). See Witzel, Michael, *Das alte Indien* (Munich: Beck, 2003), p. 11.

183. For the fantasy of finding 'white Englishmen' in a suitably remote region ('Kafiristan', modern Nuristan), see Rudyard Kipling's story, *The Man Who Would Be King* (New York, NY: Doubleday and McClure, 1899). A scholarly version of this fantasy, where the 'Aryans' are corrupted by sultry India, can be found in Lanman's popular *Sanskrit Reader* and in Oldenberg's standard introduction to Vedic religion. See Lanmann, Charles Rockwell, *A Sanskrit Reader* (Boston, MA: Ginn, Heath, and Company, 1884), pp. 352 and 357; Oldenberg: *Religion des Veda*, p. 2. Their celebration of 'Aryan' aggressiveness is typical of the late nineteenth century, though it is usually contrasted with Jewish humanitarianism rather than with Indian quietism. See Arvidsson: *Aryan Idols*, pp. 149–56 and 162–5.

184. Arvidsson: *Aryan Idols*, pp. 5–8. As Arvidsson points out, even Müller himself was to some extent creating myths for the nineteenth century as much as discovering myths from Vedic India. See Arvidsson: *Aryan Idols*, pp. 87–90. Of course Müller's myths were not racist myths.

185. Heine's poem, 'Die Götter Griechenlands', captures the romantic nostalgia for a lost world of liberated naturalness, and by its equation of the clouds and the Greek gods, it might well be classified as a typical work of the Nature School! The connection with the romantic movement can also be found on the scholarly side. In his work on the Baltic myths, Mannhardt cites German romantic poetry and European folklore as sources for ancient pagan thought! See Mannhardt, Wilhelm, 'Die lettische Sonnenmythen', *Zeitschrift für Ethnologie* 7 (1875), pp. 73–104, 209–44, and 281–329. Many nineteenth-century scholars were, however, ambivalent about the merits of the liberal romantic tradition. See Arvidsson: *Aryan Idols*, pp. 87–90.

186. Since these scholars were all men, they were naturally swept off their feet by the Vedic hymns in which the Dawn goddess reveals her breasts to a delighted humanity. See Oldenberg: *Religion des Veda*, p. 237; Macdonell, Arthur Anthony, *Vedic Mythology* (Delhi: Motilal Banarsidass. 1898 [2002]), p. 47. Oldenberg assures us that this has nothing to do with 'sultry and decadent sensuality', but I hope he did not really believe this.

187. By the twentieth century, it was quite acceptable for scholars to dismiss Roscher and Müller, two great champions of the school. 'As early as the fifth century B.C. Metrodorus of Lampsacus was putting forward the doctrine which inspires the earlier volumes of Roscher's *Lexikon*, that all Greek legend is disguised cosmological myth and consists essentially of highly obscure talk about the weather [...] people like Macrobius anticipated Max Müller in discovering the Sun God beneath every divine personage': Halliday, W.R. *Indo-European Folk-Tales and Greek Legend* (Cambridge: University Press, 1933), p. 3. For the decline and fall of the Nature School, see Arvidsson: *Aryan Idols*, pp. 129–31.

188. Erdosy: 'Ethnicity in the Rigveda', p. 45. Erdosy is criticizing the belief that the speaking of Sanskrit implies an 'Aryan' invasion of India.

189. Momigliano, Arnaldo, 'Georges Dumézil and the Trifunctional Approach to Roman Civilization', in Momigliano, Arnaldo, *On Pagans, Jews, and Christians* (Middletown, CT: Wesleyan University Press, 1987), pp. 311–12.
190. The classes do not appear until the late hymn, *RV* 10: 90. Witzel refers to this as a '*new* [my italics] stratification of society into four classes' and shows that it is an innovation of the Kuru kingdom. See Witzel, Michael, 'The Development of the Vedic Canon and its Schools: The Social and Political Milieus', in Witzel, Michael (editor), *Inside the Texts, Beyond the Texts* (Cambridge, MA: Harvard University Press, 1997), p. 295.
191. Dumézil's interest in these three classes may have been inspired by a monarchist desire to restore the three feudal estates, since he had in his youth joined the *Action Française* of the vicious traitor Charles Maurras. See Momigliano: 'Dumézil and the Trifunctional Approach', p. 293; Arvidsson: *Aryan Idols*, pp. 240–1.
192. Dumézil, Georges, *Mythe et épopée. I. L'idéologie des trois fonctions dans les épopées des peuples indo-européens* (Paris: Gallimard, 1968 [1986]), pp. 31–257. Its most exasperating flaw is the extraordinary respect it shows for Colonel de Polier's version of the *Mahābhārata*, but this demonstrates Dumézil's love for a particular telling of a story rather than for general schemata.
193. Hiltebeitel had translated Dumézil's work into English, and his *Ritual of Battle* uses Dumézil's approach to analyse the *Mahābhārata* from an Indological perspective. See Hiletbeitel, Alf, *The Ritual of Battle. Krishna in the Mahābhārata* (Albany, NY: State University of New York Press, 1990).
194. Dumézil: *M&E I. L'idéologie des trois fonctions*, pp. 259–437.
195. In the field of Classics, his work inspired the committed Marxist Vernant and the human rights activist Vidal-Naquet, neither of whom could have agreed with Dumézil's admiration for the *Action Française* or for Charles Maurras. Vernant had spent the war-years resisting the friends of Maurras, and Vidal-Naquet's parents had been sent to Auschwitz by those friends.
196. Lincoln, Bruce, *Priests, Warriors, and Cattle: A Study in the Ecology of Religions* (Berkeley, CA: University of California Press, 1981).
197. Arvidsson: *Aryan Idols*, pp. 149–56.
198. When Dumézil writes about 'epic types', he discusses the hero, the magician, and the king alone. See Dumézil, Georges, *Mythe et épopée. II. Types épiques indo-européens: un héros, un sorcier, un roi* (Paris: Gallimard, 1971 [1986]). Grotanelli notes the neglect of the third function by Dumézil and his followers. See Grotanelli, Cristiano, 'Dumézil, the Indo-Europeans, and the Third Function', in Patton, Laurie L., and Doniger, Wendy. *Myth and Method* (Charlotesville, VA: University of Virginia Press, 1996), pp. 131–2.
199. This rather obvious point was already noted in the *Taittirīya Saṃhitā*: the Vaiśyas are 'more numerous (*bhūyāṃsas*) than the others' (*TS* 7: 1, 1^5), and more famously in Periklēs' definition of Athenian democracy as 'governing in the interest of the majority' (Thucydides 2: 37, 1).

200. Yasna 29 (The Plaint of the Ox): 6. Translated and discussed at Lincoln: *Priests, Warriors, and Cattle*, pp. 140–2 and 149–51.
201. Hesiod: *Theogony* 26.
202. Hesiod: *Works and Days*, pp. 39, 221 and 264.
203. Nagy, Gregory, *Greek Mythology and Poetics* (Ithaca, NY: Cornell University Press, 1990), pp. 56–60. Impoverished poets can be intimidated by their local audience, but poets with a Panhellenic reputation are free to tell the truth. See Nagy: *Greek Mythology and Poetics*, pp. 42–6.

Chapter 2 The Family of the Aśvins

1. 'The correct etymology derives the name from the root *nes*, from which we have *neomai*, *nostos*, and *Nestor*. They are the saviours who guarantee the traveller's or warrior's safe return, whether on land or on sea.' See Skutsch, Otto, 'Helen, Her Name and Nature,' *Journal of Hellenic Studies* 107 (1987) p. 189. Mayrhofer, Wagner and Zeller also support this etymology: *EWA* (*Etymologisches Wörterbuch des Altindoarischen*), vol. 2, p. 30 under *nas* and p. 39 under *nāsatya*; Wagner, Noerber, 'Dioskuren, Jungmannschaften und Doppelkönigtum', *Zeitschrift für deutsche Philologie* 79 (1960), p. 1; Zeller: *Die Vedischen Zwillingsgötter*, p. 5.
2. Dumézil: *M&E I. L'idéologie des trois fonctions*, p. 49; *EWA*, vol. 2, p. 39 under *nāsatya*; Parpola: 'Aryans and soma', p. 18.
3. Bergaigne, Abel, *La religion védique d'après les hymnes du Rig-veda* (Paris: F. Vieweg, 1883), vol. 2, p. 434.
4. Macdonell: *Vedic Mythology*, pp. 20 and 54.
5. Macdonell: *Vedic Mythology*, pp. 20, 88 and 104.
6. Macdonell: *Vedic Mythology*, pp. 20 and 49.
7. *RV* 3: 58, 6a and 6c.
8. 'Why do the ancient poets say, o Aśvins, that you come most readily to deal with misfortune?' (*RV* 3: 58, 3cd; these lines are identical with *RV* 1: 118, 3cd).
9. Bergaigne: *La religion védique*, vol. 2, pp. 434–5. He compares their rescue operations again later in his work, this time emphasizing the similarities. See Bergaigne: *Religion védique*, vol. 2, pp. 495–8.
10. Bergaigne starts off his analysis of the Aśvins by declaring that they are 'morning gods': Bergaigne: *Religion védique*, vol. 2, p. 431.
11. Bodewitz, H.W., *The Daily Evening and Morning Offering (Agnihotra) according to the Brāhmaṇas* (Leiden: E.J. Brill, 1976), p. 3.
12. See below, Chapter 4, 'The Morning Prayer (*prātaranuvāka*)', and 'The Twilight Chant (*saṃdhistotra*) and the Aśvin Hymn (*āśvinaśastra*)'.
13. She may be their mother at *RV* 3: 39, 3, if Geldner has solved this riddle correctly: 'the twin-bearing mother has given birth to twins.' See Geldner: *Rig-Veda*, vol. 1, p. 381, translation and note to 3a. Since the Aśvins emerge from the dawn, they must be her children. There is a well-established tradition that Dyaus slept with his daughter Uṣas, so she could very well be both the mother and the sister of the Aśvins.

14. The Aśvins were usually identified as a representation of twilight. See Myriantheus, L., *Die Açvins, oder arischen Dioskuren* (Munich: Theodor Ackermann, 1876), p. 36. Other scholars identified them with the morning-star. See Oldenberg: *Religion des Veda*, pp. 210–13. Similar identifications of their 'physical basis' are discussed at Macdonell: *Vedic Mythology*, pp. 53–4, and at Hillebrandt, Alfred, *Vedic Mythology*, translated by Sreeramula Rajeswara Sarma (Delhi: Motilal Banarsidass, 1980), vol. 1, pp. 39–44.
15. These are the stages in which the universe develops, but Yaska does not present them in this order (he mentions Stage 3 between Stage 1 and Stage 2).
16. The adjective *vāsātya* means 'of Vasāti'. Böhtling's Sanskrit dictionary and its translation by Monier-Williams suggest 'dawn' as the probable meaning of Vasāti, but this would obliterate Yaska's distinction between the two Aśvins. If we derived it from the verb *vas vasati* 'dwell' rather than *vas ucchati* 'shine', Vasāti could be translated as Night, because this root means 'stay *overnight*' in Sanskrit and other Indo-European languages (*EWA*, vol. 2, p. 531 under *VAS* [3]). The related noun *vasati* can also mean 'night', though it usually means 'dwelling' and 'passing the night'.
17. This process is described in the creation hymn, *RV* 10: 129. In the beginning, the universe is like a womb filled with liquid (*ambhas*, 1d; *salila*, 3b), darkness (*tamas*, 3a), and emptiness (*tuchya*, 3c). From inside this womb emerge heat (*tapas*, 3d), desire (*kāma*, 4a), and semen (*retas*, 4b). From the interaction between the moist empty darkness and the hot desiring semen, Oneness (That One, *tad ekam*, 3d) or Being (*sat*, 4c) is born (*ajāyata*, 3d). Yaska ignores the sexual imagery, confining himself instead to moist darkness and hot light.
18. *RV* 10: 129, 1ab.
19. *RV* 10: 37, 3cd.
20. Dumézil: *M&E I. L'idéologie des trois fonctions*, p. 78.
21. Harris: *Boanerges*, p. 236; Zeller: *Die Vedischen Zwillingsgötter*, pp. 33–5.
22. 'Makha is indeed the sacrifice' (*ŚB* 6: 5, 2[1]). See Buitenen, J. A. B. van, *The Pravargya, an Ancient Indian Iconic Ritual* (Poona: Deccan College Postgraduate and Research Institute, 1968), p. 19.
23. Geldner: *Rig-Veda*, vol. 1, p. 261, translation of *RV* 1: 181, 4.
24. Zeller: *Die Vedischen Zwillingsgötter*, pp. 33 and 35.
25. Several hymns refer to the incestuous relationship between the sky god Dyaus and his daughter Uṣas (*RV* 1: 71, 5 and 8; *RV* 3: 31, 1; *RV* 10: 61, 7). See Geldner: *Rig-Veda*, vol. 1, p. 261, note to *RV* 1: 181, 4; Doniger, Wendy, *Hindu Myths* (Harmondsworth: Penguin, 1975), pp. 25–6.
26. Zeller dismisses the notion that they could be the sons of Dawn and Night. See Zeller: *Die Vedischen Zwillingsgötter*, p. 32 note 201. Yaska is not, however, presenting this as his own personal theory, he is quoting an apocryphal Vedic hymn.
27. Harris: *Boanerges*, p. 236.
28. Zeller: *Die Vedischen Zwillingsgötter*, p. 31.
29. Normally, the Aśvins are indistinguishable. 'In general, they are praised together, appear at the same time, and perform the same activities' (Yaska,

Nirukta 12, 2). 'This passage is the only example in the entire literature where the Aśvins have different functions, even though they are extremely vague ones,' Zeller: *Die Vedischen Zwillingsgötter*, p. 33.

30. Zeller: *Die Vedischen Zwillingsgötter*, p. 34.
31. The two parents appear again at at *RV* 10: 10, 4c, where they are referred to as 'the Gandharva in the waters' and 'the young woman of the waters'.
32. In the Vedic period, Indian scholars believed that if you were warned not to ask a question that surpassed your intellectual abilities, and persisted in doing so anyway, your head would explode (*Bṛhadāraṇyaka Upaniṣad* 3: 6, 1). See Witzel: 'Early Indian history', especially pp. 408–13; 'The case of the shattered head', *Studien zur Indologie und Iranistik* (1987), pp. 363–4 and 377–89.
33. Geldner, in his note on this passage, suggests that *budhne* ('bottom') should be treated as a preposition and translated as 'after'. Instead of 'at the base of the heat of the fire', these words would mean 'after the heat of the fire', Geldner: *Rig-Veda*, vol. 1, p. 381, note to *RV* 3: 39, 3d.
34. As the offspring of Dyaus and his daughter they would indeed be both the sons *and* the grandsons of Dyaus.
35. Geldner: *Rig-Veda*, vol. 3, pp. 149–50, note to *RV* 10: 17, 1ab; Jamison: 'Rigvedic Svayaṃvara', p. 303 note 1.
36. Bloomfield, Maurice, 'Contributions to the Interpretation of the Veda', *Journal of the American Oriental Society* 15 (1893), p. 175; Zeller: *Die Vedischen Zwillingsgötter*, p. 24. Technically, Vivasvant should be the only mortal at the wedding, since the ancestors of the human race have not yet been born, but the poet Devaśravas has decided to ignore this. Similarly, in the Yama–Yamī hymn, there is no other mortal for Yamī to marry apart from her brother Yama and her father Vivasvant, and yet Yama tells her, 'find another husband apart from me' (*RV* 10: 10, 10d).
37. Under the entry '*Vivasvat*', Geldner's index states, 'Name des Sonnengottes': Geldner, Karl Friedrich, and Nobel, Johannes. *Namen- und Sachregister zur Übersetzung.* (Cambridge, MA: Harvard University Press, 1957), p. 140. This is slightly misleading because Vivasvant is human throughout books 1–9; he is a sun god only at *RV* 10.39.12d, and perhaps at *RV* 10: 65, 6d, where he receives offerings along with the other gods.
38. Bloomfield: 'Interpretation of Veda', pp. 176–7; Macdonell: *Vedic Mythology*, pp. 43.
39. 'Being married' (*pariuhyamānā*) is a present participle, so it literally means 'while being married'. Zeller rather wickedly suggests that Saraṇyū was already pregnant with Yama during the wedding, Zeller: *Die Vedischen Zwillingsgötter*, p. 25. If we insisted on taking the participle literally, it would imply that Saraṇyū ran away in the middle of the wedding ceremony.
40. This ambiguity has been pointed out by modern scholars. See Bloomfield: 'Interpretation of Veda', pp. 173 and 178; Zeller: *Die Vedischen Zwillingsgötter*, p. 25–6.

41. This story lies behind *RV* 10: 10, but the hymn rejects it, because the marriage between Yama and Yamī would be incestuous. See Geldner: *Rig-Veda*, vol. 3, p. 133, introduction to *RV* 10: 10.
42. Witzel sees this story about Yama as further evidence for the newcomer status of Vasiṣṭha. See Witzel: 'Development of the Vedic Canon', pp. 289 note 145.
43. We hear of Manu Vivasvant (*manau vivasvati*, *RV* 8: 52, 1) and Manu the son of Savarṇā (*Sāvarnya* at *RV* 10: 62, 9c; *Sāvarṇi* at *RV* 10: 62, 11c). See Bloomfield: 'Interpretation of Veda', pp. 178–80; Geldner: *Rig-Veda*, vol. 2, p. 374, note to *RV* 8: 52, 1a, and vol. 3, p. 232, introduction to *RV* 10: 62. As Bloomfield points out, it does not matter greatly whether the poet was thinking of the original Manu, or a particular descendant of Manu; the important point is that in order for anyone to bear the name Manu Sāvarṇya or Manu Sāvarṇi, the original Manu must have been the son of Savarṇā. See Bloomfield: 'Interpretation of Veda', p. 180.
44. Geldner: *Rig-Veda*, vol. 3, p. 149, introduction to *RV* 10: 17.
45. As we saw, *savarṇā* is ambiguous at *RV* 10: 17, 2b. Yaska may have felt he was clarifying the intention of the poet Devaśravas, rather than giving the word a new twist.
46. Bloomfield: 'Interpretation of Veda', p. 175.
47. Bloomfield: 'Interpretation of Veda', p. 178.
48. Zeus in the form of a gander rapes Nemesis, and she gives birth to Helenē; as a swan, Zeus rapes Lēdē, who gives birth to Helenē and the horse gods; Poseidōn changes into a horse and rapes Dēmētēr or Erinus, who gives birth to the first horse. See below, Chapter 6, 'The Birth of Helenē', and '3. The Birth of the Horse'.
49. Bloomfield: 'Interpretation of Veda', pp. 178 note.
50. Geldner: *Rig-Veda*, vol. 3, p. 349, note to *RV* 10: 121, 10.
51. Notice how Vasiṣṭha denounces demons (*yātavas*, *RV* 7: 21, 5a) and phallus-worshippers (*śiśnadevās*, *RV* 7: 21, 5d). He declares that they can have no part in soma sacrifices. The earlier gods (*devās pūrve*, *RV* 7: 21, 7a) have submitted to the new order.
52. For Plato's disapproval of metamorphosis, see *Republic* 2: 380d–381d.
53. See note 43 above for Ṛgvedic references to 'Manu Vivasvant' and 'Manu the son of Savarṇā'.
54. The main body of the *Bṛhaddevatā* dates to the early Puranic period (first to fifth centuries AD), but some additions are as late as the seventh to eleventh centuries. See Patton, Laurie L., *Myth as Argument. The Bṛhaddevatā as Canonical Commentary* (Berlin: Walter de Gruyter, 1996), p. 12.
55. Bloomfield: 'Interpretation of Veda', pp. 178.
56. The name has, of course, nothing to do with the noun *nas* (nose), but is rather derived from the verb *nas* ('reach home safely'). See *EWA*, vol. 2, p. 30 under *nas* and p. 39 under *nāsatya*.
57. 'The legends of the *Nirukta* and the *Bṛhaddevatā* [. . .] on the union of Vivasvat and Saraṇyū have every appearance of having been invented, perhaps however

with pre-existing mythical elements, to explain these two stanzas', Bergaigne: *Religion védique*, vol. 2, p. 506 note 4. He is referring to *RV* 10: 17, 1–2.

58. *Taittirīya Saṃhitā* 6: 4, 9.
59. This formula 'she mounted your chariot' (*ā vāṃ rathaṃ sthā*) is found at *RV* 1: 116, 17; *RV* 1: 118, 5; *RV* 5: 73, 5; and *RV* 8: 8, 10. Slightly different versions are found at *RV* 1: 34, 5 and *RV* 6: 63, 5. See Jamison: 'Rigvedic Svayaṃvara', p. 306 for this formula. Jamison sees it as a formula for a *svayaṃvara* rather than an elopement.
60. *ā sūriyeva* [. . .] *rathaṃ gāt* (*RV* 1: 167, 5). The usual verb (*ā-sthā*) reappears in the following stanza, 'the Maruts help her to mount (*āsthāpayanta*) their chariot' (*RV* 1: 167, 6).
61. For this reversal of the normal formula, see Jamison: 'Rigvedic Svayaṃvara', p. 307 note 8.
62. *yānam yena patī bhavathaḥ sūriyāyāḥ* (*RV* 4: 43, 6).
63. 'A marriage with mutual desire (*icchayā 'nyonyasaṃyogaḥ*) of a young woman and a suitor, for sexual pleasure and arising from desire (*maithunyaḥ kāmasaṃbhavaḥ*), is known as a *gāndharva* union' (*Laws of Manu* 3: 32). See Dumézil, Georges, *Mariages indo-européens* (Paris: Payot, 1979), pp. 31–45.
64. If heat (*ghṛṇā*) is instrumental, the line would be even more explicit in blaming Sūryā's lack of concern for the poor horses of the Aśvins: 'they keep (Sūryā) away from burning them with her heat.' See Geldner: *Rig-Veda*, vol. 2, p. 78, note to *RV* 5: 73, 5d.
65. Independent heiresses were quite exceptional in Vedic India; a woman could only become an independent heiress if her father had no sons and died before marrying her off. If she followed the *Vrātyas*, her status could be reduced to that of a concubine or even a prostitute. See Witzel, Michael, 'Little Dowry, No Satī. The Lot of Women in the Vedic Period', *Journal of South Asia Women Studies* 2 (1996), pp. 162–3. For the equation of *Vrātyas* with Maruts, see Heesterman, J. C., 'Vrātya and Sacrifice', *Indo-Iranian Journal* 6 (1962), pp.16–17, and Falk: Bruderschaft und Würfelspiel, p, 190.
66. In arguing that Sūryā's wedding is a *svayaṃvara*, Geldner focuses on the competition among her suitors, Geldner: *Rig-Veda*, vol. 1, p. 264, note to *RV* 1: 184, 3a. Jamison emphasizes Sūryā's personal choice and the formulaic phrase *svayaṃ sā vṛṇite*, 'she herself chose', Jamison: 'Rigvedic Svayaṃvara', p. 304–9. Jamison is right in saying that Sūryā did indeed make her own choice, but it is not clear that she chose marriage.
67. It is true that Draupadī ends up with five husbands in the *Mahabhārata*, but that is not her fault. She chose Arjuna alone at her *svayaṃvara* and was perfectly well-behaved until her mother-in-law interfered.
68. It is unclear whether they are attracted by the splendour of Sūryā's beauty, or she is drawn by theirs. See Geldner: *Rig-Veda*, vol. 1, p. 476, note to *RV* 4: 44, 2ab. Sometimes it is clearly the splendid beauty of all three. See Geldner: *Rig-Veda*, vol. 2, p. 166, note to *RV* 6: 63, 6b. Whether the beauty is masculine, feminine,

or both, the motivation for the relationship is always the splendour of beauty (*śrī*): *RV* 1: 116, 17d; *RV* 1: 184, 3a; *RV* 4: 44, 2a; *RV* 6: 63, 5a and 6a; *RV* 7: 72, 1d.

69. Geldner: *Rig-Veda*, vol. 2, p. 150, note to *RV* 6: 49, 8b.
70. Macdonell takes *RV* 6: 58, 4 to mean that Pūṣan actually married Sūryā, Macdonell: *Vedic Mythology*, p. 35. Even if we accepted his interpretation, this strange marriage would not be a *svayaṃvara* since 'the gods gave him, overcome with desire, to Sūryā'. The marriage would be based on his choice and theirs, not on the free choice of Sūryā.
71. Compare *yad ayātaṃ vahatuṃ sūriyāyās tricakreṇa saṃsadam icchamānā* (*TS* 4: 7, 15[4]) with *yad aśvinā pṛchamānāv ayātaṃ tricakreṇa vahatuṃ sūryāyāḥ* (*RV* 10: 85, 14). The lines are identical in wording apart from the phrases *saṃsadam icchamānā*, 'wishing to sit together' and *aśvinā pṛchamānāv* 'Aśvins asking (for her)'. As friends of the groom, the Aśvins should be supporting Soma's request for Sūryā's hand, which has already been granted by her father Savitar, but perhaps they have already decided that Sūryā should run off with them instead. This is certainly implied by the phrase 'wishing to sit with (her)'.
72. 'In the wedding hymn Sūryā never chooses anyone or anything. . .,' Jamison: 'Rigvedic Svayaṃvara', p. 308.
73. The term *vara* is ambiguous, since it can mean both 'suitor' (*Freier*) and 'matchmaker' or 'spokesman for the groom' (*Freiwerber*), as Geldner points out. See Geldner: *Rig-Veda*, vol. 3, p. 268, note to *RV* 10: 85, 8c.
74. *Vadhūyu* is used in the literal sense of 'bridegroom' only of Soma here at *RV* 10: 85, 9a and of the successful suitor in a real-life *svayaṃvara* among human beings at *RV* 10: 27, 12a. See Jamison: 'Rigvedic Svayaṃvara', p. 309. The only other uses of *vadhūyu* are in metaphors comparing Indra and Agni to men who have a wife (*RV* 3: 52, 3c and *RV* 9: 69, 3a). The terms *vadhūyu* (husband, suitor) and *vadhu* (bride, young woman) come from the Indo-European root **u̯edh* meaning 'to lead' (no connection with English 'wed,' which comes from **u̯adh* meaning 'promise'). For the change in meaning from Indo-European 'lead' to Indo-Iranian 'marry,' compare the Latin verb *dūcere*, which means both 'to lead' and 'to marry'.
75. 'She mounts an even more characteristic wedding vehicle, *ánas-* "wagon"', Jamison: 'Rigvedic Svayaṃvara', p. 306. Her marriage wagon (*anas*) is also mentioned at *RV* 10: 85, 10a.
76. The *Aitareya Brāhmaṇa* explicitly dismisses the possibility of polyandry: 'therefore one man has many wives; one woman does not have many husbands' (*AB* 3: 21).
77. The bride is equated with Sūryā here at 20c, again at 35c (her wedding-dress), and 38b (the Gandharvas bring her to the husband).
78. *Aitareya Brāhmaṇa* 4: 7; *Kauṣītaki Brāhmaṇa* 18: 1.
79. Note the dual, *patī*. Both of them will be her husbands.
80. The phrasing is almost identical: *viśve devā anv amanyanta* (*RV* 1: 116, 17c), *viśve devā anu* [. . .] *ajānan* (*RV* 10: 85, 14c).

81. She chooses them for their 'beauty' (*śrī*) – *RV* 1: 117, 13d; *RV* 6: 63, 5a; *RV* 7: 69, 4a.
82. *Vahatu* implies a legitimate marriage, see Bloomfield: 'Interpretation of Veda', p. 181. In its literal sense of a real wedding, *vahatu* is used only of Vivasvant's marriage with Saraṇyū (*RV* 10: 17, 1a) and Soma's marriage with Sūryā (five times in *RV* 10: 85 and also at *RV* 1: 184, 3b). The other occurrences of *vahatu* are metaphorical.
83. *RV* 1: 34, 5; *RV* 1: 116, 17; *RV* 1: 117, 13; *RV* 1: 118, 5; *RV* 1: 119, 5; *RV* 4: 43, 2; *RV* 4: 44, 1; *RV* 5: 73, 5; *RV* 6: 63, 5; *RV* 7: 68, 3; *RV* 7: 69, 4; *RV* 8: 8, 10; *RV* 8: 22, 1.

Chapter 3 Nāsatyas – Saviour Gods

1. 'These two are impure, they associate with human beings (*manusyacarau*),' *TS* 6: 4, 9^{1-2}.
2. Indra 'comes most readily with help' at *RV* 6: 52, 5 and 6 (*avasā āgamiṣṭhaḥ*); the Aśvins 'go most readily to any misfortune' at *RV* 1: 118, 3c (*praty avartiṃ gamiṣṭhā*) and 'come most readily with help' at *RV* 5: 76, 2c (*avasā āgamiṣṭhā*). *RV* 4: 43, 2a asks 'who comes most readily?' (*katama āgamiṣṭho*) and compares the Aśvins with Indra (*RV* 4: 43, 3b). We find a strange use of the formula in two hymns. At *RV* 3: 58, 9d (*āgamiṣṭhaḥ*) the chariot of the Aśvins and at *RV* 5: 76, 2a (*gamiṣṭhā*), the Aśvins themselves 'come most readily' for offerings! This playful adaptation shows that the rescue formula was well known *RV* 5: 76, 2 has, in fact, both the new adaptation and the original formula: the Aśvins 'go most readily' for offerings (*gamiṣṭhā*, *RV* 5: 76, 2a), they 'come most readily with help' (*avasā āgamiṣṭhā*, *RV* 5: 76, 2c).
3. *RV* 1: 112, 6b and 20b; *RV* 1: 116, 3–5; *RV* 1: 117, 14–15; *RV* 1: 118, 6c; *RV* 1: 119, 4ab and 8; *RV* 1: 158, 3ab; *RV* 1: 180, 5ab; *RV* 1: 182, 5–7; *RV* 6: 62, 6; *RV* 7: 68, 7; *RV* 7: 69, 7; *RV* 8: 3, 23; *RV* 8: 5, 22; *RV* 10: 39, 4cd; *RV* 10: 40, 7a; *RV* 10: 65, 12; *RV* 10: 143, 5.
4. Böhtlingk's dictionary and its translation by Monier-Williams take *arāvā* here as a synonym of *arvan*, 'horse'. Griffith therefore translates this line as 'your horse delivered him, your devoted servant', Griffith, Ralph T.H. *The Hymns of the Rig Veda.* (Delhi: Motilal Banarsidass, 1896 [1973]), p. 369. It seems more natural to take *arāvā yaḥ yuvākuḥ* together ('the *arāvā* who was your devotee'), and since this is the only case cited by Böhtlingk where *arāvan* means 'horse,' Geldner is surely right in taking it to mean 'the malicious man who was your devotee', Geldner: *Rig-Veda*, vol. 2, p. 244, translation of *RV* 5: 68, 7 and note to *RV* 7: 68, 7c.
5. Geldner: *Rig-Veda*, vol. 2, p. 244, note to *RV* 7: 68, 7c.
6. Referring to this passage (in a comment on another hymn), Geldner remarks: 'We can conclude that there was a temporary cooling of the friendship between Tugra and the Aśvins,' Geldner: *Rig-Veda*, vol. 1, p. 158, note to *RV* 1: 117, 14. In fact, the term *arāvan* (*RV* 7: 68, 7) might suggest malice or hostility towards

the Aśvins as well as towards his son. See Geldner: *Rig-Veda*, vol. 2, p. 244, note to *RV* 7: 68, 7c.

7. *RV* 1: 116, 4d; *RV* 1: 117, 15c; *RV* 8: 5, 22c. At *RV* 1: 158, 3a, their chariot is not explicitly mentioned, but Geldner points out that the adjectives *peru*, *pajra*, and *yukta* probably refer to a chariot: *peru* = saving, *pajra* = reliable, and *yukta* = yoked (to winged horses). See Geldner: *Rig-Veda*, vol. 1, p. 216, note to *RV* 1: 158, 3ab.
8. The 'bird-horses' are usually called simply 'birds' (*vi* at *RV* 1: 119, 4a; *RV* 6: 62, 6a; *RV* 8: 3, 23c; *RV* 8: 5, 22c), or 'winged ones,' a common synonym for birds (*patratrin* at *RV* 6: 62, 6d; *RV* 7: 69, 7c; *RV* 10: 143, 5c; *pataṃga* at *RV* 1: 116, 4b).
9. *RV* 1: 116 is a little confusing on this point. We have the magic living ships at 3cd and 5d, but three chariots at 4d.
10. 'With animated ships' (*naubhir ātmanvatībhir*, *RV* 1: 116, 3c); 'an animated ship' (*plavam ātmavantam*, *RV* 1: 182, 5b). These ships have a soul (*ātman*).
11. Compare '*samudrasya dhanvan ārdrasya pāre*' ('to the shore of the ocean, on the other side of the water', *RV* 1: 116, 4c) with '*samudra ā | rajasaḥ pāra*' ('in the ocean, on the other side of the atmosphere', *RV* 10: 143, 5ab).
12. Détienne, Marcel, and Vernant, Jean-Pierre, *Cunning Intelligence in Greek Culture and Society*, translated by Janet Lloyd. (Chicago, IL: University of Chicago Press, 1991), pp. 221–2.
13. *ūhathuḥ* appears 20 times in the *Ṛgveda*, mostly in stories where the Aśvins *bring* people out of danger (ten times), or *bring* assistance to them (five times). Such help includes a horse, gods, and a wife, Kāmadyu.
14. *RV* 1: 118, 6c and *RV* 1: 182, 6d.
15. This formula, 'we have crossed to the far side of darkness' (*atāriṣma tamasas pāram asya*), occurs at *RV* 1: 92, 6a; *RV* 1: 183, 6a; *RV* 1: 184, 6a; and *RV* 7: 73, 1a.
16. *upo adṛśran tamasaś cid antāḥ*, *RV* 7: 67, 2a.
17. *RV* 1: 112, 7 and 16; *RV* 1: 116, 8; *RV* 1: 117, 3; *RV* 1: 118, 7; *RV* 1: 119, 6; *RV* 1: 180, 4; *RV* 5: 73, 6; *RV* 5: 78, 4; *RV* 7: 68, 5; *RV* 7: 69, 4; *RV* 7: 71, 5; *RV* 8: 73, 3, 7, and 8; *RV* 10: 39, 9; *RV* 10: 80, 3.
18. Jamison: *Ravenous Hyenas*, p. 229 note 149. Geldner had also considered this interpretation. 'In the Atri myth however, it means the fire (or the hot pot) into which Atri fell,' Geldner: *Rig-Veda*, vol. 1, p. 258, note to *RV* 1: 180, 4ab.
19. 'They let Atri go' (*RV* 1: 112, 16ab), 'they released Atri from the pit' (*RV* 1: 117, 3b).
20. *aṃhas* (*RV* 1: 117, 3a; *RV* 7: 71, 5c).
21. *tamas* (*RV* 7: 71, 5c).
22. Words based on the root *oman* are used almost exclusively in the Atri story (five times); otherwise they are used twice of medicines (administered by the Aśvins at *RV* 1: 34, 6c and by the Waters at 6: 50, 7a), and once of Agni's helpers (5: 43, 13b). Except for the last case, the *oman*-words will in effect mean 'cool(ing)', as Jamison points out. See Jamison: *Ravenous Hyenas*, p. 230 note 152. Geldner

refers to *oman* as 'a catch word in the Atri myth', Geldner: *Rig-Veda*, vol. 1, p. note to *RV* 1: 34, 6c.

23. Jamison: *Ravenous Hyenas*, pp. 240–1.
24. Geldner: *Rig-Veda*, vol. 1, p. 258, note to *RV* 1: 180, 4ab.
25. *RV* 5: 30, 15; *TS* 1: 6, 12^2.
26. This line could also mean, however, that they '(made) the cooking-pot sweet, and kept it away from Atri.' See Geldner: *Rig-Veda*, vol. 1, p. 259, note to *RV* 1: 180, 4ab.
27. Geldner: *Rig-Veda*, vol. 2, p. 243, note to *RV* 7: 68, 5a.
28. More properly, this early and simpler Ṛgvedic form of the *Pravargya* ritual should be called the *Gharma* ritual. See Houben, Jan E.M., 'On the Earliest Attestable Forms of the Pravargya Ritual: Ṛg-Vedic References to the Gharma-Pravargya, especially in the Atri-family Book (Book 5)', *Indo-Iranian Journal* 43 (2000), p. 2.
29. Viśvāmitra reminds Indra that his people always offer hot milk, unlike the impious Kīkaṭa people: 'What do the cows do for you among the Kīkaṭas? Those people do not draw milk to be mixed (with soma), they do not heat up the hot milk (or cooking-pot, *gharma*)', *RV* 3: 53, 14b.
30. 'Heat it up' could refer to the hymn itself, or to the sun. If it means the sun, this would support van Buitenen's view that the *Pravargya* ritual is partly designed to encourage the heat of the sun. See Buitenen: *Pravargya*, pp. 28, 30, and 37.
31. 'You released Atri from the pit with his people' (*gaṇena*; *RV* 1: 117, 3); 'you brought him up with all his people' (*sarvagaṇam*; *RV* 1: 116, 8d).
32. Buitenen: *Pravargya*, p. 102; Staal, Frits, *Agni, the Vedic Ritual of the Fire Altar* (Berkeley, CA: Asian Humanities Press, 1983), p. 368.
33. Buitenen: *Pravargya*, p. 22.
34. The same thing happened to the unfortunate Antaka, 'perishing in a pit' (*jasamānam ārane*; *RV* 1: 112, 6a), and to Vandana, whom 'you two raised from a pit' (*ṛśayād ud ūhathur*; *RV* 10: 39, 8c). Such illtreatment of travellers was common in Vedic India and elsewhere. See Rau: *Staat und Gesellschaft*, pp. 29–30, and the story of Joseph at *Genesis* 37: 23–4.
35. Jamison: *Ravenous Hyenas*, pp. 233–5.
36. This possibility is briefly mentioned by Geldner and Jamison. See Geldner: *Rig-Veda*, vol. 3, p. 192, note to *RV* 10: 39, 9cd; Jamison: *Ravenous Hyenas*, p. 229, note 150.
37. 'The story of the *ṛbīsa* is transferred to Saptavadhri of the Atri family', Geldner: *Rig-Veda*, vol. 2, p. 400, note to *RV* 8: 73, 9.
38. *RV* 1: 116, 16d; *RV* 1: 157, 6a; *RV* 8: 18, 8a; *RV* 8: 86, 1a; *RV* 10: 39, 3d; *RV* 10: 39, 5b.
39. It is found in eight hymns: *RV* 1: 116, 10d; *RV* 1: 117, 13ab; *RV* 1: 118, 6d; *RV* 5: 74, 5; *RV* 5: 75, 5; *RV* 7: 68, 6; *RV* 7: 71, 5a; *RV* 10: 39, 4ab.
40. Witzel, Michael, 'On the origin of the literary device of the 'Frame Story' in Old Indian literature', in Falk, Harry (editor), *Hinduismus und Buddhismus, Festschrift für Ulrich Schneider* (Freiburg: Hedwig Falk, 1987), pp. 386–7.

41. See *bhuvanacyavānāṃ ghoṣo devānām*, 'the noise of the earth-shaking gods' (*RV* 10: 103, 9c). In this sense of 'shaking,' *cyu* can be used of sexual activity, which may explain the name Cyavana. See Witzel: 'Origin of the Frame Story', p. 387.
42. *punar yuvānaṃ cakrathuḥ* (*RV* 1: 117, 13b and, with the same words in a different order, *RV* 1: 118, 6d); *yuvā kṛtaḥ punar* (*RV* 5: 74, 5c); and with the verb *takṣ*, which has the same meaning as *kṛ*, *punar yuvānaṃ takṣathuḥ* (*RV* 10: 39, 4b).
43. *jujuruṣo* at *RV* 1: 116, 10a and *RV* 5: 74, 5a; *jurate* at *RV* 7: 68, 6a; *jarantam* at *RV* 1: 117, 13a; and the noun *jaraso* at *RV* 7: 71, 5a.
44. *vavrim prāmuñcatam drāpim iva*, *RV* 1: 116, 10ab; *vavrim aktam na muñcataḥ*, *RV* 5: 74, 5b.
45. See the famous account of transmigration at Bhagavadgītā 2, 22.
46. Jamison: *Ravenous Hyenas*, p. 174.
47. Jamison: *Ravenous Hyenas*, pp. 190–1.
48. Jamison: *Ravenous Hyenas*, pp. 156–7.
49. Jamison: *Ravenous Hyenas*, pp. 146.
50. See below, Chapter 4, 'The *Pravargya* (Heating Ritual)'.
51. The eagle brings soma to the followers of Indra (*Indrāvataḥ*, *RV* 4: 27, 4a), just as Mātariśvan brought fire to the human race. The eagle's gift of soma and Mātariśvan's gift of fire are explicitly compared at *RV* 1: 93, 6ab.
52. When it is discussing the soma sacrifice, the *Śatapatha Brāhmaṇa* interprets honey (*madhu*) as meaning soma (ŚB 4: 1, 5^{17-18}). In its account of the *Pravargya* ritual, on the other hand, it cites *RV* 1: 116, 12cd and says that honey is the secret doctrine of the *Pravargya* (ŚB 14: 1, 1^{25-26}). Behind this second interpretation lies the later equation of the *Pravargya* with the head of Dadhyañc.
53. 'Indra is the one and only soma-drinker, Indra is the life-long juice-drinker, among gods and men' (*RV* 8: 2, 4).
54. Anthony and Vinogradov: 'Birth of Chariot', p. 41.
55. This does not imply that the Ṛgvedic story-tellers, or their predecessors, had practised or even witnessed such a ritual, but stories about it had entered their tradition.
56. Central Asian **atharwan* (priest) → Vedic *atharvan*, Avestan *athravan*. See Witzel, Michael, 'Linguistic Evidence for Cultural Exchange in Prehistoric Western Central Asia', *Sino-Platonic Papers*, 129 (Philadelphia, PA: Deptartment of East Asian Languages and Civilizations, University of Pennsylvania, 2003), p. 38; Witzel, Michael, 'Early Loan Words in Western Central Asia: Indicators of Substrate Populations, Migrations, and Trade Relations', in Mair, Victor H. (editor). *Contact and Exchange in the Ancient World.* (Honolulu: University of Hawai'i Press, 2006), p. 173.
57. Central Asian **anću* (soma plant) → Vedic *aṃśu*, Avestan *ąsu*. See Witzel: 'Linguistic Evidence', p. 27; Witzel: 'Early Loan Words', p. 173; Staal: *Discovering the Vedas*, pp. 28–9.
58. Sanskrit *hotar* is cognate with Avestan *zaotar*, and both the Indian and the Iranian priests know how to extract soma juice (Sanskrit *soma*, Avestan *haoma*)

from the soma plant (Sanskrit *aṃśu*, Avestan *ąsu*). From this shared terminology, we can conclude that the Indo-Iranian **jhautar* priests were taught by the Central Asian **atharwan* priests how to get Indo-Iranian **sauma* from the Central Asian soma plant (**anću*). This is not simply a Vedic myth. The story is Central Asian and Indo-Iranian, and it must date from before the twentieth century BC when the common Indo-Iranian language was replaced by the separate Indian and Iranian languages.

59. Witzel: 'Development of the Vedic Canon', pp. 291–3.
60. Oldenberg: *Religion des Veda*, pp. 359–60; Thite, Ganesh Umakant, 'Animal-Sacrifice in the Brāhmaṇa Texts', *Numen* 17 (1970), p. 144; Witzel, Michael, 'The case of the shattered head', *Studien zur Indologie und Iranistik* (1987), pp. 390–1; Heesterman: *Broken World*, pp. 72–3. See below, Chapter 4, 'The *Āśvinagraha* (Aśvin Cup)'.
61. Thite: 'Animal-Sacrifice', pp. 151–2. For the substitutions running from man to goat to rice, see Smith, Brian K., and Doniger, Wendy, 'Sacrifice and Substitution: Ritual Mystification and Mythical Demystification', *Numen* 36 (1989), pp. 199–203. Witzel cites the late Vedic *Vādhūla Brāhmaṇa*, which tells how the gods agreed to accept a horse instead of a man (as in the story of Dadhyañc), then a goat instead of a horse, and finally an animal figurine made of rice, barley or clay. See Witzel: 'The case of the shattered head', pp. 391–2. For a modern example of substitution (rice flour for goats) see Staal: *Agni*, vol. 1, p. 303, and vol. 2, p. 465.
62. Thite: 'Animal-Sacrifice', pp. 148–51; Witzel: 'The case of the shattered head', p. 412 note 103. We find similar substitutions elsewhere – a ram is substituted for Isaac in Israel, a deer for Iphigeneia in Greece.
63. 'The heroes (the Maruts) went to Śaryaṇāvant with its good soma' (*suṣome śaryaṇāvati*, *RV* 8: 7, 29). Indra, a connoisseur whose judgement may be trusted, enjoys drinking soma there (*RV* 8: 36, 9; *RV* 8: 64, 11; *RV* 9: 113, 1).
64. See Geldner: *Rig-Veda*, vol. 3, p. 207, note to *RV* 10: 48, 10ab.
65. See below, Chapter 4, 'The *Pravargya* (Heating Ritual)'.
66. 'Indra and the Aśvins represent the two main types of divine intervention in human affairs', Oldenberg: *Religion des Veda*, p. 56 note 1.
67. Yama and Manu are alternative ancestors of the human race, though their father, Vivasvant, is also included among 'mortals' at *RV* 10: 17, 2a. Avestan texts have Yima alone as the first human, and the *Ṛgveda* views Manu alone as the ancestor of the living. Yama, in contrast, is the first dead person, the king of all dead ancestors.
68. See the related word, *sajātya* ('man of the same family', 'clansman') at *RV* 8: 83, 7a, where Indra, Viṣṇu, the Maruts and the Aśvins are asked to look after the poet's clansmen (*sajātyānām*). The term also occurs at *RV* 10: 39, 6c, where Ghoṣā laments that she is without clansmen (*asajātyā*).
69. *RV* 8: 18, 19c says that the Kāṇva poets and the divine Ādityas belong to the 'same family' (*sajātiye*). *RV* 8: 27, 10a goes even further, because now the Kāṇvas belong to the 'same family' (*sajātiyam*) as all the gods and enjoy

'friendship' (*āpiyam*) with them. These exaggerated claims and the implicit acknowledgement that *sajātiyam* does not mean much more than 'friendship', warn us not to take too seriously any claims of belonging to the same family as the gods.

70. Geldner: *Rig-Veda*, vol. 2, p. 78, note to *RV* 5: 73, 4d.
71. This phrase 'at the criticial moment' (*paritakmiyāyām*) occurs only six times in the *Ṛgveda*. It refers to timely interventions by Indra (*RV* 4: 41, 6d; *RV* 5: 31, 11a; and *RV* 6: 24, 9d) and by the Aśvins (*RV* 1: 116, 15b; *RV* 4: 43, 3b; and *RV* 7: 69, 4b). All other instances of the word *paritakmyā* (apart from these six occurences in the locative case) refer to stories involving Indra (*RV* 5: 30, 13d and 14a; *RV* 10: 108, 1c).
72. Dadhyañc is the son of Atharvan, the first fire-priest (*dadhyaṅ* [. . .] *ātharvaṇo*, *RV* 1: 116, 12c; *ātharvaṇāya dadhīce*, *RV* 1: 117, 22; *dadhiaṅṅ ṛṣiḥ* [. . .] *atharvaṇaḥ*, *RV* 6: 16, 14ab). Dadhyañc himself is one of the first humans to offer soma (*RV* 9: 108, 4a).
73. *RV* 1: 116, 16d; *RV* 1: 157, 6a; *RV* 8: 18, 8a; *RV* 8: 86, 1a; *RV* 10: 39, 3d and 5b.
74. *RV* 8: 9, 6b; *RV* 8: 22, 10d.
75. Contrast the dangerous Rudra (*RV* 2: 33, 4ab; *RV* 5: 42, 11a; *RV* 7: 46, 3ab and d) with the healing Rudra (*RV* 2: 33, 4cd; *RV* 5: 42, 11b; *RV* 7: 46, 3c).
76. 'You two killed the son of Viṣvāc with poison' (*RV* 1: 117, 16d).
77. In the *Brāhmaṇa* period, carpenters are regarded as impure and are not allowed to perform a sacrifice. See Rau: *Staat und Gesellschaft*, p. 28.
78. The Hotar priests of the *Ṛgveda* form an alliance with the doctors of the Atharvan tradition against the Adhvaryu priests, whose Yajurvedic texts denounce medicine. See Witzel: 'Development of the Vedic Canon', pp. 292–3.
79. Agni is typically described as the divine Hotar corresponding to the human one.
80. Presumably, one of the Aśvins acts as the Adhvaryu, and the other as his assistant, the Pratiprasthātar.
81. Geldner: *Rig-Veda*, vol. 1, p. 106, note to *RV* 1: 83, 3ab.
82. Geldner: *Rig-Veda*, vol. 1, p. 202, notes to *RV* 1: 144, 3ab and 4ab. Geldner suggests that 'the two of equal age' might refer to the two arms of the priest lighting the fire (note to 3ab).
83. Oldenberg: *Religion des Veda*, pp. 388–9. The word 'Hotar' means the priest who makes libations (*hu, juhoti*). See *EWA*, vol. 2, p. 821 under *hótar-* and *hótrā*. He was later restricted to reciting Ṛgvedic verses, and his other tasks were assigned to the Adhvaryu. See Oldenberg: *Religion des Veda*, p. 386.
84. The adjective *supāṇi* occurs eight times in the *Ṛgveda*. It is used of Tvaṣṭar (three times), and also of the Aśvins (here alone) and Savitar (twice). The Aśvins and Savitar appear together in the Sāvitra formula of the Adhvaryus: 'on the impulse of Savitar, with the arms of the Aśvins, with the hands of Pūṣan.' The remaining two occurrences refer to Mitra and Varuṇa.
85. *Suhasta/suhastya* occurs 16 times in the *Ṛgveda*, six times of the Ṛbhus and eight times of an Adhvaryu priest.

86. Witzel, Michael, 'Early Sanskritization. Origins and Development of the Kuru State', *Electronic Journal of Vedic Studies* 1–4 (1995), pp. 9–10; Witzel: 'Development of the Vedic Canon', pp. 266–8.

Chapter 4 The Aśvins in Vedic Ritual

1. Witzel: 'Early Sanskritization', pp. 11–12. This division is based on culture (Witzel: *Das alte Indien*, p. 28) and on religious behaviour (Witzel: 'Early Sanskritization', p. 260 note 16). So a man with a Sanskrit name may be called an 'outsider' (*dāsa*), while someone with a non-Sanskrit name may be included as an *ārya*. See Witzel, Michael, 'Rgvedic History: Poets, Chieftains and Polities', in Erdosy, George (editor), *The Indo-Aryans of Ancient South Asia. Language, Material Culture and Ethnicity* (Berlin: Walter de Gruyter, 1995), pp. 325–6. Parpola suggests that the 'outsiders' (Dāsas, Dasyus, Paṇis) were people who spoke a different dialect of Indo-Iranian (or perhaps merely a different Sanskrit dialect) and worshipped different gods. See Parpola: 'Aryans and soma', pp. 367–9. In either case, the division between *ārya* and *dāsa* has nothing to do with race.
2. Rau: *Staat und Gesellschaft*, pp. 34–5 (the Vaiśyas are 'food'), p. 36 (the Brahmins and Kṣatriyas must co-operate because they exploit the same 'food'). See Witzel: 'Early Sanskritization', p. 9 (four classes), and pp. 5 and 9 (Brahmin-Kṣatriya alliance); Witzel: 'Development of the Vedic Canon', p. 267 (four classes), and p. 294 (Brahmin-Kṣatriya alliance).
3. Witzel: 'Early Sanskritization', pp. 8–16.
4. *Śruta* means 'heard', so the term *śrauta* means those traditional beliefs that had been handed down orally and 'heard' by each new generation.
5. Witzel: 'Origin of the Frame Story', pp. 382–4; Jamison, Stephanie, and Witzel, Michael, (www.people.fas.harvard.edu/witzel/vedica.pdf, 1992) p. 37.
6. Bloomfield, Maurice, *Hymns of the Atharva-Veda* (Delhi: Motilal Banarsidass, 1897 [2000]), pp. xxvi–xxvii; Witzel: 'Development of the Vedic Canon', p. 277 note 85. The Aṅgiras and Bhṛgu families are the most important composers of the *Ṛgveda* and of the *Atharvaveda*. See Witzel: 'Development of the Vedic Canon', p. 292; Witzel: 'Ṛgvedic history', p. 316. For the medicinal magic (*bheṣaja*) of the *Atharaveda*, see Bloomfield: *Atharva-Veda*, pp. xxviii–xxi;. The word *bheṣaja* can even be used as a synonym for the *Atharvaveda*, see Bloomfield: *Atharva-Veda*, p. xxi.
7. Witzel: 'Development of the Vedic Canon', p. 291.
8. The *Atharvaveda Saṃhitā* usually refers to itself as the 'Veda of the Atharvans and Aṅgirasas' (*atharvāṅgirasaveda*), or simply the 'Veda of the Atharvans' (*atharvaveda*). See Bloomfield: *Atharva-Veda*, pp. xvii–xviii.
9. Witzel: 'Development of the Vedic Canon', pp. 291–2.
10. Witzel: 'Development of the Vedic Canon', p. 275 and note 77.
11. Witzel: 'Development of the Vedic Canon', p. 291.

12. Caland, Willem, and Henry, Victor. *L'agniṣṭoma* (Paris: Ernest Leroux, 1906), pp. 162–4.
13. Caland and Henry: *L'agniṣṭoma*, pp. 169–81. It is called the Outdoor Chant because, unlike all the other chants, it is sung outside the Recitation Hut (*sadas*) of the priests; and it is the Purifying Chant because while the Samavedic priests are singing it, others are purifying the soma from the main vat by pouring it through a filter into a vat called the Container of the Purified (Soma), the *pūtabhṛt*.
14. Caland and Henry: *L'agniṣṭoma*, pp. 182–3.
15. *TS* 6: 4, 7–8.
16. Heesterman, J.C., 'Vrātya and Sacrifice', *Indo-Iranian Journal* 6 (1962), pp. 18–19; Heesterman: *Broken World*, p. 72; Schmidt, Hans Peter, 'Vedic *Pāthas*', *Indo-Iranian Journal* 15 (1973), pp. 35–8. The gruesome detail, that bits of flesh would stick to the post and hatchet during a beheading, is presented as perfectly normal (*RV* 1: 162, 9). See Schmidt: 'Vedic *Pāthas*', p. 37.
17. *RV* 10: 171, 2. The passage emphasizes the gory elements. See Witzel: 'Early Indian History', p. 391.
18. Oldenberg: *Religion des Veda*, pp. 359–60; Thite, Ganesh Umakant, 'Animal-Sacrifice in the Brāhmaṇa Texts', *Numen* 17 (1970), p. 144; Witzel: 'Early Indian history', pp. 390–1; Heesterman: *Broken World*, pp. 72–3.
19. This development is somewhat similar to the way in which the American and Chinese governments have adopted the discreet 'medical' procedure of lethal injection, whereas the Saudi and Iranian governments have maintained more explicit ways of killing their victims.
20. *TS* 2: 3, 11^{2-3}; *TS* 2: 6, 3^{6}; *TS* 4: 1, 7^{4}; and *TS* 5: 3, 1^{1}.
21. In the passage that describes the Aśvins as *ānujāvara*, Keith strangely translates it as 'infirm', Keith, Arthur Berriedale, *The Veda of the Black Yajus School, Entitled Taittiriya Sanhita* (Cambridge, MA: Harvard University Press, 1914), p. 578. Elsewhere, however, he translates it as 'youngest' (*TS* 6: 6, 11^{2}), 'low(est) in rank' (*TS* 2: 3, 4^{2-4}), and 'inferior' (*TS* 7: 2, 10^{2}).
22. The cup for Indra and Vayu should be first if a man wants harmony among his offspring or is ill (the Indra–Vayu cup is, of course, first in a normal soma sacrifice); the cup for Mitra and Varuṇa should be first if someone dies; and the cup for the Aśvins should be first if the sacrificer is inferior in rank (*TS* 7: 2, 7^{1-2}).
23. Immediately after the passage about Indra, we hear that if a Brahmin is lower in rank, he must offer rice-shoots to Bṛhaspati (*TS* 2: 3, 4^{4}). In this case, however, there is no suggestion that Bṛhaspati himself suffers from any feelings of inferiority, temporary or otherwise. The 'lower-ranking' Brahmin prays to him simply because he is the god of the Brahmins.
24. In the case of the 'low-ranking' Brahmin, as with Indra's 'low-ranking' warlord, Bṛhaspati leads him to the forefront *of his colleagues* (*agraṃ samānānām*), in other words, to the forefront of the *top-ranking* Brahmins.

25. The warlords and the priests were united in their contempt for the rest of the population. See Rau: *Staat und Gesellschaft,* pp. 117–18; Falk: *Bruderschaft und Würfelspiel*, p. 192. Witzel: Early Sanskritization', p. 9; Witzel: 'Development of the Vedic Canon', p. 294.
26. *TS* 2: 6, 4[1]; *TS* 6: 2, 10[1]; *TS* 6: 3, 6[3]; and *TS* 6: 4, 4[1].
27. Witzel: 'Development of the Vedic Canon', p. 267 note 46.
28. Dumézil: *M&E I. L'idéologie des trois fonctions*, pp. 48–52 and 57–9.
29. Oldenberg: *Religion des Veda*, p. 386; Jamison and Witzel: *Vedic Hinduism*, p. 37; Witzel: 'Development of the Vedic Canon', p. 291.
30. Elsewhere, *madhu* will be identified not as soma, but as the hot milk offering in the *Pravargya* ritual (*ŚB* 14: 1, 1[25]).
31. He no longer plays a role in the soma sacrifice, but he is given the new function of teaching the Aśvins about the *Pravargya* ritual (*ŚB* 14: 1, 1[25]).
32. We are promised (at *ŚB* 4: 1, 5[15]) that the explanation will come 'in the chapter on the Verses Chanted by Day' (*divākīrtyas*). In fact, it comes in the chapter on the *Pravargya* (*ŚB* 14: 1, 1).
33. In the *Ṛgveda* this right is not questioned, but in the *Śatapatha Brāhmaṇa* it has to be explained and justified, because the earlier Yajurvedic tradition represented by the *Taittirīya Saṃhitā* had already declared the Aśvins ineligible.
34. Houben: 'Earliest Pravargya Ritual', p. 2.
35. Witzel: 'Early Sanskritization', p. 15 note 93; Houben: 'Earliest Pravargya Ritual', pp. 6–7.
36. Gonda, Jaan, 'A Propos of the Mantras in the Pravargya Section of the Ṛgveda Brāhmaṇas', *Indo-Iranian Journal* 21 (1979), pp. 248 and 262.
37. Sacred grass (Sanskrit *barhiṣ*, Avestan *baresman*) was spread out on the ground in Indian and Iranian rituals.
38. The victim's omentum (the membrane protecting its stomach) was offered to the gods, both in Indian and Iranian sacrifice. See Oldenberg: *Religion des Veda*, pp. 360–1.
39. Paradoxically, but not surprisingly, the Atris themselves are ignored. See Witzel: 'Development of the Vedic Canon', p. 292 note 155.
40. Buitenen, J. A. B. van, *The Pravargya, an ancient Indian iconic ritual* (Poona: Deccan College Postgraduate and Research Institute, 1968), p. 31; Houben: 'Earliest Pravargya Ritual', pp. 3–4.
41. Gonda: 'Pravargya Mantras', pp. 249–51.
42. Houben argues that the *Pravargya* had already been incorporated into the soma sacrifice during the Early Vedic period, see Houben: 'Earliest Pravargya Ritual', pp. 3 and 13–14; Gonda is doubtful, see Gonda: 'Pravargya Mantras', p. 237; and van Buitenen believes that this does not happen till after the *Ṛgveda* and *Atharvaveda* have been compiled, see Buitenen: *Pravargya*, p. 6.
43. Witzel points out that the *Pravargya* has merged with the soma sacrifice by the time of the *Yajurveda Saṃhitās*. See Witzel: 'Origin of the Frame Story', p. 390 and note 27.

44. Buitenen: *Pravargya*, p. 6; Witzel: 'Origin of the Frame Story', p. 408.
45. Buitenen: *Pravargya*, p. 2.
46. Caland and Henry: *L'agniṣṭoma*, pp. 283; Buitenen: *Pravargya*, pp. 142–4.
47. Buitenen: *Pravargya*, p. 3.
48. Buitenen: *Pravargya*, p. 4.
49. The *Pravargya* of the Pressing Day, a tiny episode of the soma sacrifice, had merely balanced the *Dadhigharma*, another minor episode. The elaborate *Upasad Pravargya*, however, is now balancing all the episodes of the entire soma sacrifice! In each case, Indra represents the other side of the comparison (Indra's *Dadhigharma*, Indra's Soma Sacrifice).
50. Caland and Henry: *L'agniṣṭoma*, p. 55.
51. Caland and Henry: *L'agniṣṭoma*, p. 77. They aptly describe this removal (*pravargyodvāsanam*) as the 'banishment' of the *Pravargya*.
52. Caland and Henry: *L'agniṣṭoma*, p. 78.
53. Caland and Henry: *L'agniṣṭoma*, pp. 110–16.
54. Gonda: 'Pravargya Mantras', pp. 253–5 and 263. He tentatively suggests that they 'wished to bring about by means of its recitation an analogous psychical process', Gonda: 'Pravargya Mantras', p. 255.
55. The words describing their activities are almost identical (except that the verb 'put' is past with the gods and present with the priests): 'they put it together, and after having put it together they spoke.' *taṃ saṃjabhrus, taṃ sambhṛtyocur* (gods and sacrifice); *gharmaṃ sambharatas, taṃ sambhṛtyāhatur* (Adhvaryus and *Pravargya*).
56. Malamoud discusses this acquisition of a new body in the context of the soma sacrifice. See Malamoud, Charles, *Cooking the World. Ritual and Thought in Ancient India*, translated by David White (New York, NY: Oxford University Press, 1996), pp. 101 and 183.
57. Witzel: 'Early Sanskritization', p. 15 and note 93.
58. The *mahāvira* pot 'overshadows [...] the hot milk offering itself', Buitenen: *Pravargya*, p. 9.
59. *Apastambha Śrauta Sūtra* 15: 7. The *Śatapatha Brāhmaṇa* says that the *Pravargya* is the head of the sacrifice and soma is its body, so the head must be higher than the body (*ŚB* 14: 1, 3^{12}). The Emperor's Throne is higher (shoulder-high, *ŚB* 14: 1, 3^{10}) than the King's Throne (navel-high, *ŚB* 3: 3, 4^{28}), but the *Śatapatha Brāhmaṇa* uses this contrast between head and body to explain why the Emperor's Throne is placed to the north (*uttara*, geographically 'higher') rather than why it is physically higher (*uttara*) from the ground (*ŚB* 14: 1, 3^{12}).
60. 'This restriction, which is repeated throughout the texts, recalls an earlier Agniṣṭoma where the Pravargya was unheard of', Buitenen: *Pravargya*, p. 6.
61. In a *sattra*, 'they [the participants] make an agreement with him [their leader] to share all its benefits', Falk: *Bruderschaft und Würfelspiel*, pp. 34–5.
62. This part is borrowed from the explanation of the Aśvin Cup at *Taittirīya Saṃhitā* 6: 4, 9. See Witzel: 'Origin of the Frame Story', p. 391 note 29; Houben, Jan E.M., *The Pravargya Brāhmaṇa of the Taittirīya Āraṇyaka: an*

Ancient Commentary on the Pravargya Ritual (Delhi: Motilal Banarsidass, 1991), p. 106 note 8.

63. Houben: *Pravargya Brāhmaṇa*, pp. 45–8.
64. Coomaraswamy suggests that this should be translated as 'Soma-Makha' or 'Makha-Viṣṇu'. See Coomaraswamy, Ananda K., 'Angel and Titan: an Essay in Vedic Ontology', *Journal of the American Oriental Society* 55 (1935), p. 376. It is true that Soma, Makha, and Viṣṇu will be equated in the *Śatapatha Brāhmaṇa*, but it ruins the story if this is stated right from the beginning.
65. The *Śatapatha Brāhmaṇa* goes on to explain that this is the etymology of Indra's name *Maghavān* ('generous').
66. *RV* 10: 171, 2.
67. Houben: 'Earliest Pravargya Ritual', p. 17.
68. There is some dispute over whether the man to be initiated is a young student priest, learning how to perform the *Pravargya*, or a mature householder.
69. The exact same wording appears once again towards the end of Chapter 19, and also at *Apastambha Śrauta Sūtra* 15: 20, 2 and 8.
70. Witzel: 'Origin of the Frame Story', pp. 404–5.
71. Witzel: 'Origin of the Frame Story', pp. 390–1.
72. Witzel: 'Origin of the Frame Story', pp. 407–8 and 412–3.
73. If the Hotar has been trained in the Aitareya school, this prayer is 100 stanzas long; if he belongs to the Kauṣītaki school, it goes on for 360 stanzas. See Caland and Henry: *L'agniṣṭoma*, pp. 130–2 and 417–59.
74. Both the Recitation Hut (*sadas*) and the Soma Hut (*havirdhāna*) are rooms inside the Great Altar Hall (*mahāvedi*). Another exception to the general rule is the Outdoor Purifying Chant (*bahiṣpavamānastotra*), which is sung at the north-eastern corner of the Great Altar Hall (*mahāvedi*) rather than in the Recitation Hut (*sadas*).
75. *Apastambha Śrauta Sūtra* 12: 3, 14.
76. *Aitareya Brāhmaṇa* 2: 15.
77. *Aitareya Brāhmaṇa* 2: 16; *Kauṣītaki Brāhmaṇa* 11: 4.
78. *Kauṣītaki Brāhmaṇa* 11: 8.
79. *devāh prātaryāvāṇaḥ* (*Aitareya Brāhmaṇa* 2: 15).
80. Bodewitz: *Agnihotra*, pp. 2–3.
81. *Kauṣītaki Brāhmaṇa* 11: 2.
82. Usually, the three representative gods are Agni, Indra or Vāyu, and Sūrya. See *Nirukta* 7: 5; *Bṛhaddevatā* 1: 5; Macdonell: *Vedic Mythology*, p. 19.
83. *Aitareya Brāhmaṇa* 2: 15; *Jaiminīya Brāhmaṇa* 1: 211. It is very common for *Brāhmaṇas* to represent a ritual as a battle between the gods and the Asuras.
84. The chant is called the *Agniṣṭoma* chant, see Caland and Henry: *L'agniṣṭoma*, pp. 369–71; the hymn is the *Āgnimārutaśastra*, Caland and Henry: *L'agniṣṭoma*, pp. 372–9.
85. Staal: *Agni*, vol. 1, pp. 680–2.
86. *Jaiminīya Brāhmaṇa* 1: 208.
87. *Jaiminīya Brāhmaṇa* 1: 212.

88. The Morning Prayer is 100 or 360 verses long, depending on what school the Hotar belongs to, see note 74 above.
89. *Śatapatha Brāhmaṇa* 11: 5, 5^9. The Maitrāvaruṇa priest should recite the Morning Prayer under his breath while the Hotar is reciting the Aśvin Hymn (*Śatapatha Brāhmaṇa* 11: 5, 5^{10}). This will counteract the error of 'pushing the Morning Prayer from its place'.
90. *Jaiminīya Brāhmaṇa* 1: 210. It had explained the Twilight Chant in the same way.
91. In the Ṛgvedic Brāhmaṇas the married couple are Soma and Sūryā (*Aitareya Brāhmaṇa* 4: 7; *Kauṣītaki Brāhmaṇa* 18: 1); in the Samavedic Brāhmaṇa, they are Bṛhaspati and Uṣas (*Jaiminīya Brāhmaṇa* 1: 213).
92. *Jaiminīya Brāhmaṇa* 1: 213.
93. *Aitareya Brāhmaṇa* 4: 8; *Jaiminīya Brāhmaṇa* 1: 210 and 213.
94. The particular type of *surā* used in the *Sautrāmaṇī* rite may have been a stronger form of distilled alcohol, one that was almost poisonous (*viṣa*). See Oort, Marianne S., 'Surā in the Paippalāda Saṃhitā of the Atharvaveda', *Journal of the American Oriental Society* 122 (2002), pp. 355–60.
95. When it was performed on its own as a cure for soma sickness, it was called the *kaukilī-sautrāmaṇī*; when it was performed after a royal consecration, it was called the *caraka-sautrāmaṇī*.
96. 'You are soma' (*TB* 2: 6, 1), etc. See Dumont, Paul-Emile, 'The Kaukilī-Sautrāmaṇī in the Taittirīya-Brāhmaṇa', *Proceedings of the American Philosophical Society* 109 (1965), p. 311; and *ĀpŚS* 19: 1, 1 and 19: 5, 7.
97. A similar bath in broth was part of the Irish coronation ceremonies (Gerald of Wales, *Topographia Hibernica* 3: 25). Although in Ireland the victim was a horse, this part of the Irish ritual is closer to the *Sautrāmaṇī* or the *Rājāsūya* than it is to the *Aśvamedha*, with which it is often compared. This comparison with the *Aśvamedha* is rightly rejected by Zimmer. See Zimmer, Stefan, 'Die Indogermanen und das Pferd – Befunde und Probleme', in Hänsel, Bernhard, and Zimmer, Stefan (editors), *Die Indogermanen und das Pferd. Festschrift fur Bernfried Schlerath* (Budapest: Archaeolingua Alapítvány, 1994), p. 31.
98. Keith: *Religion and Philosophy*, pp. 352–4; Dumont: 'Kaukilī-Sautrāmaṇī', pp. 309–11.
99. 'The *surā* is in general not employed in *çrāuta*-practices; it is *lāukika*, not *vāidika*, and everywhere in the worst repute possible,' Bloomfield: 'Interpretation of Veda', p. 152. In the *Śatapatha Brāhmaṇa*, soma is for Brahmins (12: 7, 2^2), milk for Kṣatriyas (12: 7, 3^8), and *surā* for Vaiśyas (12: 7, 3^{15}).
100. Bloomfield translates these lines as 'you two Açvins, drinking yourselves into a surfeit of *surā* with the *āsura* Namuci', Bloomfield: 'Interpretation of Veda', pp. 148–9.
101. '*vi-pā* means: to drink one liquid alone out of a mixture of liquids', Geldner: *Rig-Veda*, vol. 3, p. 363, note to *RV* 10: 131, 4a. He mentions the belief that if

geese were presented with a mixture of milk and water, they could extract the milk, leaving the water behind.

102. Geldner says that it means 'the power (effect) of brandy' or 'having the effect of brandy, spiked', Geldner: *Rig-Veda*, vol. 3, p. 363, note to *RV* 10: 131, 4a. In effect, *surāma* is a cocktail, a mixture containing *surā* as its active ingredient.
103. 'Namuci overpowered Indra at first by means of brandy. He probably offered him soma mixed with brandy, which the god could not tolerate [...] Because of this mixture, the soma became impure [...] The weakened Indra and the contaminated soma had to be healed [...] The blended soma could only be restored, that is made drinkable, by means of *vipānam* (compare *andhasor vipānam* Śat. 12, 7, 3, 4)', Geldner: *Rig-Veda*, vol. 3, p. 363, note to *RV* 10: 131, 4a.
104. 'In like manner, too, the priest is directed to draw the cups of *soma* and of *surā* so that they shall be interlinked or "married"...,' Fowler, Murray, 'The Role of Surā in the Myth of Namuci', *Journal of the American Oriental Society* 62 (1942), p. 40. The passage he cites (*Śatapatha Brāhmaṇa* 12: 7, 3^{15}) clearly refers to milk (equated with the warlords, *kṣatra*) and *surā* (equated with the people, *viś*), not soma and *surā*.
105. Dumont: 'Kaukilī-Sautrāmaṇī', p. 310.
106. Bloomfield: 'Interpretation of Veda', pp. 151–2.
107. From Mahidhara's commentary on *Vājasaneyi Saṃhitā* 10: 33, cited at Bloomfield: 'Interpretation of Veda', p. 152.
108. The full mantras are given at *Taittirīya Brāhmaṇa* 2: 6, 1d-e. See Dumont: 'Kaukilī-Sautrāmaṇī', p. 311.
109. Compare *asyendriyaṃ vīryaṃ* [...] *harāṇi* (12: 7, 1^{10}) with *etasmāt* [...] *indriyaṃ vīryaṃ krāmati* (12: 7, 2^{1}).
110. Dumont: 'Kaukilī-Sautrāmaṇī', p. 310.
111. The priest 'makes it (*surā*) a form of soma' (*somarūpaṃ evaināṃ karoti*, 12: 7, 3^{6}).
112. 'By faith alone he makes it (*parisrut*) soma' (*śraddhayaivainaṃ somaṃ karoti*, 12: 7, 3^{11}).
113. 'This drink *surā* seems inauspicious indeed for a Brahmin; he makes it auspicious, and takes it inside himself, saying "I am drinking king soma here"' (12: 8, 1^{5}). Brahmins constantly denounced *surā*, and some Brahmins even hired a substitute to drink it for them at the *Sautrāmaṇī*', Bloomfield: 'Interpretation of Veda', pp. 152–3.
114. 'Milk is indeed soma [...] by milk alone he gets soma' (*somo vai payo* [...] *payasaiva somapītham avarunddhe*, 12: 7, 3^{8}); 'the cups of milk are soma' (*somo vai payograhāḥ*, 12: 7, 3^{17}).
115. For example, in the five mantras recorded by *Taittirīya Brāhmaṇa* 2: 6, 1, all of which speak of 'soma' alone, the first refers to *surā*, the second refers to a mixture of milk and *surā*, the third to milk, and only the fourth and fifth (which speak of vomiting and diarrhoea) refer to real soma! See Dumont: 'Kaukilī-Sautrāmaṇī', p. 311.

116. As always, 'the mantras recited for the original also remain unchanged when there is a substitute', Smith and Doniger: 'Sacrifice and Substitution', p. 204. In the *Sautrāmaṇī* soma is the 'original' and *surā* is the 'substitute'.

Chapter 5 The Cult of the Dioskouroi

1. There was a fourth child, the equally famous Klutaimnēstra, but she is not associated with the Dioskouroi in early Greek art or literature.
2. This indoctrination was called the Spartan *agōgē* (guidance, direction). The young Spartans were treated almost like slaves, and were trained to endure violence and brutality. For the training, see Plutarch, *Life of Lycurgus* 16–18 and 24–5; Forrest, W.G., *A History of Sparta* (New York, NY: W.W. Norton & Company, 1968), pp. 51–3; Cartledge, Paul, *The Spartans. The World of the Warrior-Heroes of Ancient Greece, from Utopia to Crisis and Collapse* (Woodstock, NY: The Overlook Press, 2003), pp. 69–72. For the tension between their slave-like humiliation and preparation for full citizenship, see Vernant, Jean-Pierre, *Mortals and Immortals: Collected Essays*, edited by Froma I. Zeitlin (Princeton, NJ: Princeton University Press, 1991), pp. 229–43.
3. Forrest: *History of Sparta*, pp. 30–1; Cartledge: *Spartans*, pp. 28–32 and 72–6.
4. For the gratuitous killing of Helots by young Spartans, see Plutarch, *Life of Lycurgus* 28; Vidal-Naquet, Pierre, *The Black Hunter: Forms of Thought and Forms of Society in the Greek World*, translated by Andrew Szegedy-Maszak. (Baltimore, MD: Johns Hopkins University Press, 1986), pp. 149–50; Cartledge: *Spartans*, pp. 72.
5. Burkert: *Greek Religion*, pp. 262–3; Parker, Robert, 'Spartan Religion', in Powell, Anton (editor), *Classical Sparta. Techniques Behind Her Success* (Norman, OK: University of Oklahoma Press, 1989), pp. 148–50.
6. Pausanias 3: 17, 1–2; Burkert: *Greek Religion*, p. 140; Parker: 'Spartan Religion', p. 142; Köhne: *Dioskuren in der Griechischen Kunst*, p. 156 note 590. As patron of the city, Athēna was called Athēna Protector of the City (*Athēna Polioukhos*) and Athēna of the Bronze House (*Athēna Khalkioikos*). The latter title comes from the temple itself, which was of bronze.
7. Burkert: *Greek Religion*, pp. 144–5 (Apollōn) and pp. 150–1 (Artemis); Parker: 'Spartan Religion', p. 149.
8. Pausanias 3: 18, 9–19, 5; Parker: 'Spartan Religion', p. 146.
9. Parker points out that over 100,000 votive offerings were found at the temple. See Parker: 'Spartan Religion', p. 148.
10. The altar itself commemorated his transition from hero to god with a relief showing several gods escorting Huakinthos to heaven (Pausanias 3: 19, 4).
11. Nilsson, Martin P., *Geschichte der griechischen Religion. Erster Band. Die Religion Griechenlands bis auf die griechische Weltherrschaft* (Munich: C.H. Beck'sche Verlagsbuchhandlung, 1955), pp. 316–17; Nilsson, Martin P., *The Mycenaean Origin of Greek Mythology* (Berkeley, CA: University of California Press, 1972), p. 76.

12. Pausanias 3: 19, 3; Nilsson: *Geschichte der griechischen Religion*, p. 531.
13. Originally, the boys were divided into teams. One team had to steal cheese from the altar of Artemis while a second team used whips to stop them (Xenophon, *The Spartan Constitution* 2, 9). In later times, this competition was changed into an endurance test, during which all the young men were flogged till they bled (Pausanias 3: 16, 10–11). See Nilsson: *Geschichte der griechischen Religion*, pp. 488–9; Burkert: *Greek Religion*, p. 152; Parker: 'Spartan Religion', p. 148.
14. David, Ephraim, 'Laughter in Spartan Society', in Powell, Anton (editor), *Classical Sparta. Techniques Behind Her Success* (Norman, OK: University of Oklahoma Press, 1989), pp. 11–12; Parker: 'Spartan Religion', pp. 151–2; Vernant, Jean-Pierre, and Vidal-Naquet, Pierre, *Myth and Tragedy in Ancient Greece*, translated by Janet LLoyd (New York, NY: Zone Books, 1988), pp. 199–200.
15. The word *gumnopaidiai* is usually interpreted as the Festival of Naked Boys, from *paides*, 'boys', but Parker suggests that it really means the Festival of Naked Dances, from *paidiai*, 'games'. See Parker: 'Spartan Religion', pp. 149–50. In this context the term 'naked' (*gumnos*) probably means 'unarmed', which was a common way of distinguishing a young man from a mature hoplite warrior, who would be fully clothed in armour. See Vidal-Naquet: *Black Hunter*, pp. 113 and 117.
16. Nilsson: *Geschichte der griechischen Religion*, pp. 531–3; Burkert: *Greek Religion*, pp. 234–6; Parker: 'Spartan Religion', pp. 146 and 148.
17. Nilsson: *Geschichte der griechischen Religion*, p. 531; Parker: 'Spartan Religion', p. 148.
18. Pausanias 3: 11, 9; Xenophon *Hellenica* 6: 4, 16.
19. *mimēma* [. . .] *stratiōtikēs agōgēs* (Demetrius of Scepsis fr. 1 Gaede = Athenaeus 4: 141e). The connection between the religious festival and the military training is so close that Forrest uses the Karneia to help date the constitution of Lukourgos. See Forrest: *History of Sparta*, p. 58.
20. Nilsson: *Geschichte der griechischen Religion*, p. 406; Nilsson: *Mycenaean Origin*, pp. 76–7; Burkert: *Greek Religion*, p. 212; Hermary, Antoine, 'Dioskouroi,' in *Lexicon Iconographicum Mythologiae Classicae* (Zurich: Artemis, 1981), vol. 3, part 1, p. 567.
21. Hermary: 'Dioskouroi', p. 567.
22. Burkert: *Greek Religion*, p. 212.
23. The tomb of Tundareos was on the Spartan acropolis, and he was the legendary founder of the bronze temple of *Athēna Polioukhos*, Athēna Protector of the City, also known as *Athēna Khalkioikos*, Athēna of the Bronze House (Pausanias 3: 17, 4). Tundareos therefore plays a similar role to that of Erekhtheus in Athens. Erekhtheus was likewise an ancient king and shared a temple with *Athēna Polias*, Athēna Protector of the City (Homer, *Iliad* 2: 546–551).
24. Nilsson: *Geschichte der griechischen Religion*, p. 406; Burkert: *Greek Religion*, p. 213; Parker: 'Spartan Religion', p. 147; Köhne: *Dioskuren in der Griechischen Kunst*, p. 67.

25. Parker: 'Spartan Religion', p. 149; Köhne: *Dioskuren in der Griechischen Kunst*, p. 64.
26. Nilsson: *Geschichte der griechischen Religion*, p. 408; Parker: 'Spartan Religion', p. 142; Köhne: *Dioskuren in der Griechischen Kunst*, p. 67.
27. Nilsson remarks that the Dioskouroi were 'almost national gods', Nilsson: *Geschichte der griechischen Religion*, p. 408.
28. A thousand miniature reliefs were found at the shrine of Agamemnōn and his Spartan wife Alexandra, see Parker: 'Spartan Religion', p. 147. Pausanias notes how the Spartans alter Greek myths and take over heroes from other places (Pausanias 3: 13, 2). He pointedly refers to the Spartan shrine of Agamemnōn as 'a tomb which is supposedly that of Agamemnōn' (Pausanias 3: 19, 6). Pausanias had, of course, seen the 'real' tomb of Agamemnōn at Mycenae (Pausanias 2: 16, 6).
29. Parker: 'Spartan Religion', pp. 147–8. When other Greek states turned historical figures into semi-divine heroes, it was usually athletes that they worshipped! See Parker: 'Spartan Religion', p. 167 note 30.
30. The Delphic oracle is typically ambiguous on this matter, but decides on balance that he probably was a god (Herodotus 1: 65, 3). The Spartans have no doubts, erect a temple to him, and worship him as a god (Pausanias 3: 16, 6).
31. Alkman fr. 7 Campbell; Pindar, *Pythian Ode* 11: 63; Pindar, *Nemean Ode* 10: 56. Homer, speaking more loosely, says that they come from Lakedaimōn, without specifying which part of the state they come from (*Iliad* 3: 239).
32. Pausanias 3: 20, 2. A poem by Alkman of Sparta mentions the Dioskouroi in connection with a festival called the Phoibaia (Alkman fr. 5, 1 Campbell).
33. Alkman fr. 7 Campbell; Herodotus 6: 61, 3; Pausanias 3: 19, 9.
34. Alkman fr. 7 Campbell.
35. See LSJ (Greek-English Lexicon), under *'Phoibeios'*. The entry specifically mentions the temple at Therapnē as sacred to Phoibos, citing Herodotus 6: 61, 3, which speaks of the temple of Phoibos (*Phoibēion hīron*) near the temple of Helenē (*Helenēs hīron*). *Phoibaion* is the local, Doric form of *Phoibeion*.
36. Farnell: *Greek Hero Cults*, p. 231.
37. Artemis is Phoibē, just as her brother Apollōn is Phoibos, and one of her titles is Artemis of the Wetlands (*Artemis Limnaia*). There is a sanctuary of Artemis of the Wetlands near the theatre at Sparta (Pausanias 3: 14, 2), and the famous temple of Artemis Orthia is in the Wetlands Sanctuary (*Limnaion*, Pausanias 3: 16, 7). At Troizēn, the temple of Artemis Sarōnis is in the Wetlands of Phoibē (*Phoibaia limnē*, Pausanias 2: 30, 7). This is the place where Hippolutos, the eternal adolescent, rides his horse and worships Artemis (Euripides, *Hippolytus* 228–31). Phoibē, Artemis Limnaia, and adolescence are connected in Greek thought.
38. As we saw above, the young men have to go through the flogging initiation and they also perform masked dances at the Temple of Artemis Orthia. In Greek myth, it is also the place from which Thēseus abducts Helenē. She is

dancing for Artemis (Plutarch *Theseus* 31), which suggests that young women dance there as well as young men. See Nilsson: *Geschichte der griechischen Religion*, p. 489.

39. Nilsson: *Geschichte der griechischen Religion*, p. 493–4.
40. Pausanias 3: 14, 9 and 3: 20, 2. Burkert strangely states that the young men of Sparta sacrifice a dog to Phoibē, see Burkert: *Greek Religion*, p. 213. One of the texts he cites (Pausanias 3: 14, 8f, cited at Burkert: *Greek Religion*, p. 433 n.15) says that they sacrifice a puppy to Enualios, and the other (Pausanias 3: 16, 1) speaks of young women worshipping Phoibē and Hilaeira in Sparta itself, not in the Phoibaion at Therapnē.
41. Pausanias 3: 19, 7. Köhne suggests that this ancient statue of Arēs Thēritas was in fact the statue of Enualios in the Phoibaion, see Köhne: *Dioskuren in der Griechischen Kunst*, p. 62.
42. Pausanias 3: 14, 9–10.
43. Pausanias 3: 20, 1.
44. Pausanias 3: 13, 1. The tomb reminds us that Kastōr was often regarded as the only mortal twin, but Pausanias tells us that in Sparta both twins had been mortal, and both had been elevated to divinity forty years after their death.
45. Pausanias 3: 12, 10.
46. Pausanias 3: 14, 6.
47. Nilsson: *Geschichte der griechischen Religion*, p. 532; Burkert: *Greek Religion*, pp. 234–5.
48. Nilsson: *Geschichte der griechischen Religion*, p. 499.
49. Pausanias 3: 14, 7.
50. Plato *Laws* 7: 796b.
51. Epicharmus, *Mousai* fr. 92 *PCG*.
52. Spartan Museum Inscription 544. See Tod, M.N., and Wace, A.J.B., *A Catalogue of the Sparta Museum* (Rome: 'L'Erma' di Bretschneider, 1968), p. 70.
53. Pausanias 4: 27, 2.
54. The Dioskouroi are 'the stewards of Sparta with its spacious dancing-floors', and along with the super-athlete Hēraklēs and the young god Hermēs, they 'make sure that the principles of athletic competition prevail' (Pindar, *Nemean Ode* 10: 52–53).
55. Pindar, *Olympian Ode* 3: 36.
56. Farnell: *Greek Hero Cults*, p. 230.
57. Pausanias 3: 16, 1–2.
58. Pausanias 3: 16, 1.
59. Parker: 'Spartan Religion', p. 150. The White Horse Girls and the Girls of Dionusus sacrifice to the hero who first introduced the cult of Dionusus to Sparta (Pausanias 3: 13, 7).
60. Tod and Wace: *Catalogue of the Sparta Museum*, p. 43, Spartan Museum Number 220.
61. Nilsson: *Geschichte der griechischen Religion*, p. 215. In Sparta, 'the two gods' can only be the Dioskouroi.

62. See below on the Athenian girls who served as the 'bears' of Artemis at Braurōn, and the Spartan boys who are 'bullocks' and 'foxes' in the wild countryside of Lakōnia.
63. Pausanias 3: 1, 5–6. The twins Eurusthenēs and Proklēs were the first Dorian kings of Sparta because their father, Aristodēmos, died before he saw the promised land.
64. Farnell: *Greek Hero Cults*, pp. 195–6; Nilsson: *Geschichte der griechischen Religion*, p. 410; Burkert: *Greek Religion*, p. 212; Parker: 'Spartan Religion', p. 147.
65. Herodotus 5: 75, 2.
66. Herodotus 5: 75, 2.
67. 'In Sparta, however, the Dioskouroi experienced a metamorphosis that reminds us of the one that changed the Minoan house and snake goddess into the military protector of the king and the city,' Nilsson: *Geschichte der griechischen Religion*, p. 410.
68. Pausanias 3: 13, 6.
69. Farnell: *Greek Hero Cults*, p. 192. Instead of using the generic term *boulē*, the Spartans called their council the *Gerousia*, or Council of Old Men (*gerontes*).
70. Vidal-Naquet: *Black Hunter*, pp. 113 and 141.
71. Vidal-Naquet: *Black Hunter*, p. 149 and p. 156 note 66.
72. Burkert: *Greek Religion*, p. 262; Vernant: *Mortals and Immortals*, p. 241. In the dictionary of Hesychius, the *phouaxir* is defined as 'the physical training in the countryside before they are whipped' (Hesychius, under *phouaxir*).
73. Nilsson: *Geschichte der griechischen Religion*, p. 214 and 485–6; Burkert: *Greek Religion*, p. 263. The Suidas dictionary defines this period as the 'ritual dedication of young women to Artemis Mounikhia or Artemis Braurōnia before their marriage' (Suidas, under *arkteusai*).
74. Women are under the legal control of a guardian throughout their lives. See Pomeroy, Sarah B., *Goddesses, Whores, Wives, and Slaves. Women in Classical Antiquity* (New York, NY: Shocken Books, 1975), p. 62; MacDowell, Douglas M., *The Law in Classical Athens* (Ithaca, NY: Cornell University Press, 1978), p. 84.
75. See the discussion between Sōkratēs and Iskhomakhos about training a very young wife, who is only 15 years old! (Xenophon, *Oeconomicus* 7: 4–8.)
76. Aristotle makes this quite explicit when he declares that adult men are rational creatures, but children, women and slaves are not (*Politics* 1260a12–15). Since the function of a human being is to live a rational life (*Nicomachean Ethics* 1008a7–12), children, women, and slaves cannot be fully human in his system.
77. Farnell: *Greek Hero Cults*, pp. 182–3 and 196–8.
78. Harris: *Heavenly Twins* and *Boanerges*. Farnell acknowledges his debt to the theories of Harris, see Farnell: *Greek Hero Cults*, pp. 176 and 179–80. He regrets only that Harris did not apply them consistently enough and that he had been partly seduced by the possibility that the Dioskouroi might have an Indo-European origin! See Farnell: *Greek Hero Cults*, p. 180.

79. See Chapter 1, '2. Twins'.
80. See Chapter 6, '1. The Status and Parentage of the Dioskouroi'.
81. *Iliad* 3: 243–244.
82. Pausanias 3: 13, 1.
83. 'Many leather shields and helmets / fell in the dust, as did the race of semi-divine men' (*Iliad* 12: 22–23). Homer may have felt that it would be 'anachronistic' (a violation of the epic tradition) to refer to his heroes as semi-divine. They were merely heroes (*hērōes*) in the epic tradition, even if they were half-gods (*hēmitheoi*) in the cult of Homer's contemporaries. See Nagy, Gregory, *The Best of the Achaeans* (Baltimore, MD: Johns Hopkins University Press, 1979), pp. 159–61.
84. Nilsson: *Geschichte der griechischen Religion*, p. 316–17 and 531; Nilsson: *Mycenaean Origin*, p. 76. The very tomb of Huakinthos, the proof of his mortality, depicted his introduction to Olumpos as an immortal god! (Pausanias 3: 19, 3–4.)
85. *Homeric Hymn* 33 (to the Dioskouroi): *Dios kourous* (line 1), *arnessin leukoisin* (line 10).
86. Burkert: *Greek Religion*, p. 200.
87. Pausanias uses the word 'temple' (*naos*) to describe the shrines of the Dioskouroi at Therapnē (Pausanias 3: 20, 2) and Argos (Pausanias 2: 22, 5).
88. Nilsson: *Geschichte der griechischen Religion*, p. 410.
89. Their low status as young, horse-riding messenger-boys made them barely eligible to be gods. Compare the expulsion of the deformed, working-class Hēphaistos from Olumpos (*Iliad* 18: 395–399), and the contempt he inspires in the other gods (*Iliad* 1: 599–600).
90. As pre-Greek divinities, they would not have fitted very well into the usual Greek categories of men, heroes, and gods.
91. Alkman fr. 7 Campbell.
92. *kōma siōn, asanatas teletas* (Alkman fr. 7 Campbell).
93. Pausanias 3: 20, 2.
94. Tod and Wace: *Catalogue of the Sparta Museum*, p. 66, Spartan Museum Number 447. Farnell suggests that Pleistiadas was afraid of the Dioskouroi because he had cheated at the games. See Farnell: *Greek Hero Cults*, p. 196.
95. *Homeric Hymn* 33 (to the Dioskouroi), 1–3.
96. Pausanias 3: 18, 14.
97. Pausanias 3: 18, 11.
98. Pausanias 3: 17, 3.
99. Nilsson: *Geschichte der griechischen Religion*, p. 215 note 5.
100. Spartan Museum Number 5380. See Steinhauer, George, *Museum of Sparta.* (Athens: Apollo Editions, 1975), Fig. 37; *LIMC* vol. 3, pt. 2, p. 461, Dioskouroi 58; Köhne: *Dioskuren in der Griechischen Kunst*, pp. 46–9, number A2.
101. (1) The relief set up by Plesitiadas with the inscription quoted above: Tod and Wace: *Catalogue of the Sparta Museum*, p. 178, Spartan Museum Number 447; *LIMC* vol. 3, pt. 2, p. 461, Dioskouroi 65; Köhne: *Dioskuren in der Griechischen Kunst*, pp. 51–2, number A3.

(2) A relief with two amphoras between the Dioskouroi: Tod and Wace: *Catalogue of the Sparta Museum*, p. 191, Spartan Museum Number 575; Steinhauer: *Museum of Sparta*, pp. 52–3; *LIMC* vol. 3, pt. 2, p. 461, Dioskouroi 59; Köhne: *Dioskuren in der Griechischen Kunst*, pp. 53–5, number A5.

(3) Part of a Dioskouroi relief from the Temple of Artemis Orthia: Spartan Museum Number 1991; Köhne: *Dioskuren in der Griechischen Kunst*, p. 56, number A8.

102. Tod and Wace: *Catalogue of the Sparta Museum*, p. 166, Spartan Museum Number 319; Köhne: *Dioskuren in der Griechischen Kunst*, p. 52, number A4.
103. Farnell: *Greek Hero Cults*, pp. 190 and 194–5; Tod and Wace: *Catalogue of the Sparta Museum*, p. 115.
104. Nilsson compares them with the household god, Zeus Ktēsios, who could also appear as a snake. See Nilsson: *Geschichte der griechischen Religion*, p. 409–10.
105. Burkert thinks that the snakes are participating in a *Theoxenia* festival for the Dioskouroi. See Burkert: *Greek Religion*, p. 213.
106. Tod and Wace: *Catalogue of the Sparta Museum*, p. 196, Spartan Museum Number 613; *LIMC* vol. 3, pt. 1, p. 587, Dioskouroi 226; Köhne: *Dioskuren in der Griechischen Kunst*, pp. 55–6, number A7.
107. Farnell 1921: 195; Tod and Wace: *Catalogue of the Sparta Museum*, p. 115; Köhne: *Dioskuren in der Griechischen Kunst*, p. 56.
108. 'Several monuments depict these Theoxenia of the Dioskouroi [. . .] The amphoras represent an abbreviation of the cult,' Nilsson: *Geschichte der griechischen Religion*, pp. 384–5; 'a couch with two cushions is prepared; two amphorae are set out' for the Dioskouroi, Burkert: *Greek Religion*, p. 213.
109. Nilsson: *Geschichte der griechischen Religion*, p. 409 and plate 29 number 2.
110. Tod and Wace: *Catalogue of the Sparta Museum*, p. 193, Spartan Museum Number 588; *LIMC* vol. 3, pt. 1, p. 587, Dioskouroi 224; Köhne: *Dioskuren in der Griechischen Kunst*, p. 47, number A6.
111. Plutarch *On Brotherly Love*, 478ab. Plutarch uses a description of the *dokana* to start off his essay on brotherly love.
112. 'Tombs in Lakedaimōnia; from receiving the Tundaridai, having the appearance of opened tombs,' *Etymologicum Magnum* under '*dokana*'.
113. Farnell: *Greek Hero Cults*, p. 190; Tod and Wace: *Catalogue of the Sparta Museum*, p. 115.
114. Nilsson: *Geschichte der griechischen Religion*, p. 409.
115. Burkert: *Greek Religion*, p. 213. In ancient Rome, there was a similar structure called the *Tigillum Sororium* ('the Beam of Puberty'). It consisted to two vertical posts with just one horizontal beam resting on top. The young Romans had to march under this structure in order to become adult warriors. See Scullard, Howard Hayes, *Festivals and Ceremonies of the Roman Republic* (Ithaca, NY: Cornell University Press, 1981), p. 190.
116. Köhne: *Dioskuren in der Griechischen Kunst*, pp. 50–1.
117. Pausanias 4: 27, 2–3.

118. Pausanias 4: 16, 9.
119. Plutarch, *Life of Lysander* 12, 1. Stars were not used to symbolize the Dioskouroi until the Hellenistic age. See Köhne: *Dioskuren in der Griechischen Kunst*, p. 58 note 200. They must represent St Elmo's fire in this monument. See Köhne: *Dioskuren in der Griechischen Kunst*, p. 177. In the original version of the story, the eye-witnesses must have seen flashing lights, not actual stars.
120. Pausanias 10: 9, 7.
121. Plutarch, *Life of Lysander* 18, 1.
122. Pausanias 4: 26, 6
123. The untranslateable word *xenos* means that someone is both a friend and a stranger.
124. Nilsson: *Geschichte der griechischen Religion*, p. 135; Burkert: *Greek Religion*, p. 107.
125. Aristophanes makes fun of this physical separation at *Birds* 187–193. It is precisely because the gods are so distant that the birds can impose a blockade and prevent any sacrificial aromas from being imported into heaven.
126. The gods were 'expressly entertained as guests at a meal', Burkert: *Greek Religion*, p. 107.
127. As Köhne remarks, the *Theoxenia* imply that the human host is equal to the Dioskouroi. See Köhne: *Dioskuren in der Griechischen Kunst*, p. 130.
128. Nilsson: *Geschichte der griechischen Religion*, p. 135.
129. The twin horse gods are invited to sit on the sacred grass (*barhis*) at *Ṛgveda* 1: 47, 8. This carpet of sacred grass was a regular feature of all Vedic and Persian rituals. See Oldenberg: *Religion des Veda*, pp. 341–5.
130. Burkert points this out, and he suggests that the Greek *theoxenia* and Roman *lectisternium* may have something to do with the Indo-European nature of the Dioskouroi. See Burkert: *Greek Religion*, p. 107.
131. Nilsson: *Geschichte der griechischen Religion*, p. 135; Burkert: *Greek Religion*, p. 107.
132. Burkert: *Greek Religion*, p. 107.
133. 'The real guests at the entertaining of the gods, *theoxenia*, are the Dioskouroi,' Burkert: *Greek Religion*, p. 107.
134. Nilsson: *Geschichte der griechischen Religion*, p. 410 and plate 29, number 5.
135. Pindar *Olympian Ode* 3: 1–2.
136. Tod and Wace: *Catalogue of the Sparta Museum*, p. 158, Spartan Museum Numbers 201–3; Nilsson: *Geschichte der griechischen Religion*, p. 408 and plate 29 number 1. On Spartan Museum Number 202, the Dioskouroi are standing beside their horses on either side of the statue.
137. Tod and Wace: *Catalogue of the Sparta Museum*, pp. 18–20.
138. Tod and Wace: *Catalogue of the Sparta Museum*, p. 33; Nilsson: *Geschichte der griechischen Religion*, p. 408.
139. Nilsson: *Geschichte der griechischen Religion*, p. 409; Tod and Wace: *Catalogue of the Sparta Museum*, p. 18.

140. Tod and Wace: *Catalogue of the Sparta Museum*, pp. 19 and 33–4.
141. Tod and Wace: *Catalogue of the Sparta Museum*, pp. 19 and 34.
142. Pausanias 3: 16, 2–3.
143. His son was one of the suitors for Agaristē, the daughter of Kleisthenēs, dictator of Sicyon (Herodotus 6: 127, 4).
144. Herodotus 6: 127, 4; Farnell: *Greek Hero Cults*, p. 209; Nilsson: *Geschichte der griechischen Religion*, p. 409.
145. Pindar, *Nemean Ode* 10: 49–51.
146. Pindar, *Olympian Ode* 3: 38–40.
147. Bacchylides, fr. 21 Campbell.
148. Chionides, *Ptōkhoi* fr. 7 *PCG*.
149. Köhne: *Dioskuren in der Griechischen Kunst*, p. 133.
150. *LIMC* vol. 3, pt. 2, p. 465, Dioskouroi 111; Köhne: *Dioskuren in der Griechischen Kunst*, pp. 131–2, number K1.
151. *LIMC* vol. 3, pt. 2, p. 465, Dioskouroi 112; Köhne: *Dioskuren in der Griechischen Kunst*, p. 132, number K2.
152. Nilsson: *Geschichte der griechischen Religion*, p. 410; *LIMC* vol. 3, pt. 2, p. 465, Dioskouroi 113; Köhne: *Dioskuren in der Griechischen Kunst*, p. 133, number K3.
153. Köhne: *Dioskuren in der Griechischen Kunst*, pp. 121–2.
154. Aristotle says it took place in the Thēseion (*Constitution of Athens* 15, 4), but Polyaenus, writing in the second century AD, locates the event in the Anakeion (Polyaenus 1: 21, 2).
155. Pausanias 1: 18, 1; Farnell: *Greek Hero Cults*, p. 211; Köhne: *Dioskuren in der Griechischen Kunst*, p. 123.
156. *FGrH* 328 Philochorus F73; Farnell: *Greek Hero Cults*, p. 211.
157. Köhne: *Dioskuren in der Griechischen Kunst*, p. 127. Until the fifth century BC, Athens relied mainly on Thessalian horsemen. The Athenians were forced to create a new cavalry of 300 men after they were abandoned by the Thessalians at the Battle of Tanagra in 457 BC. See Bugh, Glenn Richard, *The Horsemen of Athens* (Princeton, NJ: Princeton University Press, 1988), pp. 39–52.
158. According to Pollux, Athens used to have a small force of 96 horsemen to patrol its borders. See Bugh: *Horsemen of Athens*, pp. 4–5.
159. Köhne: *Dioskuren in der Griechischen Kunst*, pp. 126–7.
160. *LIMC* vol. 3, pt. 1, pp. 581–3 and vol. 3, pt. 2, pp. 469–70, Dioskouroi 165–73 and 179–88; Köhne: *Dioskuren in der Griechischen Kunst*, pp. 92–107, numbers A23–A28.
161. *LIMC* vol. 3 pt. 2, p. 470, Dioskouroi 165, 181 and 182; Köhne: *Dioskuren in der Griechischen Kunst*, pp. 92–3 and 99–101, numbers A23, A26, A29 and A30.
162. *LIMC*, vol. 1 pt. 2, p. 320, Aischines 1; *LIMC* vol. 3 pt. 2, p. 469, Dioskouroi 180; Köhne: *Dioskuren in der Griechischen Kunst*, pp. 93–5 and 104–5, numbers A28–A29.
163. *LIMC* vol. 3 pt. 2, pp. 469–70, Dioskouroi 166 and 183; Köhne: *Dioskuren in der Griechischen Kunst*, pp. 96–9, numbers A31–A32.

164. Köhne: *Dioskuren in der Griechischen Kunst*, pp. 92 and 102–3, numbers A23 and A25. Mounted hoplites suited the terrain of Greece better than chariots. See Worley, Leslie J., *Hippeis. The Cavalry of Ancient Greece* (Boulder, CO: Westview Press, 1994), pp. 18–19. They were also more suitable than regular cavalry. See Bugh: *Horsemen of Athens*, pp. 37–8.
165. *LIMC*, vol. 3 pt. 2, p. 469, Aischines 1; Köhne: *Dioskuren in der Griechischen Kunst*, pp. 104–5, number A28.
166. For the connotations of chariot and hoplite on vase-painting, see Köhne: *Dioskuren in der Griechischen Kunst*, p. 113. Köhne regards these paintings as 'paradigms for the aristocracy', Köhne: *Dioskuren in der Griechischen Kunst*, p. 92. The aristocratic *hippotrophoi* (horse-breeders) who entered their horses at Panhellenic games were not, however, identical with the cavalrymen who fought in wars. See Bugh: *Horsemen of Athens*, pp. 23–4 and 36–7.
167. Pausanias 2: 22, 6; Nilsson: *Geschichte der griechischen Religion*, p. 407.
168. There were horses in the sculpture group too, but it is not certain that anyone was on horseback (Pausanias 2: 22, 5).
169. The Argive story told that Thēseus had got Helenē pregnant in Attica; she escaped to Argos where she gave birth to Iphigeneia, and then she built a temple to the birth goddess, Eileithuia. See below, Chapter 6, 'The Abduction of Helenē'.
170. Nilsson: *Geschichte der griechischen Religion*, pp. 414–15.
171. Both Nilsson and Burkert regard this as the primary way in which they saved people: 'this is why they were called *soteres*', Nilsson: *Geschichte der griechischen Religion*, p. 410; 'Not least, they prove their worth in battle,' Burkert: *Greek Religion*, p. 213.
172. *Homeric Hymn* 33 (to the Dioskouroi), 6–8.
173. *Homeric Hymn* 33 (to the Dioskouroi), 12–16.
174. Alcaeus fr. 34 Campbell.
175. *LIMC* vol. 3, pt. 2, p. 456, Dioskouroi 2; Köhne: *Dioskuren in der Griechischen Kunst*, p. 146, number K19.
176. Xenophanes 21 A 39 Diels-Kranz.

Chapter 6 The Myths of the Dioskouroi

1. *Iliad* 3: 238.
2. *Iliad* 3: 243–244.
3. Gernet, Louis, and Boulanger, André, *Le génie grec dans la religion* (Paris: Albin Michel, 1932 [1970]), pp. 95–6; Burkert: *Greek Religion*, pp. 121–2. Gernet notes Homer's disrespect for the solemn ritual of throwing a sacrificed pig into the sea at *Iliad* 19: 266–267. See Gernet, Louis, *Droit et Institutions en Grèce antique* (Paris: Flammarion, 1968 [1982]), p. 60 note 167. Perhaps Homer is really the most religious poet of all – nobody thinks of Isaiah as irreligious when he mocks the practice of animal sacrifice (Isaiah 1: 11–14). Homer's apparent secularism may be a way of distancing the gods from practices that are merely

human, and his rejection of hero-cult may be his way of upholding the sanctity of the gods and ensuring that their company is not infiltrated by men.

4. Homer mentions that his heroes are semi-gods (hēmitheoi) only once, at Iliad 12: 22–23). See Nagy: *Best of the Achaeans*, pp. 159–61. Gernet and Boulanger attribute this absence to the lack of ancient hero-cults in Ionia: 'the cult of heroes did not have roots any more: the *Heros* becomes *Held* – a character in a saga. The gods tend to cut themselves off,' Gernet and Boulanger: *Génie grec*, p. 94.
5. As Akhilleus faces his own approaching death, he explicitly compares himself with the equally mortal Hēraklēs (*Iliad* 18: 117–121).
6. *Odyssey* 4: 561–569.
7. *Odyssey* 11: 601.
8. *Odyssey* 11: 601–604.
9. *Odyssey* 11: 298–300.
10. *Hōs phato, tous d' ēdē katekhen phusizoos aia* (*Iliad* 3: 243); *tous amphō zōous katekhei phusizoos aia* (*Odyssey* 11: 301).
11. *Odyssey* 11: 301–304.
12. The related adjective *isotheos* means 'godlike' and is often used in the expression *isotheos phōs*, 'a godlike human being'. It does not imply that the person is a god.
13. *Homeric Hymn* 33 (to the Dioskouroi): 10. As we saw already (Chapter 5, 'Between Gods and Men'), the sacrifice of white lambs implies that they are Olympian gods.
14. *Homeric Hymn* 33 (to the Dioskouroi): 1–5.
15. The word 'Tundaridai' does not seem to mean 'Sons of Tundareos' in this hymn.
16. IG IX 1^2, 4, 1566 = IG IX,1 649, but the second text has Eusoida(s) for Exoida(s).
17. The daughters were Timandra, Klutaimēstra, and Phulonoē (*Catalogue of Women*, fr. 23a MW = 19 Most, lines 9–10).
18. *Catalogue of Women*, fr. 24 MW = 21 Most.
19. See the chart in Chapter 1, 'Twins'.
20. According to the Spartans, the Dioskouroi were not worshipped as gods until forty years after their death (Pausanias 3: 13, 1).
21. Ibycus fr. 294 Campbell.
22. *Cypria* fr. 9 West.
23. They are differentiated in this way on the sixth-century Chest of Kupselos, but neither of them is named. See Eitrem, S., *Die göttlichen Zwillinge bei den Griechen* (Christiania [Oslo]: A. W. Brøggers Buchdruckerei, 1902), p. 6; Köhne: *Dioskuren in der Griechischen Kunst*, p. 71.
24. Pindar, *Nemean Ode* 10: 79–81.
25. Pindar, *Nemean Ode* 10: 86–88. These words are addressed to Poludeukēs, so all the occurrences of the pronoun 'you' are singular.
26. Pindar, *Pythian Ode* 11: 62–64; *Nemean Ode* 10: 55–56.
27. Pindar, *Pythian Ode* 11: 62.

28. He continues, 'they penetrate below and above, near and far; they do not elude death', Burkert, Walter, *Greek Religion*, translated by John Raffan (Cambridge, MA: Harvard University Press, 1985), p. 208. His remarks bring out their double nature excellently, but even in the cautious last words, 'they do not elude death,' he is perhaps being more definite than their ambiguity would allow.
29. *First Vatican Mythographer* 3: 201.
30. Hermary: 'Dioskouroi', p. 592.
31. Lycophron, *Alexandra* 506–507.
32. This is, of course, an argument from silence. A different pair of 'white-horsed' twins, the Moliones, are already described as 'born in a silver egg' by the sixth-century BC poet, Ibycus. See Ibycus, fr. 285 Campbell.
33. *Cypria* fr. 10 West, lines 2–12.
34. *Cypria* fr. 11 West.
35. Köhne: *Dioskuren in der Griechischen Kunst*, p. 152.
36. Sappho fr. 166 Campbell.
37. Cratinus wrote a comedy about it called *Nemesis*, which could only have raised a laugh if everyone knew the story.
38. *LIMC* vol. 3, pt. 2, p. 471, Dioskouroi 185–186; Köhne: *Dioskuren in der Griechischen Kunst*, pp. 152–9, numbers K21 and K23–35.
39. The Dioskouroi are absent from a few of the early vases with Helenē's egg (about 450 BC), but once the theme becomes really popular (430–400 BC) they are always present. See Köhne: *Dioskuren in der Griechischen Kunst*, p. 154.
40. Cratinus, *Nemesis* fr. 115 *PCG*.
41. Köhne: *Dioskuren in der Griechischen Kunst*, p. 153, numbers K22 and K36.
42. Pausanias 1: 33, 7.
43. Pausanias 1: 33, 8; Köhne: *Dioskuren in der Griechischen Kunst*, pp. 154–5.
44. Eitrem: *Die göttlichen Zwillinge*, p. 41. Eitrem himself believes that Nemesis (indignation) and Helenē at Rhamnous match Aidōs (shame) and Pēnelopē at Sparta, each pair representing modesty and abduction. See Eitrem: *Die göttlichen Zwillinge*, pp. 41 and 23–4.
45. Loraux, Nicole, *The Children of Athena: Athenian Ideas about Citizenship and the Division between the Sexes*, translated by Caroline Levine. (Princeton, NJ: Princeton University Press, 1993), pp. 57–8.
46. Aristotle, *History of Animals* 559b6–15. The Greeks did not know about the human *ovum*, which was not discovered until the nineteenth century.
47. See discussion and illustrations in Loraux: *Children of Athena*, pp. 61–4 and Plates 3–5.
48. The myth tries to eliminate the contrast between the feminine geographical land of Attica and the masculine political state of Athens. It conflates the two by the mediation of a masculine 'fatherland', *patris gaia*, and a masculine goddess, Athēna. For the 'neutralization of the power of Mother Earth by "the earth of the fathers"', see Loraux: *Children of Athena*, pp. 15–16. For the

masculinity of Athena, the 'reassuring image of femininity entirely dedicated to the service of *andreia*', see Loraux: *Children of Athena*, p. 18.

49. For an analysis of women's mobility and the virgin goddess Hestia's immobility, see Vernant, Jean-Pierre, *Myth and Thought among the Greeks*, translated by Janet Lloyd (New York, NY: Zone Books, 2006), pp. 164–5.
50. Tēlemakhos tells Athēna that no man can be sure that he is really his father's son (Homer, *Odyssey* 1: 215–216), and Helenē from Attica will give birth to a Spartan princess. Women undermine the illusion that a man has the power to produce his son and heir.
51. Euripides, *Helen* 16–21.
52. *Cypria* fr. 10 West: 6.
53. Burkert: *Greek Religion*, p. 185.
54. Dēmētēr is called *Dēmētēr Erinus* because of her 'fury' at the way Poseidōn has treated her, see Burkert: *Greek Religion*, p. 138. The feelings of Nemesis are similar, and as with *Dēmētēr Erinus*, her name ('indignation') is identical with her feelings.
55. Onkos was the local ruler, who later gave the horse Areiōn to Hēraklēs.
56. Pausanias 8: 25, 5 and 7.
57. *Thebais*, fr. 11 West. See Burkert, Walter, *Structure and History in Greek Mythology and Ritual* (Berekeley, CA: University of California Press, 1979), pp. 127–8; Burkert: *Greek Religion*, p. 138.
58. *Iliad* 9: 568–571. Aeschylus made their terror famous in the *Eumenides*, where a mother once again invokes the Furies against her own son, but Homer nicely captures the earthy (and unearthly) aspect of an Erinus.
59. The Furies are black (*melainai*) at Aeschylus, *Eumenides* 52; Dēmētēr puts on black robes (*melainan esthēta*) at Pausanias 8: 42, 2.
60. The Furies themselves make this distinction: 'We keep our hands away from the immortals, none of them / can dine or share with us. / I have no part or share in white robes' (Aeschylus, *Eumenides* 349–352).
61. Dēmētēr is filled with anger (*thumos*) and grief (*penthos*) at Pausanias 8: 42, 2. Athēna, in converting the enraged Furies into benevolent Eumenides, urges them to 'put to rest the bitter anger (*menos*) consisting of a black wave (*kelainou kumatos*)', at Aeschylus, *Eumenides* 832.
62. After putting on her black robes, 'she entered a cave (*spēlaion*)' (Pausanias 8: 42, 2); the Furies at Athens will live 'in an ancient cavern (*keuthos*) of the earth' (Aeschylus, *Eumenides* 1036).
63. Pausanias 8: 42, 1–2.
64. Pausanias 8: 42, 2–3.
65. There is something truly horrifying about the way in which Pausanias suddenly springs the bad news on us: 'She is sitting on a rock, and she looks like a woman in every way, except for the head: she has the head and mane of a horse, and there are sculptures of snakes and other creatures growing out of her hair.' (Pausanias 8: 42, 4). Snake-hair is, of course, typical of Furies.

66. Matthews, Victor J., *Antimachus of Colophon: Text and Commentary* (Leiden: E.J. Brill, 1996), p. 139, *Thebaid* fr. 31 (32 Wyss).
67. Matthews: *Antimachus of Colophon*, pp. 143–4.
68. These stories come from Ancient Greek commentaries, and are discussed at Nagy: *Greek Mythology and Poetics*, p. 232.
69. Herodotus 7: 129, 1 and 4.
70. Pausanias 1: 30, 4. At the end of his *Oedipus at Colonus*, Sophocles describes the disappearance of Oidipous at this very hill, Kolōnos.
71. The myth of Pēgasos once again has Poseidōn raping a terrifying, snake-haired goddess, Medousa, who gives birth to Pēgasos only after she has been beheaded (Hesiod, *Theogony* 279–281). West remarks that Medousa belongs to the underworld monsters that are descended from the sea (Pontos), 'not because they have any connexion with the sea, but because they could not be put among the descendants of Uranos'. See West, M.L., *Hesiod. Theogony* (Oxford: Clarendon, 1966), p. 244, commentary on lines 270–336.
72. Decker: 'Pferd im Alten Aegypten', p. 265.
73. Burkert: *Greek Religion*, p. 138.
74. Burkert: *Greek Religion*, p. 44; Plath: 'Pferd und Wagen im Mykenischen', p. 106.
75. Burkert: *Greek Religion*, pp. 44 and 139.
76. The version of the story told by Antimachus of Colophon may have been asexual, but the combination of autochthonous and sexual birth is common in myth. See the discussion of human autochthony in Lévi-Strauss, Claude, *Anthropologie structurale* (Paris: Plon, 1974), pp. 236–9; and Loraux: *Children of Athena*, pp. 57–8.
77. Détienne and Vernant: *Cunning Intelligence*, pp. 191–3.
78. Hesiod, *Theogony* 278–282.
79. The name of the spring is already known to Hesiod (*Theogony* 6); Pausanias tells the story of Pēgasos at 9: 31, 3.
80. Poseidōn created the spring on the Acropolis of Athens (Herodotus 8:55), the spring of Dirkē in Thebes (Aeschylus, *Seven against Thebes* 307–310), and others elsewhere. See Burkert: *Greek Religion*, pp. 138–9.
81. Bellerophōn is thrown by Pēgasos (Pindar, *Isthmian Ode* 7: 43–47) and spends the rest of his life wandering alone and avoiding the company of men (*Iliad* 6: 200–202).
82. This myth is already on the Throne of Amuklai, which was sculpted around 550 BC (Pausanias 3: 18, 7).
83. Pindar, *Olympian Ode* 13: 63–86. See Détienne and Vernant: *Cunning Intelligence*, pp. 187–9.
84. Pausanias 2: 4, 1; Détienne and Vernant: *Cunning Intelligence*, pp. 195–9.
85. *Homeric Hymn* 5 (to Aphroditē) 12–13. Athēna also subjects the sea to navigation, warfare to tactics, and the Erinues to the power of the court system. See Burkert: *Greek Religion*, p. 141.
86. Détienne and Vernant: *Cunning Intelligence*, pp. 203–4.

87. Détienne and Vernant: *Cunning Intelligence*, pp. 199–206.
88. Pisani, Vittore, 'Elena e l' Εδωλον', *Rivista di Filologia e di Istruzione Classica* 56 (1928), pp. 497–8; Grotanelli, Cristiano, 'Yoked Horses, Twins, and the Powerful Lady: India, Greece, Ireland and Elsewhere', *Journal of Indo-European Studies* 14 (1986), pp. 127–30; Skutsch: 'Helen, Her Name and Nature', p. 190; Jackson, Peter, *The Transformations of Helen: Indo-European Myth and the Roots of the Trojan Circle* (Dettelbach: Röll, 2006), pp. 87–8; Walker, Henry John, 'The Greek Aśvins', *Annals of the Bhandarkar Oriental Research Institute* 88 (2007), p. 112.
89. Mayrhofer rejects any connection with Helenē and derives Saraṇyū's name from *sar*, 'run' (*EWA*, vol. 2, p. 707, under *saraṇyū́*). On the other hand, he derives Sanskrit *sar* from Indo-European **sal*, 'jump' (*EWA*, vol. 2, p. 706, under *SAR*), which brings Saraṇyū's name closer to Helenē's. Pokorny and Watkins separate these roots as **ser*, 'flow', and **sel*, 'jump', which would make any etymological connection impossible. For **ser*, 'flow', see Pokorny, Julius, *Indogermanisches etymologisches Wörterbuch* (Bern: Francke, 1959), p. 909; Watkins: *Indo-European Roots*, p. 76, under *ser-* ^{2}. For **sel*, 'jump', see Pokorny: *Indogermanisches etymologisches Wörterbuch*, p. 899; Watkins: *Indo-European Roots*, p. 75, under *sel-* ^{4}. Mayrhofer's rejection of any link between Helenē and Saraṇyū is strange, given his equation of Sanskrit *sar* and Indo-European **sal*. If Sanskrit *sar* derives from **sal*, as Mayrhofer suggests, then Helenē (from **sel*) and Saraṇyū (from *sar*, **sal*, and ultimately **sel*) could well be connected.
90. Watkins: *Indo-European Poetics*, p. 49.
91. For these parallels see Pisani: 'Elena e l' Εδωλον', p. 395; Skutsch: 'Helen, Her Name and Nature', p. 189.
92. Hesiod fr. 358 MW = 298 Most.
93. Stesichorus fr. 190 Campbell.
94. Helenē explains the whole story at Euripides, *Helen* 31–55.
95. Stesichorus fr. 192 and 193 Campbell.
96. In the Indo-Iranian story of Yama and Yamī, man and woman have been created at the same time, so humans are the product of an incestuous marriage between a brother and a sister (*RV* 10: 10). In the Indian story of Manu, the first woman Īḍā is created later (*ŚB* 1: 8, 1^{7}), so humans are the product of an incestuous marriage between a father and his 'daughter,' Īḍā (*ŚB* 1: 8, 1^{10}).
97. *Cypria* fr 1 West, lines 3–5. The same reason for the war is given by Helenē at Euripides, *Helen* 40.
98. This version is first recorded by Lycophron (*Alexandra* 506–507) in the third century BC.
99. For artificial insemination in India, see the story of Vasu Uparicara and Adrikā (*Mahābhārata* 1: 57, 39–48), the ancestors of both sides in the battle at Kurukṣetra. The insemination of Adrikā may be unusual (she has been turned into a fish), but note that Vasu Uparicara wanted to artificially inseminate his wife, Girikā, rather than let his semen go to waste, so he considers it a fairly normal procedure.

100. The story of Erikhthonios is not really a case of artificial insemination, because the earth is fertilized by the semen of Hēphaistos; the goddess Gaia herself is not inseminated. It is also the earth (*khthōn*) that produces Erikhthonios; the goddess Gaia does not go through a pregnancy and does not give birth.
101. Euripides, *Hippolytus* 618–624. The dream is never fully realized, of course, because the pregnant father, Zeus, is an incubator for a prematurely born baby rather than a parent giving birth to one. The goddesses Mētis and Semelē are the real mothers, they bear the embryonic Athēna and Dionusos in their wombs, and Zeus only takes over this role after he has killed the mothers.
102. There is, however, the strange birth of Vasiṣṭha and Māna Agastya (*RV* 7: 33, 11–13), discussed above at Chapter 1, 'Twins'. The gods Mitra and Varuṇa are sexually aroused by the Apsaras Urvaśī, just as Hēphaistos was aroused by Athēna; they ejaculate into a pot, and he ejaculates onto the earth; Vasiṣṭha and Māna Agastya are born from the pot, just as Erikhthonios is born from the earth.
103. Zeus often adopts the form of an animal to mate with women or goddesses, who produce sons and daughters for him in the usual way. In India, the metamorphoses of Prajāpati and his consort give rise to the various species, but the offspring are produced in the usual way: 'he mated with her, and *x* was born' (*Bṛhadāraṇyaka Upaniṣad* 1: 4, 4).
104. Aeschylus, *Agamemnon* 415–416.
105. *Ṛgveda* 10: 10, 4c.
106. *poluanoros amphi gunaikos* (Aeschylus, *Agamemnon* 62).
107. *Cypria* fr. 1 West, lines 1–7, especially line 4: 'he planned to relieve the all-nourishing earth of men.' See Euripides, *Helen* 40.
108. Aphroditē brutally reminds Helenē how unimportant she is at *Iliad* 3: 414–417.
109. Homer, *Iliad* 3: 125–128 (*hethen heineka*, 128).
110. Saraṇyū gives birth to Yama and Yamī, and the rules (*vratāni*) of Tvaṣṭar command the twins to sleep together so that the human race will continue (*RV* 10:10, 5). The plan (*boulē*) of Zeus ordains that Helenē's abduction must lead to war and lower the population of the earth (*Cypria* fr. 1 West, line 7).
111. Nilsson: *Geschichte der griechischen Religion*, pp. 476–7; Nilsson: *Mycenaean Origin*, pp. 170–1; West, M.L., *Immortal Helen* (London: Bedford College, 1975), pp. 5–6; Köhne: *Dioskuren in der Griechischen Kunst*, p. 159.
112. Kearns, Emily, *The Heroes of Attica* (London: Institute of Classical Studies, 1989), p. 158.
113. Stesichorus fr. 191 Campbell.
114. Pausanias 2: 32, 7.
115. Köhne: *Dioskuren in der Griechischen Kunst*, p. 159, number K 39.
116. West, M.L., *Hesiod. Works and Days* (Oxford: Clarendon Press, 1978), p. 213, commentary on lines 225–247. See Hesiod, *Works and Days* 226–237 and Homer, *Odyssey* 19: 109–114.
117. From the roots *is* (power) and *gen* (birth).

118. Burkert: *Greek Religion*, p. 244.
119. Pausanias 2: 35, 1.
120. Pausanias 7: 26, 5.
121. *Catalogue of Women*, fr. 23a MW = 19 Most, lines 25–26.
122. *Catalogue of Women*, fr. 23b MW = 20 Most.
123. Pausanias 1: 33, 1.
124. Pausanias 3: 16, 7.
125. Plutarch, *Life of Theseus* 31.
126. Dēmētēr's daughter, Korē, never completes the transition to womanhood either. She is, of course, abducted by Hadēs and lives with him, but she always remains Korē, the adolescent girl, and never has any children.
127. Pausanias 2: 22, 6.
128. *LIMC* vol. 3, pt. 1, p. 582, Dioskouroi 179; Köhne: *Dioskuren in der Griechischen Kunst*, pp. 80–2, number A 18. Since the husband is not identified by name, there is a remote possibility that this vase might represent the marriage of Thēseus and Helenē. See Köhne: *Dioskuren in der Griechischen Kunst*, p. 81.
129. *Catalogue of Women* fr. 197 MW = 154(b) Most, lines 3–5; fr. 198 MW = 154(c) Most, lines 5–8; fr. 199 MW = 154(d) Most, lines 1–3.
130. Theocritus 18: 13–14.
131. West: *Immortal Helen*, p. 17 note 5.
132. Theocritus 18: 39.
133. Theocritus 18: 40–41.
134. Theocritus 18: 43–48.
135. The girls emphasize this by repeating the word *pratai* ('first') at the beginning of the lines where they describe their ritual actions (Theocritus 18: 43 and 45).
136. West: *Immortal Helen*, pp. 5 and 12.
137. The son of Orestēs and Hermionē is Tisamenos (Pausanias 2: 18, 6).
138. Nilsson: *Mycenaean Origin*, pp. 170–1.
139. Nilsson: *Mycenaean Origin*, pp. 74–6.
140. West: *Immortal Helen*, pp. 4–5, 7–8, and 13–14.
141. Euripides, *Helen* 44–48.
142. *Iliad* 3: 144.
143. *Cypria* fr. 12 West
144. *Ilious Persis* fr. 6 West.
145. Pausanias 5: 19, 3; Köhne: *Dioskuren in der Griechischen Kunst*, p. 71.
146. Alcman fr. 21–22 Campbell.
147. Köhne: *Dioskuren in der Griechischen Kunst*, p. 120.
148. Köhne: *Dioskuren in der Griechischen Kunst*, pp. 82–3, number A 19.
149. *FGrH* 323a (Hellanicus) fr. 18.
150. Plutarch, *Life of Lycurgus* 15, 3.
151. Cartledge, Paul, *Spartan Reflections* (Berkeley, CA: University of California Press, 2001), p. 116.

152. Nilsson: *Mycenaean Origin*, pp. 172–4
153. Apollodorus, *Library. Epitome* 1: 24. Plutarch presents us with a historicized version at *Life of Theseus* 31: 4.
154. West: *Immortal Helen*, pp. 9–13, West, M.L., *Indo-European Poetry and Myth* (New York, NY: Oxford University Press, 2007), pp. 230–2.
155. In some Latvian songs (*daina* 33794 Barons = 416 Jonval), Saule's Daughter marries both the Sons of Dievs, which Biezais explains by arguing that they are the Morning Star and the Evening Star, and therefore only one god, so this is not a case of bigamy. See Biezais, Haralds, *Die himmlische Götterfamilie der alten Letten* (Uppsala, Sweden: Almqvist & Wiksells, 1972), pp. 446–5.
156. Eitrem: *Die göttlichen Zwillinge*, pp. 31–3; Clader, Linda Lee, *Helen. The Evolution from Divine to Heroic in Greek Epic Tradition* (Leiden: E.J. Brill, 1976), pp. 50–3. Eitrem regards the sons of Atreus as a divine pair of brothers, like the Dioskouroi themselves.
157. Helenē appears both as *Helenē* and *Whelenē* in Homer, but the ratios are the opposite to what we would expect if her name were originally *Whelenē* alone: 32 per cent with 'W', 68 per cent without, whereas the usual ratio of words with a 'w' (digamma) is 85 per cent with 'w', 15 per cent without. Her double name in Homer suggests that she is a conflation of two different persons, **Swelenā* (sun goddess) and **Selenā* (literally, 'jumping woman').
158. *mēlōn henek' Oidipodao* (Hesiod, *Works and Days* 163).
159. *Helenēs henek' ēükomoio* (Hesiod, *Works and Days* 165).
160. 'Kastōr the tamer of horses and Poludeukēs the athletic champion' (*Cypria* fr. 11 West, line 6).
161. *Iliad* 3: 237, identical with Odyssey 11: 300.
162. According to Stesichorus, Leukippos is the brother of Tundareos, so the goddesses would be first cousins of the Dioskouroi (Stesichorus fr. 227 Campbell).
163. *Cypria* fr. 15 West. Stasinus must have equated 'White Horse' Leukippos with Apollōn, and felt that Phoibē could only be the daughter of Phoibos Apollōn. See Farnell: *Greek Hero Cults*, p. 228.
164. A papyrus fragment has the words 'Poludeukēs', 'Kastōr', 'fleeing' and 'sister'. It is probably from a commentary on a poem about the abduction (Alcman fr. 5, papyrus fr. 1a Campbell)
165. A papyrus fragment gives their name on one line and Apollōn's on the next (Alcman fr. 8 Campbell).
166. Pausanias 3: 17, 3 and 3: 18, 11.
167. Bacchylides, fr. 61 Campbell.
168. Burkert: *Greek Religion*, pp. 150–1.
169. Anacreon, fr. 417 Campbell.
170. The Greek root *dam* (English 'tame') means to tame a horse or other animal, to marry a woman, and to kill a man in battle. The root *zeug* (English 'yoke') means to yoke a horse or other animal, to marry a woman (the man 'yokes the woman to marriage'), or to fight as a team (*zeugitēs*, 'hoplite warrior,' *zugon*,

'battle line'). As always, 'what marriage is for a girl, war is for a boy'. See Vernant, Jean-Pierre, *Problèmes de la guerre en Grèce ancienne* (Paris: Mouton, 1968), p. 15.

171. There is one archaic vase and eleven from the fifth century BC with this theme. See Köhne: *Dioskuren in der Griechischen Kunst*, pp. 72–4 and 135–41, numbers A15 and K7–K17.
172. *LIMC* vol. 3, pt. 2, p. 473, Dioskouroi 201–202; Köhne: *Dioskuren in der Griechischen Kunst*, pp. 134–5, number K16.
173. Köhne: *Dioskuren in der Griechischen Kunst*, p. 139.
174. *LIMC* vol. 3, pt. 2, p. 472, Dioskouroi 197; Köhne includes this mixing-bowl in his list, but does not discuss it, see Köhne: *Dioskuren in der Griechischen Kunst*, p. 134, number K13.
175. *LIMC* vol. 3, pt. 2, p. 472, Dioskouroi 199; Köhne: *Dioskuren in der Griechischen Kunst*, p. 139, number K15.
176. Köhne compares it with Amazon scenes, but he believes it is so violent that it cannot represent the abduction of the Leukippides. See Köhne: *Dioskuren in der Griechischen Kunst*, p. 139.
177. Plutarch, *Life of Lycurgus* 15, 3.
178. *LIMC* vol. 1, pt. 2, p. 699, Apharetidai 4; Köhne: *Dioskuren in der Griechischen Kunst*, p. 30, number A1.
179. Pausanias 3: 13, 1. Pausanias did not believe his tour-guides and says the battle must have taken place in Messenia (Pausanias 3: 13, 2).
180. Pausanias 3: 14, 7.
181. The Spartans told the story to Pausanias (Pausanias 3: 13, 1), and the battle with the Apharētidai may also have appeared in Alcman fr. 7 Campbell. The fragment only has the first letters of their name 'apha. . .'.
182. Stasinus of Cyprus, *Cypria* fr. 16 West.
183. Stasinus of Cyprus, *Cypria* fr. 17 West.
184. Pindar, *Nemean Ode* 10: 55–90. This is similar to the arrangement in the *Odyssey*, where they are dead and alive every second day, but in the *Odyssey* it seems that they spend their living days in the grave rather than on Olumpos.
185. Köhne: *Dioskuren in der Griechischen Kunst*, pp. 30–6, number A1.
186. The episode appears on a Corinthian vase. See Köhne: *Dioskuren in der Griechischen Kunst*, pp. 69–70, number A13. Apollonius of Rhodes has Phineus lamenting that his blindness is incurable (*Argonautica* 2: 444–445).
187. This episode appears on three vase paintings from the fifth century BC – *LIMC*, vol. 3, pt. 2, p. 475, Dioskouroi 220; *LIMC*, vol. 7, pt. 2, p. 583, Talos 4–5; Köhne: *Dioskuren in der Griechischen Kunst*, p. 163, numbers K41–43. Apollonius of Rhodes tells the story of Talōs at *Argonautica* 4: 1659–1688, but in this version the Dioskouroi play no part in his death; Mēdeia kills him from on board the ship with long-range magic spells.
188. Köhne: *Dioskuren in der Griechischen Kunst*, p. 70, number A14.
189. Pausanias 5: 17, 9.

190. The boxing-match appears on a fifth-century BC vase painting, Köhne: *Dioskuren in der Griechischen Kunst*, pp. 162–3, number K40. It is also described by Apollonius of Rhodes at *Argonautica* 2: 35–97.
191. See Chapter 5 pages 129–130 and note 41 for the possible identification of this statue of Arēs Thēritas with the statue of Enualios in the sanctuary of the Dioskouroi at Therapnē.
192. On two archaic Athenian vases they drive a spear or trident into the animal's bottom, *LIMC*, vol. 6, pt. 2, pp. 208–9, Meleagros 7 and 13; Köhne: *Dioskuren in der Griechischen Kunst*, pp. 85–6, numbers A20–21. On another Athenian vase, they attack him from the front, *LIMC*, vol. 6, pt. 2, p. 209, Meleagros 19; Köhne: *Dioskuren in der Griechischen Kunst*, pp. 85–6, number A22.
193. Köhne: *Dioskuren in der Griechischen Kunst*, p. 89.
194. Their battle alongside Hēraklēs against the family of Hippokoōn is shown on two fifth-century BC Athenian vases, Köhne: *Dioskuren in der Griechischen Kunst*, pp. 165–7, numbers K49–50.
195. Pausanias 3: 1, 5. Hēraklēs had a private grievance against them (Pausanias 3: 15, 3–6).
196. Plato, *Republic* 380d–381e.
197. The fourth-century historian Timaeus (*FGrH* 566 F 11) wrote that slaves took over the tasks originally performed by young men, *tous neōterous*. See Vidal-Naquet: *Black Hunter*, p. 170. In Sparta, adolescents were treated like slaves. See Vernant: *Mortals and Immortals*, p. 235.
198. Vernant: *Mortals and Immortals*, pp. 231–9. The young men are between slaves and citizens, between *Helots* and *Homoioi*.
199. Plato, *Republic* 523Bb–524d.
200. Plato, *Republic* 479a–e.

Chapter 7 The Greek Horse Gods in Italy

1. At this time, Sparta was involved in a long war against Argos over the disputed territory of Tegea. See Bicknell, Peter, 'The Date of the Battle of the Sagra River', *Phoenix* 20 (1966), p. 298 note 20.
2. 580–570 BC, Bicknell: 'Date of Battle of Sagra', pp. 295–8; 560 BC, Poulsen, Birte, 'Ideologia, mito e culto dei Castori a Roma: dall'età repubblicana al tardo-antico', in Nista, Leila (editor), *Castores. L'immagine dei Dioscuri a Roma* (Roma: Edizioni de Luca, 1994), p. 91; mid-sixth century, Sourvinou-Inwood, Christiane, 'The Votum of 477/6 B.C. and the Foundation Legend of Locri Epizephyrii', *Classical Quarterly* 24 (1974), pp. 189–92. According to Strabo the Lokrians were outnumbered by 130,000 to 10,000! (Strabo 6:1,10).
3. Sourvinou-Inwood: 'Foundation Legend of Locri Epizephyrii', pp. 191–2.
4. Strabo 6: 1, 10.
5. Sourvinou-Inwood: 'Foundation Legend of Locri Epizephyrii', p. 190; Guzzo, Pier Giovanni, 'I Dioscuri in Magna Grecia', in Nista, Leila (editor), *Castores. L'immagine dei Dioscuri a Roma* (Roma: Edizioni de Luca, 1994), p. 27. One set of

statues shows the Dioskouroi with the sea-god Tritōn. This may celebrate their arrival across the sea from Sparta, see Sourvinou-Inwood: 'Foundation Legend of Locri Epizephyrii', p. 190.

6. *FGrH* 115 (Theopompos) F 392. See Bicknell: 'Date of Battle of Sagra', 295–296.
7. He had supposedly been wounded by no less a person than the hero Aias.
8. Pausanias 3: 19, 12–13. This story also helps to date the battle, since Stesichorus was dead by the middle of the sixth century BC. See Bicknell: 'Date of Battle of Sagra', 296–297.
9. Stesichorus came from Himera on Sicily (Stesichorus T1 Campbell), or from Metauros (Stesichorus T1, T9 Campbell), which was near Lokroi Epizephurioi.
10. Chapter 6, 'Goddesses on the Run'.
11. Bicknell: 'Date of Battle of Sagra', 296–297.
12. Guzzo: 'Dioscuri in Magna Grecia', pp. 27–9.
13. Pedley, John Griffiths, *Paestum. Greeks and Romans in Southern Italy* (London: Thames and Hudson, 1990), p. 97.
14. Wonder, John W., 'What happened to the Greeks in Lucanian-occupied Paestum? Multiculturalism in Southern Italy', *Phoenix* 56 (2002), p. 40 note 2.
15. Guzzo: 'Dioscuri in Magna Grecia', p. 30. Both Guzzo and Wonder date these coins to the fourth century BC, see Guzzo: 'Dioscuri in Magna Grecia'; Wonder: 'Greeks in Lucanian-occupied Paestum'. Horsnaes dates them to the period of the Roman colony of Paestum, after 273 BC. See Horsnaes, Helle W., *The cultural development in North-Western Lucania: c.600–273 B.C.* (Rome: L'Erma di Bretschneider, 2002), p. 22. The new Latin name *Paestum* or *Paistom* usually appears as *Pais* on Roman coins.
16. Sanza di Mino, Maria Rita, 'Il culto dei gemelli divini in ambito medio-italico', in Nista, Leila (editor), *Castores. L'immagine dei Dioscuri a Roma* (Roma: Edizioni de Luca, 1994), p. 53.
17. Weinstock, Stefan, 'Two Archaic Inscriptions from Latium', *Journal of Roman Studies* 50 (1960), p. 112.
18. Starzzulla, Maria Josè, 'Attestazioni figurative dei Dioscuri nel mondo etrusco', in Nista, Leila (editor), *Castores. L'immagine dei Dioscuri a Roma* (Roma: Edizioni de Luca, 1994), pp. 40–3.
19. Grummond, Nancy Thomson de, *Etruscan Myth, Sacred History, and Legend* (Philadelphia, PA: University of Pennsylvania Museum of Archaeology and Anthropology, 2006), pp. 189–93.
20. Starzzulla: 'Dioscuri nel mondo etrusco', p. 39; Grummond: *Etruscan Myth*, pp. 188–90.
21. *LIMC* Vol. 3, Pt. 1, p. 598; Starzzulla: 'Dioscuri nel mondo etrusco', pp. 48–9; Grummond: *Etruscan Myth*, p. 189.
22. *LIMC* Vol. 3, Pt. 1, p. 606.
23. Grummond: *Etruscan Myth*, p. 190 (shields); *LIMC* Vol. 3, Pt. 1, p. 607 (horses).
24. *LIMC* Vol. 3, Pt. 1, pp. 607–8; Starzzulla: 'Dioscuri nel mondo etrusco', pp. 44–5; Grummond: *Etruscan Myth*, p. 191.

25. Grummond: *Etruscan Myth*, pp. 125–6.
26. While Thēseus (Etruscan *These*), the future abductor of Helenē, looks on, the god Hermēs (Etruscan *Turms*) gives the egg to *Urphea*. See Grummond: *Etruscan Myth*, p. 130, Figure VI.19.
27. Starzzulla: 'Dioscuri nel mondo etrusco', p. 45; Grummond: *Etruscan Myth*, pp. 126 and 128.
28. Bottini, Angelo, 'I Dioscuri e il mito: la nascita di Elena tra Atene e occidente', in Nista, Leila (editor), *Castores. L'immagine dei Dioscuri a Roma* (Roma: Edizioni de Luca, 1994), pp. 34–5.
29. Grummond: *Etruscan Myth*, pp. 192–3 and 194, Figure VIII.23.
30. Grummond: *Etruscan Myth*, p. 31.
31. This is 'the Etruscan ritual pose' for prophets, and de Grummond has several illustrations of such prophets. They include Pava Tarchies (Latin *Tages*) who taught prophecy to the Etruscans, see Grummond: *Etruscan Myth*, pp. 24–7 and 24, Figure II.2; the divine winged prophet Chalchas (Greek *Kalkhas)*, see Grummond: *Etruscan Myth*, pp. 30–2, and 32, Figure II.9; Odysseus 'with left leg raised in the prophecy pose', see Grummond: *Etruscan Myth*, pp. 37, Figure II.15; and the prophet Umaele, see Grummond: *Etruscan Myth*, p. 39 and Figure II.17.
32. Grummond: *Etruscan Myth*, pp. 33–7.
33. Grummond, Nancy Thomson de, 'For the Mother and for the Daughter: Some Thoughts on Dedications from Etruria and Praeneste', in Chapin, Anne P. (editor), *ΧΑΡΙΣ. Essays in Honor of Sara A. Immerwahr. Hesperia Supplement 33* (Athens: The American School of Classical Studies at Athens, 2004), p. 364.
34. Wiseman, T.P., *The Myths of Rome* (Exeter: University of Exeter Press, 2004), p. 93.
35. Wiseman: *Myths of Rome*, p. 114.
36. Weinstock: 'Two Archaic Inscriptions', pp. 112–14; Dumézil, Georges, *Archaic Roman Religion*, translated by Philip Krapp (Chicago, IL: Chicago University Press, 1970), pp. 413–14; Bertinetti, Marina, 'Testimonianze del culto dei Dioscuri in area Laziale', in Nista, Leila (editor), *Castores. L'immagine dei Dioscuri a Roma* (Roma: Edizioni de Luca, 1994), pp. 59–60.
37. Dumézil: *Archaic Roman Religion*, p. 414.
38. Bertinetti: 'Dioscuri in area Laziale', p. 60.
39. Weinstock: 'Two Archaic Inscriptions', p. 113 and Plate XIII.1; Scullard, Howard Hayes, *Festivals and Ceremonies of the Roman Republic* (Ithaca, NY: Cornell University Press, 1981), pp. 65–6.
40. Timaeus used the phrase 'Trojan pottery' (*keramon Trōikon*) for this practice at Lavinium, *FGrH* 566 (Timaeus) F 59; Livy and Plutarch used the word 'jars' (*doliola* and *duo pithous* respectively) in speaking of the *Penates* at Rome. See Weinstock: 'Two Archaic Inscriptions', pp. 113–14.
41. Weinstock: 'Two Archaic Inscriptions', pp. 113–14 and Plates XII.3 and XIII.2–5.

42. Cancellieri, Margherita, 'Le *aedes Castoris et Pollucis* in Lazio: una nota', in Nista, Leila (editor), *Castores. L'immagine dei Dioscuri a Roma* (Roma: Edizioni de Luca, 1994), p. 65.
43. Cancellieri: 'Le *Aedes Castoris*', pp. 65–6.
44. Cancellieri: 'Le *Aedes Castoris*', pp. 66–7.
45. Cicero, *De Natura Deorum* 2: 2; Dionysius of Halicarnassus, 6: 13; Valerius Maximus 1: 8, 1. See Dumézil: *Archaic Roman Religion*, p. 412; Scullard: *Festivals and Ceremonies*, pp. 65–6.
46. Dionysius of Halicarnassus, 6: 13. See Scullard: *Festivals and Ceremonies*, p. 164.
47. Dumézil: *Archaic Roman Religion*, pp. 412–13; Guzzo: 'Dioscuri in Magna Grecia', p. 29; Poulsen: 'Ideologia dei Castori', p. 91. Cicero mentions the Battle on the River Sagra (but not the intervention by the Dioskouroi) immediately after he tells about the apparitions of Castor and Pollux at Lake Regillus and after the Battle of Pydna (Cicero, *De Natura Deorum* 2: 2), so Cicero felt there was some connection between these events.
48. The original temple of 484 BC was rebuilt several times (first half of the second century BC, 117 BC, and finally AD 6). For the first three temples, see Nielsen, Inge, 'Il tempio del Foro Romano: l'età repubblicana', in Nista, Leila (editor), *Castores. L'immagine dei Dioscuri a Roma* (Roma: Edizioni de Luca, 1994), pp 106–12. For the final version, see Sande, Siri, 'Il tempio del Foro Romano: l'età augustea', in Nista, Leila (editor), *Castores. L'immagine dei Dioscuri a Roma* (Roma: Edizioni de Luca, 1994), pp. 113–18. The three pillars that still survive are from the Augustan version, which was dedicated by the future emperor Tiberius. The temple honoured Tiberius himself and his recently deceased brother Drusus. See Sande: 'Tempio del Foro: Età Augustea', p. 113.
49. The phrase *Aedes Castoris* ('the temple of Castor') in the Latin *Res Gestae* of the Emperor Augustus is translated as ναὸς τῶν Διοσκούρων ('the temple of the Dioskouroi') in Greek versions of the *Res Gestae.* See Bertinetti: 'Dioscuri in Area Laziale', p. 61.
50. Cult not supervised by *Decemviri*, see Scullard: *Festivals and Ceremonies*, p. 66; Bertinetti: 'Dioscuri in Area Laziale', p. 59. Temple inside *pomerium*, see Dumézil: *Archaic Roman Religion*, p. 412; Cancellieri: 'Le *Aedes Castoris*', p. 63; Bertinetti: 'Dioscuri in Area Laziale', p. 59.
51. Dionysius of Halicarnassus 6: 13; Scullard: *Festivals and Ceremonies*, pp. 164–5.
52. Taylor, Lily Ross, *Party Politics in the Age of Caesar* (Berkeley, CA: University of California Press, 1966), pp. 25–8; Scullard: *Festivals and Ceremonies*, p. 66–7.
53. Poulsen: 'Ideologia dei Castori', pp. 93–4.
54. The other god they swore by was Hercules (*hercle*, 'by Hercules') He was another Greek god who had been accepted as fully Latin within the *pomerium*, and he too was popular with ordinary people, especially merchants.
55. He was the grandfather of the future Caesarian, also called Publius Vatinius, who would be elected Tribune in 59 BC and Consul in 47 BC.
56. Cicero, *De Natura Deorum* 2: 2; Valerius Maximus 1: 8, 1.

57. Valerius Maximus 1: 8, 1.
58. Pope Gelasius I, *Adversus Andromachum Senatorem* (Migne, *Patrologia Latina*, vol. 59, col. 114A).
59. Parisi Presicce, Claudio, 'I Dioscuri Capitolini e l'Iconografia dei Gemelli Divini in Età Romana', in Nista, Leila (editor), *Castores. L'immagine dei Dioscuri a Roma* (Roma: Edizioni de Luca, 1994), pp. 156–7.
60. Parisi Presicce: 'Dioscuri capitolini', pp. 157–60.

Conclusion

1. *attā vai kṣatriyo, 'nnaṃ viḍ* (*Śatapatha Brāhmaṇa* 6: 1, 2^{25}). Similar phrases date back to the mantra period. See Rau: *Staat und Gesellschaft,* p. 34. Under the Kuru kings, the warlords and brahmins unite against the rest of the people. See Witzel: 'Early Sanskritization', p. 9, and 'Development of the Vedic Canon', p. 294.
2. *dōrophagoi basilēes* (Hesiod, *Works and Days* 39, 221, and 264).
3. *dēmoboros basileus* (Homer, *Iliad* 1: 231). Akhilleus is probably thinking of his peers alone when he speaks of the 'people', but we do not find the dangerous term *dēmoboros* again for almost a millennium, when it is used to attack the Emperor Caligula (Philo, *Embassy to Gaius* 108).
4. *somo 'smākaṃ brāhmaṇānāṃ rājā* (*Taittirīya Saṃhitā* 1:8,10^2).
5. *Whitaker's Almanack* (London: A & C Black, 2010), p. 42.
6. Lincoln: *Priests, Warriors, and Cattle*, pp. 47–8. Note that the Nuer have the moral right to raid the Dinka, because they are superior warriors; the Dinka can only retaliate by 'stealing' cattle from the Nuer in an underhand fashion. See Lincoln: *Priests, Warriors, and Cattle*, pp. 21–2 and 27–8.
7. Witzel: 'Rgvedic history', pp. 333–4.
8. In Latvia, the sons of Dievs travel with Saule's daughter in a sleigh across the snow (*daina* 34011 Barons = 417 Jonval).
9. Agni is the Hotar priest of the gods, Indra is their king. The Aśvins do not belong to this lofty sphere, and when they are finally accepted as soma-drinking gods, they are equated with the lowly Adhvaryu priests. These priests do the hard physical work of the sacrifice at the command of the Hotar priest and under the patronage of the king.

BIBLIOGRAPHY

Alföldy, Géza. *The Social History of Rome*. Translated by Braund, David, and Pollock, Frank (Baltimore, MD: The Johns Hopkins University Press, 1988).

Anthony, David W. 'Horse, Wagon and Chariot: Indo-European Languages and Archaeology.' *Antiquity* 69 (1995), pp. 554–65.

——— *The Horse, the Wheel, and Language* (Princeton, NJ: Princeton University Press, 2007).

Anthony, David W. and Brown, Dorcas R. 'The Origins of Horseback Riding.' *Antiquity* 65 (1991), pp. 22–38.

Anthony, David W. and Vinogradov, Nikolai B. 'Birth of the Chariot.' *Archaeology* 48 (1995), pp. 36–41.

Arvidsson, Stefan. *Aryan Idols* (Chicago, IL: University of Chicago Press, 2006).

Ball, Helen L., and Hill, Catherine M. 'Reevaluating "Twin Infanticide".' *Current Anthropology* 37 (1996), pp. 856–63.

Benveniste, Émile, *Indo–European Language and Society*. Translated by Elizabeth Palmer (Coral Gables, FL: University of Miami Press, 1973).

Bergaigne, Abel. *La religion védique d'après les hymnes du Rig-veda* (Paris: F. Vieweg, 1883).

Bertinetti, Marina. 'Testimonianze del culto dei Dioscuri in area Laziale.' In Nista, Leila (editor), *Castores. L'immagine dei Dioscuri a Roma* (Rome: Edizioni de Luca, 1994), pp. 59–70.

Bianchi, Ugo. 'Twins.' In Jones, Lindsay (editor), *Encyclopedia of Religion* (Detroit, OH: Macmillan, 2005), vol. 14, pp. 9411–19.

Bicknell, Peter. 'The Date of the Battle of the Sagra River.' *Phoenix* 20 (1966), pp. 294–301.

Biezais, Haralds. *Die himmlische Götterfamilie der alten Letten* (Uppsala, Sweden: Almqvist & Wiksells, 1972).

Bloomfield, Maurice. 'Contributions to the Interpretation of the Veda.' *Journal of the American Oriental Society* 15 (1893), pp. 143–88.

——— *Hymns of the Atharva–Veda* (Delhi: Motilal Banarsidass, 1897 [2000]).

Bodewitz, H.W. *The Daily Evening and Morning Offering (Agnihotra) according to the Brāhmaṇas* (Leiden: E.J. Brill, 1976).

Bottini, Angelo. 1994. 'I Dioscuri e il mito: la nascita di Elena tra Atene e occidente.' In Nista, Leila (editor), *Castores. L'immagine dei Dioscuri a Roma* (Rome: Edizioni de Luca, 1994), pp. 33–7.

Boyce, Mary. 'Priests, Cattle and Men.' *Bulletin of the School of Oriental and African Studies* 50 (1987), pp. 508–26.

Bryant, Edwin F., and Patton, Laurie L. *The Indo–Aryan Controversy. Evidence and Inference in Indian History* (London: Routledge, 2005).

Bugh, Glenn Richard. *The Horsemen of Athens* (Princeton, NJ: Princeton University Press, 1988).

Buitenen, J.A.B. van. *The Pravargya, an Ancient Indian Iconic Ritual* (Poona: Deccan College Postgraduate and Research Institute, 1968).

Burkert, Walter. *Structure and History in Greek Mythology and Ritual* (Berekeley, CA: University of California Press, 1979).

——— *Greek Religion*. Translated by John Raffan (Cambridge, MA: Harvard University Press, 1985).

Caland, Willem, and Henry, Victor. *L'Agniṣṭoma* (Paris: Ernest Leroux, 1906).

Campbell, David A. *Greek Lyric* (Cambridge, MA: Harvard University Press, 1982–1993).

Cancellieri, Margherita. 1994. 'Le *aedes Castoris et Pollucis* in Lazio: una nota.' In Nista, Leila (editor), *Castores. L'immagine dei Dioscuri a Roma* (Rome: Edizioni de Luca, 1994), pp. 63–70.

Cartledge, Paul. *Spartan Reflections* (Berkeley, CA: University of California Press, 2001).

——— *The Spartans. The World of the Warrior-Heroes of Ancient Greece, from Utopia to Crisis and Collapse* (Woodstock, NY: The Overlook Press, 2003).

Chadwick, John. *The Mycenean World* (Cambridge: Cambridge University Press, 1976).

Chemery, Peter C. 'Meteorological Beings.' In Jones, Lindsay (editor), *Encyclopedia of Religion* (Detroit, OH: Macmillan, 2005), vol. 9, pp. 5992–6.

Clader, Linda Lee. *Helen. The Evolution from Divine to Heroic in Greek Epic Tradition* (Leiden: E.J. Brill, 1976).

Coomaraswamy, Ananda K. 'Angel and Titan: an Essay in Vedic Ontology.' *Journal of the American Oriental Society* 55 (1935), pp. 373–419.

David, Ephraim. 'Laughter in Spartan Society.' In Powell, Anton (editor), *Classical Sparta. Techniques Behind Her Success* (Norman, OK: University of Oklahoma Press, 1989), pp. 1–25.

Decker, Wolfgang. 'Pferd und Wagen im Alten Aegypten.' In Hänsel, Bernhard, and Zimmer, Stefan (editors), *Die Indogermanen und das Pferd. Festschrift fur Bernfried Schlerath* (Budapest: Archaeolingua Alapítvány, 1994), pp. 259–70.

Delebecque, Edouard. *Le cheval dans l'Iliade* (Paris: Klincksieck, 1951).

DELG = Chantraine, Pierre, et al *ii. Dictionnaire étymologique de la langue grecque* (Paris: Klinksieck, 2009).

Détienne, Marcel, and Vernant, Jean-Pierre. *Cunning Intelligence in Greek Culture and Society*. Translated by Janet Lloyd (Chicago, IL: University of Chicago Press, 1991).

Dickinson, Oliver. *The Aegean Bronze Age* (Cambridge: Cambridge University Press, 1994).

Doniger, Wendy. *Hindu Myths* (Harmondsworth: Penguin, 1975).

Drews, Robert. *The Coming of the Greeks* (Princeton, NJ: Princeton University Press, 1988).

——— *The End of the Bronze Age* (Princeton, NJ: Princeton University Press. 1993).

——— *Early Riders: the Beginnings of Mounted Warfare in Asia and Europe* (New York, NY: Routledge, 2004).

Dumézil, Georges. *Mythe et épopée. I. L'idéologie des trois fonctions dans les épopées des peuples indo-européens* (Paris: Gallimard, 1968 [1986]).

——— *Archaic Roman Religion*. Translated by Philip Krapp (Chicago, IL: Chicago University Press, 1970).

——— *Mythe et épopée. II. Types épiques indo-européens: un héros, un sorcier, un roi* (Paris: Gallimard, 1971 [1986]).

——— *Mariages indo-européens* (Paris: Payot, 1979).

Dumont, Paul-Emile. 'The Kaukilī-Sautrāmaṇī in the Taittirīya-Brāhmaṇa.' *Proceedings of the American Philosophical Society* 109 (1965), pp. 309–41.

Edelstein, Emma J., and Edelstein, Ludwig. *Asclepius* (Baltimore, MD: The Johns Hopkins University Press, 1998).

Eitrem, S. *Die göttlichen Zwillinge bei den Griechen*. (Christiania [Oslo]: A. W. Brøggers Buchdruckerei, 1902).

Erdosy, George. 'Ethnicity in the Rigveda and its Bearing on the Question of Indo-European Origins.' *South Asian Studies* 5 (1989), pp. 35–47.

——— *The Indo-Aryans of Ancient South Asia. Language, Material Culture and Ethnicity* (Berlin: Walter de Gruyter, 1995).

EWA = Mayrhofer, Manfred. *Etymologisches Wörterbuch des Altindoarischen* (Heidelberg: Universitätsverlag C. Winter, 1986–2001).

Falk, Harry. *Bruderschaft und Würfelspiel. Untersuchungen zur Entwicklungsgeschichte des vedischen Opfers* (Freiburg: Hedwig Falk, 1986).

——— 'Das Reitpferd im vedischen Indien.' In Hänsel, Bernhard, and Zimmer, Stefan (editors), *Die Indogermanen und das Pferd. Festschrift fur Bernfried Schlerath* (Budapest: Archaeolingua Alapítvány, 1994), pp. 91–101.

Farnell, Lewis Richard. *Greek Hero Cults and the Ideas of Immortality* (Oxford: Clarendon Press, 1921).

FGrH = *Die Fragmente der griechischen Historiker*. Edited by Felix Jacoby (Leiden: E.J. Brill, 1957–1969).

Forrest, W.G. *A History of Sparta* (New York, NY: W.W. Norton & Company, 1968).

Fowler, Murray. 'The Role of Surā in the Myth of Namuci.' *Journal of the American Oriental Society* 62 (1942), pp. 36–40.

Geldner, Karl Friedrich. *Der Rig-Veda, aus dem Sanskrit ins Deutsche übers. und mit einem laufenden Kommentar versehen von Karl Friedrich Geldner* (Cambridge, MA: Harvard University Press, 1951).

Geldner, Karl Friedrich and Nobel, Johannes. *Namen-und Sachregister zur Übersetzung* (Cambridge, MA: Harvard University Press, 1957).

Gernet, Louis. *Droit et Institutions en Grèce antique* (Paris: Flammarion, 1968 [1982]).

Gernet, Louis and Boulanger, André. *Le génie grec dans la religion* (Paris: Albin Michel, 1932 [1970]).

Gonda, Jaan. *The Dual Deities in the Religion of the Veda* (Amsterdam: North-Holland Publishing Company, 1974).

——— 'A Propos of the Mantras in the Pravargya Section of the Ṛgveda Brāhmaṇas.' *Indo-Iranian Journal* 21 (1979) pp. 235–71.

Griffith, Mark, 'Horsepower and Donkeywork: Equids and the Ancient Greek Imagination.' *Classical Philology* 101 (2006), pp. 185–246 and 307–58.

Griffith, Ralph T.H. *The Hymns of the Rig Veda.* (Delhi: Motilal Banarsidass, 1896 [1973]).

Grotanelli, Cristiano. 'Yoked Horses, Twins, and the Powerful Lady: India, Greece, Ireland and Elsewhere.' *Journal of Indo-European Studies.* 14 (1986) pp. 125–52.

——— 'Dumézil, the Indo–Europeans, and the Third Function.' In Patton, Laurie L., and Doniger, Wendy, *Myth and Method* (Charlotesville, VA: University of Virginia Press, 1996), pp. 128–46.

Grummond, Nancy Thomson de. 'For the Mother and for the Daughter: Some Thoughts on Dedications from Etruria and Praeneste.' In Chapin, Anne P (editor), *ΧΑΡΙΣ. Essays in Honor of Sara A. Immerwahr. Hesperia Supplement 33* (Athens: The American School of Classical Studies at Athens, 2004), pp. 351–360.

——— *Etruscan Myth, Sacred History, and Legend* (Philadelphia, PA: University of Pennsylvania Museum of Archaeology and Anthropology, 2006).

Guzzo, Pier Giovanni. 1994. 'I Dioscuri in Magna Grecia.' In Nista, Leila (editor), *Castores. L'immagine dei Dioscuri a Roma* (Roma: Edizioni de Luca, 1994), pp. 26–31.

Halliday, W.R. *Indo-European Folk-Tales and Greek Legend* (Cambridge: at the University Press, 1933).

Harris, James Rendel. *The Dioscuri in the Christian legends* (London: C.J. Clay, 1903).

——— *The Cult of the Heavenly Twins* (Cambridge: University Press, 1906).

——— *Boanerges* (Cambridge: University Press, 1913).

Heesterman, J.C. 'Vrātya and Sacrifice.' *Indo-Iranian Journal* 6 (1962) pp. 1–37.

——— *The Broken World of Sacrifice: An Essay in Indian Ritual* (Chicago, IL: University of Chicago Press, 1993).

Hermary, Antoine. 'Dioskouroi.' In *Lexicon Iconographicum Mythologiae Classicae* (Zurich: Artemis, 1981), vol. 3, part 1, pp. 567–93.

Hillebrandt, Alfred. *Vedic Mythology.* Translated by Sreeramula Rajeswara Sarma (Delhi: Motilal Banarsidass, 1980).

Hiletbeitel, Alf, *The Ritual of Battle. Krishna in the Mahābhārata* (Albany, NY: State University of New York Press, 1990).

Hobson, John. The *Eastern Origins of Western Civilization* (Cambridge: Cambridge University Press, 2004).

Hodges, Henry. *Technology in the Ancient World* (New York, NY: Barnes and Noble, 1970).

Hopkins, Edward W. 'The Social and Military Position of the Ruling Caste in Ancient India, as Represented by the Sanskrit Epic.' *Journal of the American Oriental Society* 13 (1889), pp. 57–376.

Horsnaes, Helle W. *The Cultural Development in North-Western Lucania:* c. *600–273 B.C* (Rome: L'Erma di Bretschneider, 2002).

Houben, Jan E.M. *The Pravargya Brāhmaṇa of the Taittirīya Āraṇyaka: an Ancient Commentary on the Pravargya Ritual* (Delhi: Motilal Banarsidass, 1991).

——— 'On the Earliest Attestable Forms of the Pravargya Ritual: Ṛg–Vedic References to the Gharma–Pravargya, especially in the Atri-family Book (Book 5).' *Indo-Iranian Journal* 43 (2000), pp. 1–25.

Hyland, Ann. *The Horse in the Ancient World* (Westport, CT: Praeger, 2003).
Jackson, Peter. *The transformations of Helen: Indo-European myth and the roots of the Trojan Circle* (Dettelbach: Röll, 2006).
Jamison, Stephanie. *The Ravenous Hyenas and the Wounded Sun. Myth and Ritual in Ancient India* (Ithaca, NY: Cornell University Press, 1991).
——— 'The Rigvedic Svayaṃvara? Formulaic Evidence.' In *Vidyārnavandanam; Essays in Honour of Asko Parpola* (Helsinki: Finnish Oriental Society, 2000), pp. 303–15.
Jamison, Stephanie and Witzel, Michael. *Vedic Hinduism* (www.people.fas.harvard.edu/~witzel/vedica.pdf, 1992).
Kearns, Emily. *The Heroes of Attica* (London: Institute of Classical Studies, 1989).
Keith, Arthur Berriedale. *The Veda of the Black Yajus School, Entitled Taittiriya Sanhita* (Cambridge, MA: Harvard University Press, 1914).
——— *The Religion and Philosophy of the Veda and Upanishads* (Cambridge, MA: Harvard University Press, 1925).
Kipling, Rudyard. *The Man Who Would Be King* (New York, NY: Doubleday and McClure, 1899).
Köhne, Eckart. *Die Dioskuren in der Griechischen Kunst von der Archaik bis zum Ende des 5. Jahrhunderts v. Chr* (Hamburg: Verlag Dr. Kovač, 1998).
Krappe, Alexandre Haggerty. *Mythologie universelle* (Paris: Payot, 1930).
Kuhrt, Amélie. *The Ancient Near East* (London: Routledge, 1995).
Lanman, Charles Rockwell. *A Sanskrit Reader* (Boston, MA: Ginn, Heath, and Company, 1884).
Lawal, Babatunde. 'Sustaining the Oneness in Their Twoness: Poetics of Twin Figures (Ère Ìbeji) among the Yoruba.' In Peek, Philip M. *Twins in African and Diaspora Culture. Double Trouble, Twice Blessed.* (Bloomington: Indiana University Press, 2011), pp. 81–98.
Leis, Philip E. 'The Nonfunctional Attributes of Twin Infanticide in the Niger Delta.' *Anthropological Quarterly* 38 (1965) pp. 97–111.
Lévi-Strauss, Claude. *Anthropologie structurale* (Paris: Plon, 1974).
Levine, Marsha. 'The Origins of Horse Husbandry on the Eurasian Steppe.' In Levine, Marsha et al, *Late Prehistoric Exploitation of the Eurasian Steppe* (Cambridge: McDonald Institute for Archaeological Research, 1999), pp. 5–58.
LIMC = *Lexicon Iconographicum Mythologiae Classicae* (Zurich: Artemis, 1981).
Lincoln, Bruce. *Priests, Warriors, and Cattle: a Study in the Ecology of Religions* (Berkeley, CA: University of California Press, 1981).
Littauer, M.A. and Crouwel, J.F. *Wheeled Vehicles and Ridden Animals in the Ancient Near East* (Leiden: E.J. Brill, 1979).
Loraux, Nicole. *The Children of Athena: Athenian Ideas about Citizenship and the Division between the Sexes*. Translated by Caroline Levine (Princeton, NJ: Princeton University Press, 1993).
LSJ = *A Greek–English Lexicon.* Edited by Henry George Liddell, Robert Scott, and Sir Henry Stuart Jones (Oxford: Oxford University Press, 1968).
Ludwig, Arne et al. 'Coat Color Variation at the Beginning of Horse Domestication.' *Science* 324 (2009), p. 485.
Macdonell, Arthur Anthony. *Vedic Mythology* (Delhi: Motilal Banarsidass. 1898 [2002]).
MacDowell, Douglas M. *The Law in Classical Athens* (Ithaca, NY: Cornell University Press, 1978).

Malamoud, Charles. *Cooking the World. Ritual and Thought in Ancient India.* Translated by David White (New York, NY: Oxford University Press, 1996).

Mannhardt, Wilhelm. 'Die lettische Sonnenmythen.' *Zeitschrift für Ethnologie* 7 (1875), pp. 73–104, 209–44, and 281–329.

Matthews, Victor J. *Antimachus of Colophon: Text and Commentary* (Leiden: E.J. Brill, 1996).

Merkelbach, R. and West, Martin Litchfield. *Hesiodi. Fragmenta Selecta* (Oxford: Clarendon Press, 1983).

Momigliano, Arnaldo. 'Georges Dumézil and the Trifunctional Approach to Roman Civilization.' In Momigliano, Arnaldo, *On Pagans, Jews, and Christians* (Middletown, CT: Wesleyan University Press, 1987), pp. 289–314.

Myriantheus, L. *Die Açvins, oder arischen Dioskuren* (Munich: Theodor Ackermann, 1876).

Nagy, Gregory. *The Best of the Achaeans* (Baltimore, MD: Johns Hopkins University Press, 1979).

——— *Greek Mythology and Poetics* (Ithaca, NY: Cornell University Press, 1990).

Nielsen, Inge. 1994. 'Il Tempio del Foro Romano: l'età Repubblicana.' In Nista, Leila (editor), *Castores. L'immagine dei Dioscuri a Roma* (Roma: Edizioni de Luca, 1994), pp. 106–12.

Nilsson, Martin P. *Geschichte der griechischen Religion. Erster Band. Die Religion Griechenlands bis auf die griechische Weltherrschaft* (Munich: C.H. Beck'sche Verlagsbuchhandlung, 1955).

——— *The Mycenaean Origin of Greek Mythology* (Berkeley, CA: University of California Press, 1972).

Oldenberg, Hermann. *Die Religion des Veda* (Berlin: Hertz, 1894).

Oort, Marianne S. 'Surā in the Paippalāda Saṃhitā of the Atharvaveda.' *Journal of the American Oriental Society* 122 (2002), pp. 355–60.

Outram, Alan K. et alii. 'The Earliest Horse Harnessing and Milking.' *Science* 323 (2009), p. 1332–5.

Parisi Presicce, Claudio. 'I Dioscuri Capitolini e l'Iconografia dei Gemelli Divini in Età Romana.' In Nista, Leila (editor), *Castores. L'immagine dei Dioscuri a Roma* (Roma: Edizioni de Luca, 1994), pp. 153–91.

Parker, Robert. 'Spartan Religion.' In Powell, Anton (editor), *Classical Sparta. Techniques Behind Her Success* (Norman, OK: University of Oklahoma Press, 1989), pp. 142–72.

Parpola, Asko. 'The problem of the Aryans and the Soma: Textual–linguistic and archaeological evidence.' In Erdosy, George, *The Indo-Aryans of Ancient South Asia. Language, Material Culture and Ethnicity* (Berlin: Walter de Gruyter, 1995), pp. 353–81.

——— 'The Nāsatyas, the Chariot and Proto-Aryan Religion.' *Journal of Indological Studies.* 16–17 (2004–5), pp. 1–63.

Patton, Laurie L. *Myth as Argument. The Bṛhaddevatā as Canonical Commentary* (Berlin: Walter de Gruyter, 1996).

PCG = *Poetae Comici Graeci*. Edited by R. Kassel and C. Austin (Berlin: de Gruyter, 1983).

Pedley, John Griffiths. *Paestum. Greeks and Romans in Southern Italy* (London: Thames and Hudson, 1990).

Peek, Philip. 'Introduction: Beginning to Rethink Twins.' In Peek, Philip M. *Twins in African and Diaspora Culture. Double Trouble, Twice Blessed.* (Bloomington: Indiana University Press, 2011), pp. 1–36.

Piggott, Stuart. *Wagon, Chariot and Carriage. Symbol and Status in the History of Transport* (London: Thames and Hudson, 1992).

Piontelli, Alessandra. *Twins in the World. The Legends They Inspire, the Lives They Lead* (New York: Palgrave Macmillan, 2008).

Pisani, Vittore. 'Elena e l' Εδωλον.' *Rivista di Filologia e di Istruzione Classica*. 56 (1928), pp. 476–99.

Plath, Robert. 'Pferd und Wagen im Mykenischen und bei Homer.' In Hänsel, Bernhard, and Zimmer, Stefan (editors), *Die Indogermanen und das Pferd. Festschrift fur Bernfried Schlerath* (Budapest: Archaeolingua Alapítvány, 1994), pp. 103–14.

Pokorny, Julius. *Indogermanisches etymologisches Wörterbuch* (Bern: Francke, 1959).

Poliakov, Léon. *The Aryan Myth. A History of Racist and Nationalist Ideas in Europe*. Translated by Edmund Howard (New York, NY: Basic Books, 1974).

Pomeroy, Sarah B. *Goddesses, Whores, Wives, and Slaves. Women in Classical Antiquity* (New York, NY: Shocken Books, 1975).

Poulsen, Birte. 'Ideologia, Mito e Culto dei Castori a Roma: dall'età Repubblicana Tardo-Antico.' In Nista, Leila (editor), *Castores. L'immagine dei Dioscuri a Roma* (Roma: Edizioni de Luca, 1994), pp. 91–100.

Rau, Wilhelm. *Staat und Gesellschaft im alten Indien. Nach den Brāhmaṇa–texten dargestellt* (Wiesbaden: Otto Harrassowitz, 1957).

Renne, Elisha P. Renne. 'The Ambiguous Ordinariness of Yoruba Twins.' In Peek, Philip M. *Twins in African and Diaspora Culture. Double Trouble, Twice Blessed.* (Bloomington: Indiana University Press, 2011), pp. 306–26.

Sande, Siri. 'Il Tempio del Foro Romano: l'età Augustea.' In Nista, Leila (editor), *Castores. L'immagine dei Dioscuri a Roma* (Rome: Edizioni de Luca, 1994), pp. 113–18.

Sanza di Mino, Maria Rita. 'Il Culto dei Gemelli Divini in Ambito Medio–italico.' In Nista, Leila (editor), *Castores. L'immagine dei Dioscuri a Roma* (Rome: Edizioni de Luca, 1994), pp. 53–8.

Schmidt, Hans Peter. 'Vedic *Pāthas*.' *Indo-Iranian Journal* 15 (1973), pp. 1–39.

Schulman, Alan Richard. 'Egyptian Representations of Horsemen and Riding in the New Kingdom.' *Journal of Near Eastern Studies* 16 (1957), pp. 263–71.

Scullard, Howard Hayes. *Festivals and Ceremonies of the Roman Republic* (Ithaca, NY: Cornell University Press, 1981).

Sidney Hartland, Edwin. 'Twins.' In the *Encyclopaedia of Religion and Ethics* (New York, NY: Charles Scribner's Sons, 1955), pp. 491–500.

Skutsch, Otto. 'Helen, Her Name and Nature.' *Journal of Hellenic Studies* 107 (1987), pp. 188–93.

Smith, Brian K., and Doniger, Wendy. 'Sacrifice and Substitution: Ritual Mystification and Mythical Demystification.' *Numen* 36 (1989), pp. 189–224.

Sourvinou–Inwood, Christiane. 'The Votum of 477/6 B.C. and the Foundation Legend of Locri Epizephyrii.' *Classical Quarterly* 24 (1974), pp. 186–98.

Spence, I.G. *The Cavalry of Classical Greece* (Oxford: Clarendon Press, 1993).

Staal, Frits. *Agni, the Vedic Ritual of the Fire Altar* (Berkeley, CA: Asian Humanities Press, 1983).

——— *Discovering the Vedas. Origins, Mantras, Rituals, Insights* (New Delhi: Penguin Books India, 2008).

Starzzulla, Maria Josè. 'Attestazioni Figurative dei Dioscuri nel Mondo Etrusco.' In Nista, Leila (editor), *Castores. L'immagine dei Dioscuri a Roma* (Roma: Edizioni de Luca, 1994), pp. 39–52.

Steinhauer, George. *Museum of Sparta* (Athens: Apollo Editions, 1975).

Sternberg, Leo. 'Der antike Zwillingskult im Lichte der Ethnologie.' *Zeitschrift für Ethnologie* 61 (1929), pp. 152–200.

Taylor, Lily Ross. *Party Politics in the Age of Caesar* (Berkeley, CA: University of California Press, 1966).

Tewari, Premvati. *Āyurvedīya Prasūti-Tantra Evaṃ Strī-Roga. Part I. Prasūti–Tantra (Obstetrics)* (Delhi: Chaukhambha Orientalia, 1986).

Thite, Ganesh Umakant. 'Animal-Sacrifice in the Brāhmaṇa Texts.' *Numen* 17 (1970) pp. 143–58.

Tod, M.N., and Wace, A.J.B. *A Catalogue of the Sparta Museum* (Rome: 'L'Erma' di Bretschneider, 1968).

Turner, Victor W. 'Paradoxes of Twinship in Ndembu Ritual.' In *The Ritual Process* (Chicago, IL: Aldine Publishing Company, 1969), pp. 44–93.

Vernant, Jean-Pierre. *Problèmes de la guerre en Grèce ancienne* (Paris: Mouton, 1968).

——— *Mortals and Immortals: Collected Essays*. Edited by Froma I. Zeitlin (Princeton, NJ: Princeton University Press, 1991).

——— *Myth and Thought among the Greeks.* Translated by Janet Lloyd (New York, NY: Zone Books, 2006).

Vernant, Jean-Pierre and Vidal-Naquet, Pierre. *Myth and Tragedy in Ancient Greece.* Translated by Janet Lloyd (New York, NY: Zone Books, 1988).

Vidal-Naquet, Pierre. *The Black Hunter: Forms of Thought and Forms of Society in the Greek World.* Translated by Andrew Szegedy-Maszak (Baltimore, MD: Johns Hopkins University Press, 1986).

Wagner, Noerber. 'Dioskuren, Jungmannschaften und Doppelkönigtum.' *Zeitschrift für deutsche Philologie* 79 (1960), pp. 1–17.

Walker, Henry John. 'The Greek Aśvins.' *Annals of the Bhandarkar Oriental Research Institute* 88 (2007), pp. 99–118.

Ward, Donald. *The Divine Twins* (Berkeley, CA: University of California Press, 1968).

Watkins, Calvert. 'New Parameters in Historical Linguistics, Philology, and Culture History.' *Language* 65 (1989), pp. 783–99.

——— *How to Kill a Dragon: Aspects of Indo-European Poetics* (New York, NY: Oxford University Press, 1995).

——— *The American Heritage Dictionary of Indo-European Roots* (Boston, MA: Houghton Mifflin, 2000).

Weinstock, Stefan. 'Two Archaic Inscriptions from Latium.' *Journal of Roman Studies* 50 (1960), p. 112–18.

West, M.L. *Hesiod. Theogony* (Oxford: Clarendon Press, 1966).

——— *Immortal Helen* (London: Bedford College, 1975).

——— *Hesiod. Works and Days* (Oxford: Clarendon Press, 1978).

——— *Indo-European Poetry and Myth* (New York, NY: Oxford University Press, 2007).

Whitaker's Almanack (London: A & C Black, 2010).

Wiseman, T.P. *Remus: A Roman Myth* (New York, NY: Cambridge University Press, 1995).

——— *The Myths of Rome* (Exeter: University of Exeter Press, 2004).

Witzel, Michael. 'The case of the shattered head.' *Studien zur Indologie und Iranistik* (1987), pp. 363–415.

——— 'On the Localisation of Vedic Texts and Schools.' In Pollet, Gilbert (editor), *India and the Ancient World: History, Trade, and Culture Before A.D. 650* (Leuven: Departement Oriëntalistiek, 1987), pp. 173–213.

——— 'On the origin of the literary device of the 'Frame Story' in Old Indian literature.' In Falk, Harry (editor), *Hinduismus und Buddhismus, Festschrift für Ulrich Schneider* (Freiburg: Hedwig Falk, 1987), pp. 380–414.

——— 'Early Indian history: Linguistic and textual parameters.' In Erdosy, George (editor), *The Indo-Aryans of Ancient South Asia. Language, Material Culture and Ethnicity* (Berlin: Walter de Gruyter, 1995), pp. 85–125.

——— 'Early Sanskritization. Origins and Development of the Kuru State.' *Electronic Journal of Vedic Studies* 1–4 (1995), pp. 1–26.

——— 'Rgvedic History: Poets, Chieftains and Polities.' In Erdosy, George (editor), *The Indo-Aryans of Ancient South Asia. Language, Material Culture and Ethnicity* (Berlin: Walter de Gruyter, 1995), pp. 307–52.

——— 'Little Dowry, No Satī. The Lot of Women in the Vedic Period.' *Journal of South Asia Women Studies* 2 (1996), pp. 159–69.

——— 'The Development of the Vedic Canon and its Schools: The Social and Political Milieus.' In Witzel, Michael (editor), *Inside the Texts, Beyond the Texts* (Cambridge, MA: Harvard University Press, 1997), pp. 257–348.

——— *Das alte Indien* (Munich: Beck, 2003).

——— 'Linguistic Evidence for Cultural Exchange in Prehistoric Western Central Asia.' *Sino-Platonic Papers* 129 (Philadelphia, PA: Department of East Asian Languages and Civilizations, University of Pennsylvania, 2003).

——— 'Early Loan Words in Western Central Asia: Indicators of Substrate Populations, Migrations, and Trade Relations.' In Mair, Victor H. (editor), *Contact and Exchange in the Ancient World* (Honolulu: University of Hawai'i Press, 2006), pp. 158–90.

Wonder, John W. 'What happened to the Greeks in Lucanian-occupied Paestum? Multiculturalism in Southern Italy.' *Phoenix* 56 (2002), pp. 40–55.

Worley, Leslie J. *Hippeis. The Cavalry of Ancient Greece* (Boulder, CO: Westview Press, 1994).

Zeller, Gabriele. *Die Vedischen Zwillingsgötter. Untersuchungen zur Genese ihres Kultes* (Wiesbaden: Otto Harrassowitz, 1990).

Zimmer, Stefan. 'Die Indogermanen und das Pferd – Befunde und Probleme.' In Hänsel, Bernhard, and Zimmer, Stefan (editors), *Die Indogermanen und das Pferd. Festschrift fur Bernfried Schlerath* (Budapest: Archaeolingua Alapítvány, 1994), pp. 29–35.

INDEX

Lightning Source UK Ltd.
Milton Keynes UK
UKHW020924251122
412689UK00027B/394

9 781350 197800